This innovative book is essential reading for anyone seeking a rich social scientific understanding of ethics in this current era.

*Walter DeKeseredy, Anna Deane Carlson Endowed
Chair of Social Sciences and Director of the
Research Center on Violence at
West Virginia University, USA*

Sharon Hayes provides a fresh, new approach to teaching criminal justice ethics. Beginning with strong foundational material covering what is ethics and why we should be ethical, she then moves on to societal ethics and morality. In contrast to most ethics textbooks, it is only after giving the reader this essential baseline that she then addresses situational ethics for law enforcement, courts and corrections. In a society that frequently questions individual and group ethics, this book helps bring much needed clarity and understanding.

*Michael B. Shapiro, J. D.,
Clinical Instructor and Criminal Justice
Coordinator at the Alpharetta Center,
Georgia State University, USA*

Hayes' *Criminal Justice Ethics* text offers instructors of undergraduate criminal justice ethics courses the ability to provide students with a dynamic understanding of ethics by illustrating its evolution throughout humanity and how that history has informed ethical principles within the field of criminal justice.

*Elizabeth Quinn, Ph.D., Associate Professor,
Department of Criminal Justice,
Fayetteville State University, USA*

Criminal Justice Ethics

It is essential for those employed within the justice system to be able to competently and confidently work at the borders between ethics and the law. *Criminal Justice Ethics* offers a fresh new approach to considering ethical issues in a criminal justice context. Rather than simply offering a range of ethical dilemmas specific to various justice professionals, it provides extensive discussion of how individuals develop their 'moral imaginations' using ethical perspectives and practices, both as citizens of the world and as practitioners of justice.

Starting from a consideration of the major ethical theories, this book sets the framework for an expansive discussion of ethics by moving from theory to consider the just society and the role of the justice professional within it. Each chapter provides detailed analysis of relevant ethical issues and activities to engage students with the content, as well as review questions which can be used for revision or examination. This book will help students to:

- understand the various theoretical approaches to ethics;
- apply these understandings to issues in society and the justice process;
- assist in developing the ability to investigate, discuss, and analyze current ethical issues in criminal justice;
- appreciate the diverse nature of ethical systems across cultures;
- outline strategies for detecting and resolving ethical dilemmas.

Rich with examples and ethical dilemmas from a broad range of contexts, this book's multicultural approach will appeal not only to criminal justice educators, but also to academics, students, and practitioners approaching criminal justice from sociological, psychological, or philosophical perspectives.

Sharon Hayes is Associate Professor in Justice at Queensland University of Technology (QUT) where she teaches *Social Ethics and the Justice System* and *Sex and Crime*. Her background in ethics and justice spans twenty-five years, including a Masters in Philosophy from Tulane University, and a PhD in Social Philosophy from QUT. Sharon was a founding lay member of the Queensland Legal Practice Tribunal and has provided advice on public sector ethics to the Crime and Misconduct Commission. Sharon's recent research interests include sex crimes and domestic violence and her recent publications include *Sex, Crime and Morality* (2012, Routledge), *The Politics of Sex Trafficking: A moral geography* (2013, Palgrave), and *Sex, Love and Abuse: Discourses on domestic violence and sexual assault* (2014, Palgrave).

Criminal Justice Ethics

Cultivating the moral imagination

Sharon Hayes

Routledge
Taylor & Francis Group

LONDON AND NEW YORK

First published 2015
by Routledge
2 Park Square, Milton Park, Abingdon, Oxon, OX14 4RN

and by Routledge
711 Third Avenue, New York, NY 10017

Routledge is an imprint of the Taylor & Francis Group, an informa business

British Library Cataloguing in Publication Data
A catalogue record for this book is available from the British Library

Library of Congress Cataloging-in-Publication Data
A catalog record has been requested for this book

ISBN: 978-1-138-77696-8 (hbk)
ISBN: 978-1-138-77697-5 (pbk)
ISBN: 978-1-315-77289-9 (ebk)

Typeset in Bembo
by Swales & Willis Ltd, Exeter, Devon, UK

For my parents, Richard William Beattie and
Aileen Joan Beattie.

Contents

Figures

Tables

Acknowledgments

This book could not have been written without the input of the many students to whom I have taught ethics over the past twenty years. The lively class discussions have assisted in honing and enriching both content and style, and I thank them with all my heart. I'd like to thank my tutors, Bridget Thomas, Bethney Baker, Luke Trantor, Carol Quadrelli, and Rob Robertson for their invaluable input. I'm also appreciative of discussions about the material with Matthew Ball, who co-taught it with me from 2010 through 2012. Thanks also to Olivia Hayes for keeping me updated on ethics in the media, and to Cathy Rayner for transcribing some of my lectures. Extra thanks must also go to Cathy and Olivia who, as my family, have provided invaluable support and cups of tea during the writing of this book. Thanks also to OUP for their kind permission to reproduce some of my previous work in Chapter 12 and to Sage for allowing us to reproduce an extract from one of their journals in Chapter 13. Finally, thanks to the editors at Routledge, particularly Heidi Lee, for their ongoing patience and unfailing good humor!

Chapter 1

Introduction

This book is about the ethical and moral issues that impact upon those who work in, and those who access, the criminal justice system. It is more than just a professional code of conduct or even an exploration of how ethics can be applied to professional roles, although those are important parts. This text aims to broaden your thinking about the criminal justice system, how it is structured and how it fits into society at large. It introduces the term 'social ethics,' which illustrates the impact of the criminal justice system on specific populations, particularly those who are disadvantaged. It also demonstrates how public and private morality play such a large role in conceptualizations of ethics.

Social ethics is also concerned with the moral rules and values that relate to the internal operations of groups of people. There are any number of social groups comprising the criminal justice system, including for example, lawyers, police officers, correctional officers, and judges, each of which operates within a particular culture. Those officials and professionals entrusted with the administration of justice in our community are expected not only to carry out the tasks of their profession with competence and diligence, but also to base their professional behavior on strong moral and ethical grounds. Despite the fact that all the justice professions may claim to be sound repositories of public trust, this is not always the case. There is a clear and marked power imbalance between those with specialist knowledge, legislative powers and discretions who administer the justice system, and those who are simply subjected to it. This chapter discusses the nature of 'social ethics' and the 'moral imagination,' and why they are important for the study of criminal justice ethics.

The moral imagination

Imagine a world in which everyone was completely truthful all the time, where lying had never even been conceived as a possibility. Without the ability to lie, there would also be no stealing, cheating, corruption, or indeed, secrets—crime would be minimal because offenders would be obliged to own up. A recent film, *The Invention of Lying* (Warner Brothers 2009) starts from that very premise: no one lies, even by omission, and people are compelled to state the truth.

While this seems like an idyllic state of affairs, in fact it leads to some very inter-esting (and funny) outcomes. The male protagonist in the film, Mark Bellison, is a relatively mediocre writer of television documentaries—there is no fiction, and therefore no fictional films, because no one understands the concept. His life is fairly lacklustre, which becomes clear when he dates a beautiful woman, Anna, who informs him over dinner that he is really not in her league because he is fat and plain-looking. Apparently his gene pool excludes him from being husband material because she does not want fat, ugly kids. Not long after, he loses his job. When he attempts to draw the last of his cash out of the bank to pay his overdue rent, the bank teller advises that the system is down, and asks him how much he has in his account. On the spur of the moment, Mark tells a huge fib, claiming he has $800, more than double his actual amount. The system comes back on and the teller notices he only has $300 in his account, but since he says he has $800, the system must be corrupt—so she gives him the $800! Having invented lying, Mark tries to explain it to his friends with hilarious results—no matter what he tells them, they believe him. Cynically, Mark uses his new-found ability to lie to his own advantage, ending up rich and famous—and, of course, getting the girl.

What is most interesting about the film, however, is how starkly it high-lights just how often we lie to each other, not only for our own benefit, but to spare others' feelings and to help them through pain and grief. For example, Mark's neighbor is suicidal, believing himself to be worthless. Once Mark dis-covers lying, he is able to convince his neighbor he has numerous wonderful traits. Similarly, when his mother expresses fear on her death-bed, he concocts a comforting story about "the man in the sky" and heaven, where everyone lives happily ever after. On the flip side, earlier in the film we laugh at truths that most of us would never tell—that our date is fat and snubby-nosed, or that we are running late because we were masturbating. The first most of us would keep to ourselves out of pity or empathy; the second out of embarrassment (or because it is just a little 'too much information'). In short, *The Invention of Lying* cleverly highlights the ambivalent nature of truth and the importance we place on sometimes trading truth off for a more palatable outcome.

Indeed, it is the fact that lying is so ubiquitous in our society that makes the film so humorous, and that points up the common assumption that sometimes lying is a good thing to do. When my partner spends long hours cooking a meal, which turns out to be rather tasteless, rather than pointing out its faults, I eat it with a smile and even compliment the effort. When someone asks, "Does this dress make my arse look fat?" we deny it vehemently, regardless of whether it does or not. And such lies of 'good intention' are not always only trivial. Keeping bad news to ourselves (or lying about it), for example, is quite common—when I was away overseas, my mother was ill in bed for six weeks, but didn't tell me because she didn't want me to worry. A doctor might not tell a cancer patient that his illness is terminal because the loss of hope would only add more pain. Sometimes when I am marking student assignments, I come across one that is so bad I want to scream, but instead of writing a long list of scathing comments, I try to find some positives and then couch the criticisms in kind language so the student will not become discouraged (it is a shame reviewers of books are not always so kind). Such lies are meant to spare feelings, to encourage, and to comfort.

Acknowledging the ambivalence of 'truth' helps us to understand the challenge of ethics: that there are many grey areas, and sometimes a solution might mean trading off one evil for another in order to achieve a better outcome. Acknowledging the complexity of ethical dilemmas and decisions provides a starting point for using our moral imaginations to explore our interactions with others and with society at large. C. Wright Mills (1957) conceptualized the idea of the *sociological* imagination as the ability to "think yourself away from the familiar routines of everyday life" and look at them from an entirely new perspective. In ethics, this is even more important. Ethics is concerned with how we interact with and treat each other, and therefore requires an ability and propensity to see things from another person's perspective. The *moral imagination*, then, describes the ability to step back, to look at situations from an impartial point of view, and to think outside the box, so to speak. We use our moral imaginations when we tell little white lies to protect others from what might otherwise be painful truths. In other words, in such instances we are putting ourselves in others' shoes, imagining what it might be like to be them.

But even then, it is more than this—our moral imagination asks us to stand outside ourselves, not just for our friends, but generally. Although his is a much more substantive view, David Bromwich (2014) talks about the moral imagination in this way. He suggests that we exercise it when we move out of our own natures to take in the suffering and pain of others who are not like us. Bromwich cites Wordsworth's poem called "The Idiot Boy," in which a mother sends her intellectually challenged child, Johnny, out to find a doctor for her friend and then becomes anxious when he does not return. He describes the kind of imagination it takes as a reader to feel the mother's pain for an aberrant son, something that is quite outside most people's experience:

> To sympathise with someone like myself is commendable, perhaps, but it shows nothing much . . . But to feel with the mother who has lost her idiot boy, or, as in *Frankenstein*, with a monstrous creature who must learn humanity from people even as he finds that people turn away in horror and disgust—these are truer tests of a "going out of our nature."
>
> (Bromwich 2014: 12)

Bromwich argues that whatever dignity I accord to Johnny and his mother ultimately says more about me than it says about them. He cites Shelley: "The great secret of morals . . . [is] a going out of our nature, and the identification of ourselves with the beautiful which exists in thought, action or person, not our own" (cited in Bromwich 2014: 12). To identify with others like ourselves is a doddle; to identify and embrace that which is almost completely different to us, and then to see the humanity and agency in them, is an achievement of the moral imagination.

We use our moral imagination to imagine ourselves into the perspectives of those with whom we cannot normally identify, in order to actually recognize how like us they really are—that is, as moral agents; autonomous decision-makers who are wired, like us, to seek to make an impact on the world. While some crime is committed by what used to be called psychopaths, but today are referred to as 'anti-social personalities,' the percentage of psychopaths in the general population is only about five percent (Ronson 2012). A psychopath cannot put himself in another's shoes, for he lacks the psychological capacity to do so, and this makes him very different to the rest of us. Not all psychopaths commit crimes, of course—or at least, not all get caught—and this means that most offenders are indeed people just like us, at least in the sense I am speaking of. This in turn means that somewhere, something has gone wrong for offenders, and their efforts to make an impact on their world in legal ways have failed, so they seek illegal means. Using our moral imaginations in thinking about criminal justice, then, means understanding the humanity and moral agency underlying every offender and would-be offender, as well as victims and those caught in the collateral damage of a crime. Criminal justice ethics requires that we be the kind of person who is disposed to using our moral imaginations in this way.

In this book, I will show you how to also use your moral imaginations to imagine yourselves into the perspectives of entire groups of people—this is the 'social' of social ethics. This is important for the study of criminal justice ethics because criminal justice professionals—police, lawyers, judges, social workers, youth workers, prison officers, and so on—face on a daily basis situations involving individuals or groups with whom they share little in the way of culture, history, language, age, race, and sexuality. Dealing with such situations requires that they use their moral imaginations to ensure that justice is done, and that people are treated fairly and equally under the law, even those to whom they feel antagonistic. Given the extent of prejudice in our society, this is much easier said than done. For this reason, we will be drawing on a lot of story-telling throughout this book, through the use of case studies and hypotheticals—true and invented stories of ethical dilemmas and situations that provide a rich context for comparing and contrasting ethical theories, personal and societal assumptions, and their practical applications.

How to use this book

This book is written as a process from theory to practice, and for that reason should be studied consecutively chapter by chapter. Part I conceptualizes the ethical project and explores some theoretical frameworks for discussing ethics. It then moves on to applying those theoretical concepts to ethical decision-making. Part II explores ethics in public life and how we move from the ethics of the personal to the ethics of the social. Part III specifically addresses criminal justice professionals, incorporating the discussions in Parts I and II, to assist in conceptualizing how the theoretical can be applied in more practical terms in criminal justice contexts.

Structure of the text

This text is divided into three sections or Parts. Part I defines ethics and morality and explores a range of ethics theories, their historical development and contemporary applications, and how they might be applied to everyday life. It provides insight into the different ways that people think about and resolve ethical dilemmas, and highlights the importance of appreciating other perspectives. Chapter 2 discusses the philosophical foundations of ethics and the nature of ethical dilemmas and provides an introduction to ethical theory. It explores ethical relativism, subjectivism and meta-ethics, and provides a brief overview of consequentialist and non-consequentialist theories. Chapter 3 explores consequentialist theories in more depth, with a particular focus on ethical egoism and utilitarianism. It draws on the work of historically well-known utilitarian philosophers such as Jeremy Bentham, John Stuart Mill, G. E. Moore, and Kenneth Arrow, and egoist theorists such as Friedrich Nietzsche and Ayn Rand. Examples of ethical dilemmas are drawn from seminal works by theorists such as Bernard Williams and J. J. C. Smart, as well as current events around the globe. Chapter 4 explores non-consequentialist theories in depth, focusing on deontology and virtue ethics. It draws on historically well-known deontological philosophers such as Immanuel Kant and John Rawls, and theorists of Virtue Ethics such as Aristotle, Alastair MacIntyre, and Philippa Foot. It also explores seminal ethical dilemmas posed by these philosophers, such as whether it is ever ethical to lie, steal, or kill. The theories outlined in Chapters 3 and 4 provide frameworks for ethical decision-making processes. It is essential that we are able to fully justify an ethical decision and defend a particular course of action against critique, not only by using these theories, but also by supporting our position with facts and logical arguments. Chapter 5 explores what constitutes critical thinking, how to assess the theories, and ethical discussion-making. It describes and explains deductive logic and three ethical decision-making methods: the Utilitarian Calculus, Noel Preston's Ethic of Response, and Stanley Benn's Rationalist Model.

Part II discusses the importance of maintaining a distinction between our private morality and the morality we express in public or as professionals. It also explores how society ought to be organized to produce the maximum benefit to its members. This is truly a question of *social* ethics, and is essential for justice professionals to consider, given that their professional activities encompass the realm of the social. Chapter 6 considers what characterizes the good society, and asks how our ability to choose between right and wrong might be affected by the kind of society in which we live. It examines how issues of individual moral responsibility are related to social responsibilities, as well as various understandings of how society should be organized. Chapter 7 describes the difference between procedural and distributive justice, then proceeds to focus on distributive justice and how it impacts our thinking about how to produce a just society. It compares various theoretical frameworks for considering justice, including libertarian, utilitarian, contractarian, and socialist perspectives. Chapter 8 discusses the various forms of justice that are sought in the application of the law, and applies the ethical theories in the context of achieving justice in the legal system. It also provides examples of how ethical issues, theories, and decisions play out in this context. It considers the relationship between justice and law, and the ways in which justice is sought through the law. This chapter also explores the concepts of natural rights and legal rights, due process and how it might be violated, and whether justice may be tempered by mercy. Finally, Chapter 9 compares and contrasts the adversarial and inquisitorial systems as a starting point for examining the relationship between law and morality. Moving from the procedures of the law and the way in which ethical perspectives are enshrined within them, this chapter considers the purposes of the law, and the ways in which the law expresses particular forms of morality. It also examines the historical influence of morality on the law and on society in general.

Part III examines ethical issues specific to a range of justice professions and institutions, including lawyers, policing, and punishment. Chapter 10 explores issues in public sector ethics, corruption and official misconduct. It examines ethical issues such as conflicts of interest, fraud and bribery, and the cultural characteristics of organizations that foster corruption. This chapter explores the notions of public trust and public good, how corruption occurs and strategies for prevention. It also examines Whistleblower legislation and application and the development of official codes of conduct. Chapter 11 explores issues in legal ethics and the legal profession. Traditionally, legal professionals have been subject to higher standards of conduct than most other professionals, for example, by being subject to stringent admission requirements such as requiring full disclosure of any criminal history including even minor traffic offences (Thomas 2006). Nevertheless, the legal profession is fraught with ethical dilemmas. Issues such as client confidentiality, duties owed to the court, duties owed to clients, conflicts of duty and negligence will be covered in this chapter. Comparisons will be made between professional practice in Australia, the UK, Canada, and the USA. Chapter 12 focuses on the role of police in the criminal justice system and discusses the ethical issues related to policing. Police bear an important and demanding duty: to protect the community against crime. It is often said that they are the 'thin blue line' between order and chaos. Police officers are permitted certain powers that other 'regular' citizens do not possess so that they can carry out their job. They are able to detain, question and charge citizens if they are suspected of committing a crime. This chapter explores the ethical issues facing law enforcement officers, comparing and contrasting how various jurisdictions in Western countries deal with corruption and misconduct. It also examines police oversight and the impact of independent oversight bodies on levels of corruption and misconduct. Finally, Chapter 14 summarizes the main themes of the text and identifies future directions for theoretical, empirical and professional work.

I have tried to lay the chapters out in a way that is easily accessible. A list of keywords and concepts is provided at the beginning of each chapter, definitions are highlighted, and case studies and hypotheticals appear in boxes for easy identification. Key phrases and sentences are also highlighted throughout and linked to the review questions at the end of each chapter. In this way you can quickly find the answers to the review questions, which will help scaffold your learning for the next chapter. In addition, weekly test questions are provided on the companion website, along with summaries and further resources. It is hoped that this journey into your moral imagination will prove both illuminating and fruitful.

References

Bromwich, David (2014) *Moral Imagination*. Princeton: Princeton University Press.

Mills, C. Wright (1957) *The Sociological Imagination*. Oxford: Oxford University Press.

Ronson, John (2012) *The Psychopath Test: a journey through the madness industry*. London: Picador Trade.

Thomas, Mark (2006). Legal Ethics: regulation of the legal profession. In S. Hayes, N. Stobbs, and M. Lauchs (Eds.) *Social Ethics for Legal and Justice Professionals*. Sydney: Pearson Education, pp. 43–58.

Warner Brothers (2009) *The Invention of Lying*. Directed by Ricky Gervais and Matthew Robinson.

Part I

Ethical theory

Part I explores the major ethical theories, their historical development, and contemporary applications. It gives you insight into the different ways that people think about and resolve ethical dilemmas, and highlights the importance of appreciating other perspectives.

Chapter 2

What is ethics?

Key terms: moral judgments; ethical theory; social ethics; ethical dilemma; justified belief; theory of knowledge; role of the media; meta-ethics; normative ethics; applied ethics

Introduction

Ethics is the study of right and wrong; that is, what is the right thing to do in a given situation. Ethics is often conflated with the notion of morality, and often the two terms are used interchangeably to mean the same thing. There is, however, some difference between them. When we use the term 'morality' we are usually talking about social mores or personal convictions about certain kinds of behavior that people in a society should engage in. In other words, morality is a set of beliefs about what is good and bad—for example, being pro-choice or pro-life in the abortion debate, or whether you support gay marriage or freedom of speech. Ethics, on the other hand, is a set of rules or guidelines for a particular group or class of actions, which are usually codified either formally or conventionally. 'Medical ethics,' for example, describes the set of rules and guidelines for doctors when dealing with patients in their care. Similarly, 'criminal justice ethics' describes the set of rules and guidelines justice professionals must adhere to when performing their official roles. Ethics requires that we sometimes put aside our personal morality in order to conform to our professional code of conduct. If a nurse is anti-abortion, for example, he or she is still ethically required to attend to a patient in their care who has had an abortion. Similarly, if a teacher is homophobic, they must put aside their personal views and treat lesbian, gay, bisexual, transgender, and intersex (LGBTI) students the same as any other student. However, life is not always so clear-cut, even if we do have ethical rules and guidelines.

For example, lying is generally unacceptable in most societies—except perhaps for those little white lies discussed in Chapter 1. However, I could find myself in a situation where I have to make a choice between lying and, say, saving a life. Imagine, for example, finding yourself in a situation where you are held at gunpoint and asked to reveal the whereabouts of a close friend who owes money to your attacker. Do you reveal your friend's whereabouts or do you lie in the hope that you will put the attacker off track? Does it depend on the situation? Or are there rules that we can draw on when making such decisions? The study of ethics reveals several competing ideas about how we should go about making decisions when confronted by such 'ethical dilemmas.' Most of the ethical dilemmas we confront in our everyday lives are far less demanding than our example, however. Dilemmas might arise in the form of such mundane problems as deciding whether or not to take a 'sickie,' or whether to run a red light. In the following two chapters we will explore four ethical theories, comparing and contrasting them to ascertain whether we can, indeed, find an ethical basis for making such decisions.

Apart from guiding individuals' actions, ethics also has a broader application. Before we can understand what a code of ethics is, we must understand the underlying theory and assumptions that dictate them. Since before the first millennia of the common era, philosophers were proposing rules for living ethically in society. In Plato's *Republic*, which was written in 360 BCE, Thrasymachus argues that justice will always be in the interests of the mighty few who are strong enough and capable enough to rule over other weaker members of society. Glaucon, on the other hand, suggests that the role of justice is to keep good order, and that all we need do is get together as a group and agree on a set of rules that everyone can live by. Socrates rejects both stances, arguing that ethical principles underlying justice can be drawn from universal objective standards. Many contemporary philosophers also theorize why certain sets of principles and guidelines should be applied over others, and whether they should apply universally. As we shall see in the following chapters, while there is no neat delineation between them, they tend to fall into two camps—consequentialism and non-consequentialism. Chapter 3 discusses the first, while Chapter 4 explores the second.

Personal moral judgments are also underpinned by one or another ethical theory, though most people have not and probably will never reflect on, or learn what theory or theories they live by. Nevertheless, we have to live in a particular society; we have to live and associate with other people in our everyday lives at work and at home. Ethical theories provide a useful framework for understanding why people have different perspectives. As mentioned in Chapter 1, ethics requires that we put ourselves in another's shoes, at least where our professional role is concerned, but arguably also in our personal relationships as well as in how we relate to others in the broader social context. 'Social ethics' is a set of rules or guidelines for deciding how society should be structured in the fairest and most morally defensible and just manner. We will discuss the notion of social ethics further in Part II. For now, though, we will concentrate on some key ethical concepts before moving on to discuss consequentialism and non-consequentialism.

Meta-ethics, normative ethics, and applied ethics

Ethics is commonly divided into three categories: meta-ethics, normative ethics, and applied ethics. While meta-ethics studies the origin and meaning of ethical theories and concepts, normative ethics "involves arriving at moral standards that regulate right and wrong conduct" (Fieser 2006). Applied ethics works to consider the application of ethical theory to real-life ethical dilemmas (Fieser 2006).

The term 'meta' means 'abstract higher level analysis,' so the term 'meta-ethics' refers to an abstract higher level analysis of ethical concepts (Sayer-McCord 2012). Normative ethics provides a prescription for action—in other words, it tells us what we should do in a given situation, or provides a list of rules to guide our behavior. The theories covered in the following two chapters are normative theories. So, while normative ethics tries to answer the question, "What should I do?," meta-ethics asks questions such as "What is goodness?" or "How can we tell right from wrong?" or even "What is truth?" (Sayer-McCord 2012). The discussion about truth in Chapter 1 is a relatively simple meta-ethical analysis of the concept. Applied ethics, as the name suggests, applies the normative ethical theories and assumptions of ethics to real life, most often in the form of professional ethics, such as medical ethics and criminal justice ethics. Such applications generally lead to the construction of codes of ethics and codes of conduct. A code of ethics is a statement of values, while a code of conduct specifies what conduct is acceptable and what is not. Sometimes a combination of both is used, as in the Queensland public sector, which has outlined its code of ethics and guidelines for ethical conduct by public officials in the *Public Sector Ethics Act 1994 (Qld)*. The values espoused therein include "integrity and impartiality," "promoting the public good," "commitment to the system of government," and "accountability and transparency." It then specifies how public sector agencies are to apply these values in preparing codes of conduct, as well as what the general content of a code of conduct should contain.

Many people, including academics, think that applied ethics is the only useful form of ethics. However, ethical values such as those outlined in the Queensland legislation must be based upon some theoretical understanding of ethics, or at the very least they can be shown to illustrate a particular ethical viewpoint. We will examine in more detail how this happens in Chapter 10. In the meantime, let us examine some key meta-ethical concepts.

What do we mean by 'right' and 'wrong'?

There are two senses in which we can say something is right. There is a practical sense and a moral sense. Let me use the example of abortion to explain. If you tell me you want children, I could say that having an abortion is not the right thing to do. "If you want kids, don't have an abortion" makes common sense. In the moral sense, however, if I say, "It's never right to have an abortion," I am making a moral judgment about what I think you should do, because it covers all contexts, not just the specific context in which you in particular want to have children—as opposed to someone else who might not. These quite different meanings of "right" serve very different purposes. Nevertheless, many people get them mixed up.

Social ethics is about moral judgments that we make as a society or world, about how our society or world should be structured—how the system should be structured, how the citizens who participate within that system ought to act, how different groups of individuals should be treated within the system, in various situations. This is very important for every person who lives in the society, because we all belong to various groups—ethnic, racial, gender, sexuality, age, ability, and so on, but also any of the various types of workplaces, places of education, and places of worship. There are certain general principles which most people in Western society would agree were the right principles to live by—do not kill, steal or cheat, for example—but there is a lot of grey area around many other aspects of our daily lives, many of which we, as a society, find it difficult to agree upon. In this book, then, you will encounter a lot of grey areas—issues that you will find difficult to solve. This book provides no right answers to those difficult questions, but it will equip you to approach ethical dilemmas and other aspects of moral judgments in an informed and fruitful way.

Sometimes it is obvious what is the right thing to do in a given situation—do not steal, for example. Stealing is against the law, and it is fairly obvious that we should not engage in any illegal activities (except perhaps under extraordinary circumstances—more on this later). But what about cheating on your girlfriend, or 'trolling' someone you don't like on Twitter? Or running a red light because it is three o'clock in the morning and there is no one else around? These are the kinds of ethical dilemmas we encounter in everyday life. We do not often stop to think about our response, but the fact is that the way we respond tells a lot about who we are as an individual.

Activity 2.1: Ethical dilemmas in everyday life

Think about your recent experience. Can you remember one or two instances when such an ethical issue cropped up? For example, were you given too much change at the grocery store? What did you do? Take a moment to write down your answers.

Whose truth, whose justice?

There is another important meta-ethical question we should ask before we plunge ourselves into discussions about ethical dilemmas and theories, and that is: who sets the moral agenda? Who decides at the macro level how society should be organized? Our initial answer would probably be 'politicians' and, by extension, the people who vote for them. However, a more thorough examination of this issue reveals that there are many other players in the organizational game. The media, for example, play a huge part in deciding what information comes to our attention and how we interpret that information. When you read a story in a newspaper, you are getting one perspective on the events in the story. If you read an article in *The Guardian* or *The Australian*, for example, you will be exposed to one perspective, but if you read the same story in the *Daily Mail* or the *Telegraph*, you will undoubtedly read something quite different. Similarly, the *New York Times* will report on a political decision in one way, while *USA Today* will present it most likely in a completely contrary manner. The media tell us what news is happening, but they are necessarily selective, so when a headline appears on the front page of a newspaper, it is telling us what its editors think is most important today. When we look at the media, then, we must ourselves be carefully selective about what we take from their perspective. As we move through the chapters of this book, we will be looking at media articles, news clips, advertisements, popular culture, and social media as a way of understanding the nature of competing perspectives, with a view to trying to understand who sets our moral agenda. In this way, you will learn to evaluate differing perspectives without necessarily taking on any of them, and eventually deciding on your own perspective as informed readers.

What can we know?

Understanding differing perspectives and deciding which, if any, to adopt requires a lot of rational thinking. As rational individuals, we believe certain things to be true based on a variety of factors, including factual evidence, experience, perception, hearsay, logic, and faith. An ideally rational person— that is, an individual who has perfect reasoning capacity coupled with perfect knowledge of the facts and foresight into the future—will always know the truth about any given situation or phenomenon. However, real individuals such as ourselves are neither particularly good reasoners, nor do we ever have 'all the facts.' The most we can do is develop a belief based on our best (flawed) judgment, given the available evidence and other relevant beliefs that we already have. What this means is that the 'truth' on which our beliefs rest may be shaky at best, or at worst, completely misguided. How can we make decisions about what to do if we will never have a sound basis for making decisions?

To see how someone is justified in holding a particular belief will better help us to understand how that person might rationally act on that belief, or at least how that person might be rationally committed to acting on that belief, even if it is based on misguided notions of the facts. Theories of justified belief are typically located within a broader theory of knowledge, in which, for example, we would be able to determine what it means for a person to actually *know* something, as opposed to simply believing it. If a person has a particular belief—let us say, for example, a belief that it is raining in New York—she necessarily assumes it is true. Yet if her belief is based on mistaken evidence—for example, yesterday's forecast rather than today's, which says New York has clear skies—she does not *know* that it is raining in New York, despite having a justified belief that it is raining.

A distinction needs to be made between a theory of knowledge and a theory of truth. Whereas a theory of knowledge purports to tell us how a person knows it is (to carry on our example) raining in New York, a theory of truth explicates what the truth about today's weather in New York amounts to. Stanley Benn maintained that rational individuals are disposed to seek coherence in their system of beliefs. He claims that, "a disposition to consistency is, in general, a condition for understanding and dealing efficiently with the world" (Benn 1986: 20). It is basic to the forming and executing of projects for rational believers that they pursue consistency in their beliefs. What this means is that, if an individual is faced with an inconsistency in her beliefs or actions, she would be regarded as irrational if she chose to ignore the inconsistency rather than reconsidering the contradictory beliefs. Similarly, when someone is deciding which course of action to take, she considers appropriate alternatives and what reasons she might have for choosing one over the other. As long as we maintain consistency among our beliefs, we are acting rationally. But this means that it is perfectly reasonable—indeed, it is highly probable—that we often act on untrue beliefs.

If at least some of my beliefs are not based on factual evidence, how do I know that what I believe is true and that beliefs that contradict mine are false? If I believe I know the truth, and you believe you know the truth, then who is right? As you work through this book you will learn to recognize that one person's 'truth' is not necessarily the same as another's, and how to determine what is true for you. This is not to argue for a 'relativist' view of ethics by any means; rather, it is to recognize that, often, moral agendas are set according to a particular set of beliefs that might not cohere with everyone, or even the majority. But it is important to find an answer to "How can we ever know what the truth is?" If we cannot know how to find the truth of a matter, how can we ever arrive at a solution to an ethical dilemma? Obviously, we all have beliefs and many of them probably differ, so how do we decide? In his Nobel Prize speech in 1970, Russian author Alexander Solzhenitsyn remarked that, "one word of truth outweighs the entire world." Truth is so hard to pin down for us mere mortals that any grain of truth or fact that can be established beyond any doubt must be worth a million worlds. Indeed, truth seems so hard to find that some people, including many academics, have declared that it cannot be found, no matter what we do. To these people, truth is dependent upon the reality perceived by each person.

And this does seem to make sense. For example, when I look at Van Gogh's *Irises* (see Figure 2.1), I see beauty and sadness, because there is one lonely white iris in a bed of otherwise beautiful blue irises. To me the painting creatively reflects the tortured life of the artist and this, along with its technical excellence and beauty, makes it very valuable and highly prized. To my friend

Figure 2.1 Van Gogh's *Irises*

Jerry, however, the painting is just a bunch of flowers that could easily be replaced by any number of still life paintings by artists at the local market. In fact, Jerry says that what I really mean when I say the painting is beautiful and valuable, is simply that I like it. "I think it's boring and ugly," he states categorically. What do you think? Figure 2.2 provides a more mundane example.

I firmly believe that toilet paper should always be hung like the roll on the right. The roll on the left is just wrong. First of all, with the roll on the right there will be less sheet overhang after tearing off, not to mention the one-handed sheet tear-off issue, which is much easier to do with the roll on the right as well. One-handed tearing of the roll on the left will always end up leaving a long trail of paper on the ground (if you do not believe me, see the science of loo paper hanging provided by Essential Life Lessons (2005)—or try it for yourself). Of course, many of you will not care which way the toilet paper hangs. The hanging of toilet paper is not a moral issue (well, actually, it is in my house), but the point is that people disagree about things all the time. And the things we disagree about might be really important, such as whether abortion should be legalized, or euthanasia, or the death penalty. These are huge issues because lives (or potential lives) are at stake, so we must be careful in undertaking how we decide what is right. The following chapters will help

Wrong   Right

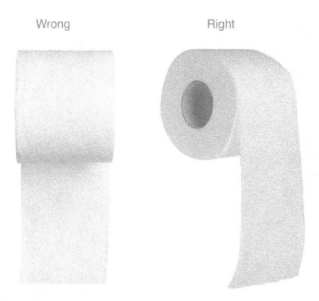

Figure 2.2 Toilet rolls

you to understand that we do not necessarily need to find the truth to achieve justice or to act ethically.

Dead white philosophers

In this book, I am going to be mentioning a lot of (what I call) "dead, white guys." Unfortunately, these are the only ones that history has recorded as the most important philosophers and ethicists from the last two millennia or so. I do my best to provide alternative perspectives where possible, but most of these are more recent and less influential in some senses. Basically, the big-name philosophers *are* dead, white males. But before we get into that, here is a famous example of differing perspectives from sport—baseball, in fact. In the game of baseball, as you are probably aware, there are balls and there are strikes, and a count records the number of balls and strikes for any one batter. The referee calls the points, and in this example, there are three referees, each of which has a different perspective on the topic.

Ref. 1:   There's balls and there's strikes and I call them the way they are.

Ref. 2:   There's balls and there's strikes and I call 'em as I see 'em.

Ref. 3:   There's balls and there's strikes and they ain't nothin' 'til I call 'em.

(Caton 2012)

Ref. 1 is really saying, "I'm the umpire, you hit a ball or a strike, I see what it is and I identify it"—in other words, he is saying that he calls what actually exists. Ref. 2, on the other hand, infers that it depends on his interpretation—it is his perspective that decides the call. Finally, Ref. 3 argues that balls and strikes are actually created by his calling of them. This example shows that although we might all be playing the same game, how very differently many of us think the game is being played. An important question when it comes to ethics is: can we decide what is ethical if we are not all on the same page—that is, have the same understanding and interpretation? Ref. 3 is arguing that we make our own reality, that truth is a social construction, and that we create reality by naming something.

Activity 2.2: How do you look at things?

Everyone has a particular way of looking at things, and most people have beliefs, which they obviously regard as true. Talk to some friends or family members and find some issues on which you disagree. Look at both sides of the argument. Can you justify your viewpoint? Can they?

Perhaps it is not a case of "is it true?" but rather, "whose truth is it?" When we read an article in the media, what we are actually reading is an account of events with a particular spin. We need to look past that to form our own viewpoint. In the fourth century BCE, Plato told a fable called "The Allegory of the Cave" (Plato 2009). The story likens the general population to prisoners in a cave. The prisoners are chained so that they are faced away from the mouth of the cave and they cannot move their heads to look around. Behind them is a fire that lights up the cave, and puppeteers move around the fire casting shadows on the wall of the cave for the prisoners to see. When one sees the shadow of a book, he calls it "book," but it is not really a book, it is just a shadow. We are, says Plato, just like the prisoners in that we name things around us, but often what we name is just a shadow, not the real thing. The prisoners think the shadows are reality, just as we might think a description of events in the newspaper is reality. We read a story and think A is A and B is B, when in reality, the story is just one person's perspective of the events. Shadows can be distorted, just like our perceptions. In the allegory, one prisoner is freed and when he turns around and walks out of the cave, at first he is overwhelmed by the light, but once his eyes adjust he can finally see things as they really are. Similarly, until we learn to open our eyes and understand how reality is created through different perspectives, we too will be fooled. As you start to work through this book, your heads might hurt (just like the freed prisoner) with all the theoretical and conceptual material in the next few chapters. Do not worry—again like the freed prisoner, your thinking will eventually adjust to them and you will gain a better understanding of ethics and ethical theory, and learn to become more critical of what is presented to you as truth.

Nazi military leader, Joseph Goebbels once said, "We do not talk to say something, but to obtain a certain effect" (Ellul 1973). I think this is fairly representative of most people. We all manipulate our self-images; we all want to appear in a certain way, to present a certain type of image. People can manipulate the truth in various ways, depending on how they want to present it to you or what it is they want you to know. The adversarial legal system is a good example of this. Is a barrister's goal to establish the truth or to win the case? While these two goals are not necessarily mutually exclusive, the main goal of course is to win the case. A client might tell his lawyer that he is guilty, but choose to plead not guilty. Lawyers are legally bound by confidentiality rules that prevent them from revealing anything a client says that the client wishes to remain confidential. So in this system, the lawyer's duty is not to establish the facts of the case; rather, it is to represent the client's case to the best of his or her ability. This is not necessarily a bad thing, and we will discuss the implications of various legal systems in more detail in Chapters 8 and 11. Meanwhile, it serves to illustrate that, in our society, powers of persuasion are often more valued than the facts.

Many philosophers believe that we can arrive at the truth through reason, and we will be discussing some of those in the next few chapters. Immanuel Kant, for example, believed that the truth is objective—it is something that exists 'out there'—and it is our purpose to discover it. Most religions are based on this assumption, though they generally rely on the writings of a divine being to help guide them toward enlightenment, but even atheists and agnostics often believe this is so. I want to challenge this view—not to condemn it as wrong necessarily, but to challenge you to question and to debate important issues, rather than simply taking them as given because some expert said so. Another corollary of the argument that the truth is out there, is that there is a definitive right and wrong thing to do in a given situation.

Activity 2.3: What do you think?

Take the following quiz and find out. Do you believe that:

1 no one has the right to judge what is right or wrong for another person?
2 no one has the right to intervene when they think someone has done something morally wrong?
3 it is hopeless to try to arrive at a final answer to ethical questions?
4 there is one and only one right standard of moral evaluation?
5 what is right depends upon which culture you are in?

(Hinman 2005)

If you answered 'yes' to questions 1, 2, 3 and 5, and 'no' to question 4, you are likely a moral relativist. The next section will explain what moral relativism is, along with some other essential terms in ethics.

Moral relativism and subjectivism

There are many forms of relativism, but its basic premises are threefold. First, relativists argue that there are no moral truths—rather, something is judged as ethical relative to a particular viewpoint. Second, there are many such viewpoints. Finally, no viewpoints are privileged above others (Westacott 2005). The relativist argues that just because this is the case, we should all decide what is right for ourselves and refrain from judging others. You might be thinking that the foregoing discussion leads directly to relativism, because it all depends upon perspectives. However, that is not necessarily what I am arguing. What I have tried to demonstrate is that we are faced daily with many variations of the truth, and we need to sift through the evidence carefully in order to form our own opinions. Such a stance does not infer that we must all be relativists; rather, it just means that getting to the facts or the truth might be more difficult than we at first believe.

Moral subjectivism is slightly different to relativism, although the two are often confused. The subjectivist also claims that there are no universal moral truths. However, where the relativist argues that morality is judged relative to a particular viewpoint, the subjectivist states that no viewpoint is moral—there just is no morality. Moral rules are mere inventions (Mackie 1977). As a theory, subjectivism has three versions—linguistic, conceptual, and ontological. The linguistic version states that what is right or wrong simply reflects our feelings about the issue. From this view, "X is unethical" is reflected in the sentence "I don't like X." The conceptual version of the theory states that all ethical rules are constructed by people, are inherently arbitrary, and that we therefore have no obligation to abide by them. Finally, the ontological version states that there are no such things as objective rules. People can agree on standards, but they are not objective in the sense of being some truth that exists in the world that we have uncovered or brought to light. The term 'ontological' just refers to 'what exists.' However, for our purposes we need only understand the subjectivist claim that there is no such thing as morality, and that what we take to be morality is really just a set of rules we agreed to abide by.

Case Study: *Breaking Bad*[1]

Walter White is a high school science teacher somewhere in the US Midwest. One day he finds out he has inoperable and incurable cancer. Worried about his wife and children and how they will make ends meet without him,

(continued)

(continued)

he decides to go into partnership with an ex-student to produce Crystal Methamphetamine—or Crystal Meth—an illegal but highly sought after recreational drug. Apparently Walter makes the best Crystal Meth in town and very soon he is in great demand and makes a lot of money. He uses the money to help his family and to help pay for his medical bills.

A relativist might argue that Walter's behavior was ethical if it did not hurt anyone else, and that it is nobody's business whether other people take recreational drugs. People should be allowed to do whatever they want—who are we to tell others what to do with their lives? It could be argued, in fact, that what Walter did was a good thing because it helped out his family, as well as the drug users he sold to. A subjectivist might argue that what Walter does in his spare time is none of our business and that if you are personally against recreational drug use, then that is your decision, but keep others out of it. On the other hand, because subjectivists believe that there is no morality, they could argue that we could have laws against recreational drugs as long as everybody agreed to it. Subjectivists, then, do not agree that one person's viewpoint is as good as any other's, as does the relativist.

The problem with relativism is that it has an essential flaw. If relativism is true, then why would we ever care about what other people think about us?—and yet we do! Why would anyone be motivated to pursue science or beauty or achievement of any kind? While we might concede that some things are relative—beauty, perhaps, or a taste for chocolate—clearly there is an issue with inferring that from some relative things we can deduce that all is relative. Indeed, it has been argued that relativism is a 'slippery slope,' one that will eventually cause us to lose faith in everything we once believed in (Gibson n.d.). While subjectivism might still result in workable systems of rules for ordering society, relativism appears to have no real practical application. Relativism is also internally inconsistent, because it would be perfectly logical to say that if relativism is true, then relativism itself might be relative.

Conclusion

Now that your head is spinning from all this theoretical discussion, we will move on to look at some ethical theories that are workable. The following chapters are divided into three modules. The rest of Part I discusses ethical theories with a view to providing some conceptual frameworks for making ethical decisions. It explores the four major ethical theories, their historical development and contemporary applications. It will provide insight into the different ways that people think about and resolve ethical dilemmas, and highlight further the importance of appreciating other perspectives.

Part II discusses ethics in public life. It examines the importance of maintaining a distinction between our private morality and the morality we express in public or as professionals. It also explores how society ought to be organized to produce the maximum benefit to its members. This is truly a question of *social* ethics, and is essential for justice professionals to consider, given that their professional activities surround the very idea of justice.

Part III examines ethical issues specific to a range of justice professions and institutions, including the legal profession, policing, and punishment.

Review questions

1　Discuss Walter White's behavior in the *Breaking Bad* example. Can he justify his illegal activity in any way?
2　An ethical dilemma often involves a problem in which the person facing the dilemma feels 'torn' between two or more courses of action. What is special or unusual about ethical dilemmas compared to other kinds of dilemmas that we face and resolve every day?
3　What is the difference between ethics and morality?
4　What is the difference between meta-ethics and normative ethics?
5　Do a Google search of 'ethics' and see what you can come up with. What competing definitions can you find of the term 'ethics'? Do any of them differ from the explanation and definition provided in this chapter? Which do you like the best and why?
6　What kind of viewpoint would you have if you were a subjectivist?
7　What is an amoral point of view? Give an example.
8　Find an article on the same story or event in two or more different newspapers/sites and examine how they differ in telling the story. What is the emphasis for each? What impression do you get?
9　What is a 'justified belief'? What happens when people hold different beliefs that conflict with one another? For example, I believe chocolate is good for me, but I also believe it will make me put on weight, which is bad for me.
10　Keep a diary for a day of all the ethical dilemmas you come across, either in your own experience, in the media, or otherwise. How many did you identify? Did the exercise change the way you think about ethics?

Note

1　*Breaking Bad* is a US television crime drama series produced by Vince Gilligan, 2008–2013. High Bridge Entertainment and Gran Via Productions, Albuquerque, New Mexico.

References

Benn, Stanley I. (1986). Persons and Values: reasons in conflict and moral disagreement. *Ethics*, 95(1): 20–37.

Caton, Karuna (2012). *The Misleading Mind*. New World Library.

Ellul, Jacques (1973). *Propaganda: the formation of men's attitudes*. Translated by Konrad Kellen & Jean Lerner. New York: Vintage Books.

Essential Life Lessons (2005). *Lesson 1: Over is Right, Under is Wrong*. Available at http://currentconfig.com/2005/02/22/essential-life-lesson-1-over-is-right-under-is-wrong/ (accessed June 27, 2014).

Fieser, J. (2006). *Internet Encyclopedia of Philosophy: ethics*. Available at http://www.iep.utm.edu/e/ethics.htm#H2 (accessed June 27, 2014).

Gibson, Peter (n.d.). *The Problem of Moral Relativism*. Available at www.philosophyideas.com (accessed February 19, 2014).

Hinman, Lawrence (2005) *Ethics Updates*. Available at http://ethics.sandiego.edu/ (accessed September 11, 2014).

Mackie, J. L. (1977). *Inventing Right and Wrong*. London: Penguin.

Plato (2009). *The Republic*. Translated by Benjamin Jowett. Available at http://classics.mit.edu/Plato/republic.html.

Sayer-McCord, Geoffrey (2012). Metaethics. *The Stanford Encyclopedia of Philosophy*. Available at http://plato.stanford.edu/entries/metaethics? (accessed June 27, 2014).

Westacott, Emrys (2005). Relativism. *The Internet Encyclopedia of Philosophy*. Available at http://www.iep.utm.edu/relativi/ (accessed October 25, 2014).

Chapter 3

Consequentialism

Key terms: consequentialism; utilitarianism; egoism; selfless good deed; intrinsic value; instrumental value; hedons and dolors; utilitarian calculus

Introduction

Consequentialism is a class of ethical theories that seek to make ethical decisions based on the best outcome; that is, they seek to *maximize* the outcome. The consequentialist argues that the outcome often justifies the means used to achieve it, so in order to make the right decision about what to do, we must carefully consider all the possible outcomes for each action, and then do the action that gives us the best outcome. If, for example, I were trying to decide whether to give $20 to a large global charity, or spend it on beer, I would be required to think about the outcome of each action. What outcome will it have for the charity if I donate $20? Obviously it would be a good thing for them, and I would also benefit by feeling good about myself. On the other hand, I could argue that $20 is not going to make much difference to a big organization such as theirs, while I would certainly feel pretty good about drinking some beer. If it were also my birthday, then that surely would weigh the odds in favor of beer, wouldn't it? After all, a birthday deserves a celebration! The problem is, deciding which outcome is the best is not always as easy as this simple example. In this chapter we will explore two consequentialist theories, each of which differ in how they go about choosing the best outcome. The second theory discussed, ethical egoism, maintains that the only ethical method of decision-making is to put one's own self-interest first. However, the theory we will discuss first, utilitarianism, argues that we should choose the best outcome *for all concerned*. That means that there might be times when we have to put aside our own personal interests to achieve a better outcome. But would such behavior be required—that is, morally obligatory—or would it be classed as a selfless good deed—a nice thing to do, but beyond what is morally required? The main task of this and the following chapter (Chapter 4) is to critically analyze each of the theories in order to determine whether there might be times when in fact we are morally required to put aside our own personal interests in making ethical decisions.

So, is there such a thing as a selfless good deed? An episode of the 1990s television series, *Friends*, asks that very question. In the episode, Phoebe believes in good deeds, while Joey adamantly disagrees (Curtis 1998). Joey is hired by PBS television for a telethon, but instead of being the host, he is asked to answer phones. Prior to going on the show, Joey and Phoebe argue about whether Joey doing the telethon is a good deed. Phoebe accuses him of just wanting to be on TV, arguing that it is just selfishness masked as a good deed. In return, Joey points out that there *are* no good deeds—that *everyone* acts selfishly. He says that even Phoebe's acting as surrogate for her brother's triplets was selfish because it made her happy. Phoebe decides to prove that there is such a thing as a good deed. She makes various attempts without success then, suddenly inspired, she donates $200 to Joey's telethon. Phoebe hates PBS and says that, therefore, donating to their telethon is proof of a good deed. But her donation leads to a new record in donations, which gets Joey recognized and finally on TV. But this makes Phoebe happy, so she is foiled again!

When I asked my first year Social Ethics class whether they thought there was such a thing as a good deed, they came up with some interesting suggestions. Here are some of them:

1 organ donation;
2 volunteer work for a charity;
3 voluntarily going to war as a soldier;
4 working overtime and not getting paid for it;
5 looking after someone disabled.

Last semester one student even suggested that sex-slaves were selfless—but I am pretty sure they do get something out of that! Let us look at each of these seemingly selfless good deeds and see what we come up with.

Organ donation certainly seems selfless. We could be saving someone's life by donating some or all of our organs, which in itself need not be selfless, since presumably we would be already dead, making our self-interests a moot point. Nevertheless, perhaps you or your family have a personal or religious preference for keeping your body intact post-mortem. It is for this reason that we are required to give consent to organ donation—in our society we respect an individual's wishes concerning arrangements for the disposal of their body after death. But does giving consent constitute a selfless good deed? Considering that we will cease to be consciously aware after our death, it could be argued that giving consent while alive is relatively easy and does not require a great deal—if any—sacrifice, so as a general rule, the answer would probably be "no." However, there might be certain extenuating circumstances where the answer might still be "yes." Imagine a situation where an Orthodox Jewish woman called Anna has been given a diagnosis of inoperable, terminal cancer with only weeks to live. As time goes by, she gets her affairs in order and prepares to be taken to hospital as her illness begins causing her much pain.

While in hospital, Anna is placed in a ward with another woman who has had multiple heart attacks, and is in dire need of a transplant. Although she believes it is against her religion to do so, Anna takes pity on her roommate, who is otherwise comparatively young and strong and would survive with the transplant. She secretly signs a consent form for organ donation before slowly losing consciousness and dying a few days later.

Is Anna acting selflessly in consenting to donate her organs? Considering she is dying, going against her religion for the sake of saving another is completely irreversible—she will have no opportunity to repent or seek absolution after the event and she will no doubt cause much pain to her family and religious compatriots. It seems that Anna's act might be a selfless good deed.

What about volunteering for a charity, say, to help disabled individuals one afternoon a week? It would depend on what your motivation was—if you were doing it for work experience or because you felt obligated, then it would not be selfless, but if you were genuinely empathic, seeking to better the lives of others rather than relax and enjoy yourself in some other way, then it might. Again there are many possible extenuating circumstances, motivations, and outcomes. Some people who volunteer might be selfless while others might not. However, there is one argument that always seems to rear its ugly head when talk about selfless deeds is being tossed around. And it is no surprise that after some discussion, my students came to it.

That argument says that we are all motivated to perform good deeds by feeling good, getting respect, or for some other personal 'benefit.' Eighteenth-century Scottish philosopher, David Hume, made this argument famous, widely claiming to be skeptical of the ability to make ethical decisions based on reason (and a good many other things) in his *Treatise on Human Nature* (1739). For Hume, "moral distinctions are derived from the moral sentiments: feelings of approval (esteem, praise) and disapproval (blame) felt by spectators who contemplate a character trait or action" (Cohon 2010). In other words, Hume argued that morality is not based on reason, but rather on our sentiments or emotions. Thus, we only ever act ethically because we want to feel good and/or avoid pain, and there can therefore be no selfless good deeds.

Have you ever done something for somebody that you really, really did not want to do? For example, a 4 a.m. drop-off at the airport? Not many people would prefer to be driving than sleeping at 4 a.m., which means that the act of driving someone to the airport at that time certainly constitutes a good deed—but is it selfless? Perhaps the person is your partner or child and you are worried about their safety, or perhaps you are too cheap to spring for a cab. In either case, you have an ulterior motive. David Hume suggests that all action is intended to satisfy some desire (1739). Let us look at some of the other things that we do for others which, if given the option, we would rather not, to see if we can prove him wrong.

What if, for example, someone who clearly does not speak your language stops you in the street and by showing you a name on a card, asks you for directions. You are in a hurry to get to the train station on time but you find it so difficult to make yourself understood that you end up walking with them to where they need to go, consequently missing your train. Would that be a self-less good deed? Hume, of course, would say we are merely seeking the visitor's approval, or trying to avoid feeling guilty, or perhaps we will use the situation to prove how nice we are to our significant other. However, this method of always reducing every action to sentiment or emotion is not helpful because human behavior, motivation, and reason are extremely sophisticated processes. Simply reducing them to one very minor human characteristic is to ignore the rich complexity of our human character.

Utilitarianism

Could it be that the 'feeling good' bit is just a by-product of the action, at least in some cases? This line of thought is interesting because consequentialists argue that the most important thing in life is to create happiness, but as mentioned above, at least one form of consequentialism—called utilitarianism—requires that we sometimes sacrifice our own happiness to achieve a greater benefit for others. In general, consequentialists believe that people tend to be self-interested. However, they differ over how society should best be organized to achieve the best outcomes for individuals. Utilitarians argue that the best way to organize society is to create the greatest benefit for the greatest number of people, which means that individual preferences will be overridden on a regular basis. Egoists, on the other hand, argue that society is far better off if every person looks out for themselves—that is, left to pursue our own interests in the best way we can, we are bound to achieve the best results for each individual.

Hypothetical: lost at sea

Imagine you and four other people are lost at sea in a lifeboat for 20 days, no food, only a little tiny amount of water . . . What do you do? Someone suggests that it might be better if at least some of you survive rather than all of you perish, and that perhaps killing and eating one or more passengers would be the thing to do. Do you kill and eat the weakest or the oldest or the sickest person so that the rest of you can survive?

Interestingly, this scenario actually happened, though not with a boat. In October of 1972 a Uruguayan aircraft was carrying forty passengers including a rugby team from Montevideo in Uruguay, to Santiago, Chile, when it crashed into a mountain in the Andes. Sixteen passengers died in the initial crash or very shortly thereafter, and another eight also lost their lives in an avalanche a few days later. The sixteen remaining survivors managed to stay alive for over two months by eating the flesh of the dead passengers. Eventually, two of the group trekked ten days across the mountain to seek help, and they were finally rescued in December. While this real-life scenario is similar to our hypothetical above, the most important difference is that they ate the flesh of those who had already died, which arguably is quite a different matter to actually killing someone. In the lifeboat scenario, we might not have time to wait for someone to die. Would it be better to kill the weakest person and eat them than let everyone die? A utilitarian is compelled to agree that it is permissible to sacrifice one person to save a larger group. However, does it condone killing to do so? How can we decide?

Once people in the boat had decided to sacrifice one or more to save the others, the best overall outcome would be for them to draw straws, or to find some other way of deciding who should provide the nourishment—or to ask for volunteers. However, it could also be argued that this endangers all their lives and that not all lives are necessarily of equal value in situations such as these. What if one of the passengers was the prime minister or president? What if some others were criminals, or close to dying already—either from illness or old age? Should children be included in drawing straws? If not, at what age would you draw the line?

But perhaps there are many people on the boat who are unwilling to consider killing someone and eating them to survive. Of course, there is the "Ewww" factor, but it is not difficult to imagine there would be many people who would also refuse on point of principle. However, there is also the fact that were you actually stuck in the middle of the ocean and confronted with death, you might think differently.

Let us go back to the selfless good deed—would offering yourself up to be eaten be considered a selfless good deed? If you agree with Hume, what sentiment would be pushing you to do so—what exactly would you be "getting out of it"? Another eighteenth-century philosopher, Immanuel Kant, suggests that people can put aside their emotions and be rational about such sacrifices because as moral agents we are able to put ourselves in others' shoes, to be empathic. Unless we are psychopaths, we know what it feels like to need help. And this is what Kant argues—that it is a uniquely human characteristic to be able to put oneself into another person's shoes and to understand what it feels like to be in their situation. A utilitarian, on the other hand, is not really concerned with empathy, or with intention at all. The utilitarian's only concern is consequences.

Utilitarianism is an ethic of conduct or action, and like all consequentialists, utilitarians try to achieve the best outcome in a given situation. The unique characteristic of this theory, however, is that it seeks to find *the best outcome overall, for all stakeholders*. This is the way many of us look at decision-making. For example, when we are faced with a decision (not necessarily an ethical one), we might make a list of the pros and cons. "What are the good things

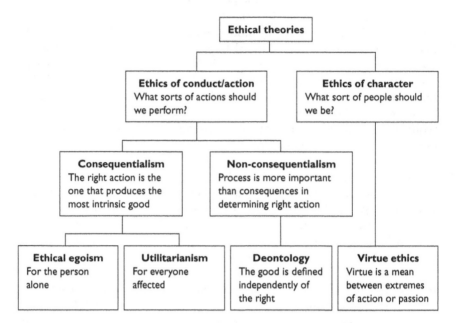

Figure 3.1 Relation between ethical theories

about taking this job? What are the bad things about taking this job? Moving to Sydney? Not moving to Sydney? What about my family?" etc., etc.

So, many of us are using utilitarian decision-making in our everyday lives—it is a common way of looking at the world. It is also the way many governments work, especially liberal-democracies. Democracy is built around creating the most amount of happiness for the greatest number of people. In fact, that is how voting works—crudely. Obviously it is much more complicated than simply trying to achieve a majority, but in all cases democratic structures attempt to give citizens the government that the highest number of people prefer. It is a fairly common way of thinking and making decisions, but it does mean that some people's preferences will be overridden for the greater good. It is a matter of expediency that a government cannot satisfy *everyone's* preferences. Utilitarians argue that the end can justify the means; that sometimes it is permissible to sacrifice someone or something for a *greater good*. The greater good, then, is another key characteristic of utilitarianism.

Wars are utilitarian. We sacrifice a few or even many soldiers and citizens so that the greater society can benefit by retaining its chosen way of life. Utilitarians go by the axiom: the greatest good for the greatest number. 'Utility,' the basis of the term 'utilitarianism,' just means 'purpose,' or a sense of being practical. It is called utilitarianism because it aims to achieve the best 'overall utility' in any given situation. But how do we measure utility? Utilitarians argue that utility is increased when something that has intrinsic value for the majority of people—happiness, for example, or material wealth—is increased. Intrinsic value is defined as something that has value in and of itself, rather than being purely instrumental. Some of the things that have been proposed by philosophers as the basis for intrinsic value—that is, ways of measuring intrinsic value—in the 'utilitarian calculus' include: happiness, pleasure and material wealth. These and others will be discussed in the next section.

Utilitarianism is quite a morally demanding position to take because the minimum standard is requiring you to *maximize* utility (Hinman 1994). In other words, it is asking you to put aside your own self-interest and do what is best for the whole, for the 'common good.' So, in a sense, utilitarianism often asks you to engage in a selfless good deed, where society as a whole benefits from the action. Utilitarianism asks you to think about not just what is good for *you*, but what is good for everybody.

Utilitarian philosophers and candidates for intrinsic value

Jeremy Bentham, another eighteenth-century philosopher, was what you could call the 'father of utilitarianism.' He argued that the best outcome can be calculated based on the most amount of *pleasure* being experienced by the greatest number of people. Pleasure and pain, states Bentham, "govern us in all we do, in all we say, in all we think" (Bentham 1781: 1). Bentham defines pleasure as "the enjoyable feeling we experience when a state of deprivation is replaced by fulfilment" (Hinman 1994). He claimed that because pleasure is a bodily state, it is easy to quantify. Thus all actions of governments and individuals should be directed toward increasing pleasure and reducing pain, and our common goal should be the promotion of overall happiness. Bentham introduced the notion of utility as a measure of achievement.

Bentham's godson, John Stuart Mill, however, regarded pleasure as too crude to measure utility because it ignored higher values and ideals. Mill argued that using pleasure to quantify utility was more or less like regarding people as self-indulgent hedonists. Indeed, it has been suggested that if pleasure is all we need care about, then we might as well just be a brain in a jar hooked up to a pleasure machine (Hinman 1994). Mill therefore suggested that *happiness* is a better measure because in its ideal state it takes account of more than just the pleasure of the moment; it also takes into account one's long-term interests and goals; whatever leads to a 'happy' life. He argued that we should consider the best long-term outcome of our actions and behaviors, rather than just immediate gratification (Mill 2014). However, critics of Mill's theory argue that both long-term goals and 'happiness' are difficult to measure, and that it would be difficult to settle on one definition of happiness.

A more recent (early twentieth-century) British philosopher, G. E. Moore, suggested that, rather than focusing on individual happiness, the best way to maximize overall benefit was to base the calculation on shared social ideals. Ideal candidates he identifies include abstract concepts such as justice, knowledge, freedom, and beauty (Moore 1903).

> Moore's normative view again comprised two main theses. One was impersonal consequentialism, the view that what is right is always what produces the greatest total good impartially considered, or counting all people's good equally. The other was the ideal or perfectionist thesis that what is good is not only or primarily pleasure or desire-satisfaction, but certain states whose value is independent of people's attitudes to them. Moore recognized several such states, but in *Principia Ethica* said famously that "by far the most valuable things . . . are certain states of consciousness, which may roughly be described as the pleasures of human intercourse and the enjoyment of beautiful objects" (237). According to his ideal consequentialism, what is right is in large part what most promotes loving personal relationships and aesthetic appreciation by all persons everywhere.
>
> (Hurka 2010)

Unfortunately, Moore's theory suffers the same or similar criticisms as Mill's. For example, how do we decide whose definition of these ideals is to be used? Who decides the definition of beauty, freedom, or justice?

Kenneth Arrow, a more contemporary theorist of economics, came up with a very elegant solution to the problem of what to measure in the utilitarian calculus. Arrow, who was a co-winner of the Nobel Prize in Economics in 1972 (with Thomas Hicks), suggested that the best measure was the satisfaction of individual preferences. In other words, the best way to get the best overall outcome is to satisfy as many individual preferences as possible. This is an excellent solution for utilitarians because people will always differ in their wants, needs, and goals—thus, what I prefer might differ hugely from what you prefer. I like chocolate ice cream, for example, whereas you might like vanilla or rocky road. We all have different wants and desires, and we all have different roles in life. Preference satisfaction does not discriminate between people's preferences; rather, it allows each person to choose for themselves what has intrinsic value. Intrinsic value is defined as whatever satisfies an individual's preferences.

How utilitarians make ethical decisions?

The utilitarian calculus is really just a sophisticated cost–benefit analysis, where you weigh the pros and cons against each other to come up with a viable solution. However, it is much more complex than merely making a list of fors and againsts, because it must take into account the preferences of more than one person, and often on a very large scale. In addition, it must calculate the weight and intensity of each factor for each individual or group. The mathematical equation for the calculus is shown in the box below.

Bentham's utilitarian calculus

$(Hin \times Hdu) \times HN - (Din \times Ddu) \times DN$

Definitions
- **Hedons** (H) are the standard measurement units of pleasure—every episode of pleasure contains some number of hedons
- **Dolors** (D) are standard measurement units of pain—every episode of pain contains some number of dolors
- **Intensity** (in) is the depth of pain or pleasure felt
- **Duration** (du) is the length of time the pleasure or pain is experienced
- **N** is the number of people affected
- The **hedonistic utility** of an act, X (HuX), is the result of subtracting the total number of dolors that X would cause from the total number of hedons that X would cause
- **Maximum utility** (MU): An act, X, **maximizes** hedonistic utility if and only if no alternative to X has a higher hedonistic utility than X has.

(Bentham 1781)

When performing the calculus, a utilitarian is guided by the following principles:

1 An act is morally right if and only if it maximizes hedonistic utility.
2 All consequences must be weighed.
3 If two episodes of pleasure (or pain) are alike in intensity, but one lasts longer than the other, then the longer one contains more hedons (or dolors) or pleasure (or pain).
4 If two episodes of pleasure (or pain) are alike in duration, but one is more intense than the other, then the more intense one contains more hedons (or dolors) or pleasure (or pain).

The problem, of course, is that at least in some cases, intensity and weight will be difficult to calculate. The following classic ethical dilemma was first devised by philosopher Philippa Foot in her 1967 essay, "The Problem of Abortion and the Doctrine of the Double Effect." Since then, philosophers have continued to discuss the problem it presents for utilitarianism.

Activity 3.1: the Trolley Problem

Suppose you are the driver of a trolley. The trolley rounds a bend, and there come into view ahead five track workmen, who have

(continued)

(continued)

> been repairing the track. The track goes through a bit of a valley at that point, and the sides are steep, so you must stop the trolley if you are to avoid running the five men down. You step on the brakes, but alas they don't work. Now you suddenly see a spur of track leading off to the right. You can turn the trolley onto it, and thus save the five men on the straight track ahead. Unfortunately, . . . there is one track workman on that spur of track. He can no more get off the track in time than the five can, so you will kill him if you turn the trolley onto him.
>
> (Thomson 1985: 1395)

What do you do? What would a utilitarian do? Try to apply the utilitarian calculus to see what you come up with. What are the issues or problems you found?

It looks like a complicated equation, but in reality it is quite simple. H stands for hedons—hedons are things that are good. Dolors are things that are bad. Hedons are 'pros' and dolors are 'cons.' So it's pros versus cons. The complexity arises because it is difficult to assign measures to each parts of the equation. The Trolley Problem demonstrates just how difficult it really is to put together. Not only do you have to identify all the possible outcomes of a particular course of action, but you need to assign a weight to each component to measure the intensity of the good or the bad outcome. We also have to measure the duration of the hedons and dolors—how long is this outcome likely to last? For example, if taking action A will achieve a positive outcome—make people happy, say—for ten minutes, it might be overridden by a less positive outcome that made people happy for ten years. Then you have to work out the number of people who are experiencing happiness (or the relevant outcome). Once you have worked out the number of people achieving relatively positive outcomes, have weighted and calculated the duration of them accordingly for each person, then you need to perform the same calculation for each pro and con—each hedon and dolor—in the equation. Quite a complex calculation.

So it seems that there are three distinct issues. The first is that not everything can be quantified, for example, love, friendship, family. This means that other more quantifiable aspects such as material good, money, and productivity might be emphasized more in the calculus, leaving the less quantifiable aspects out. Second, even quantifiable goods are not necessarily commensurable, for example, a good dinner and a good night's sleep (Hinman 2012: 126). To correctly perform the calculus we must be able to trade off one good against another. Finally, there is the problem of prediction. In the case above, we can probably predict fairly accurately the effect of being hit by the trolley for any people on the track. However, we cannot predict what would happen if no one was hit. Perhaps the lone man on the side track is studying at night to be a doctor and, if allowed to live, might invent a life-saving vaccine. Or perhaps, unbeknown to him, he has a terminal illness and will be dead in a year anyway. On the other hand, perhaps the group of five have been conspiring to break into their head office and steal the payroll. Predicting the future is very tricky. Even highly qualified economists fail to predict disruptions in financial markets, even though they have studied trends and other quantifiable goods. The utilitarian, then, often must take a huge leap of faith, even after carefully considering each variable and assigning a number to it.

Act and rule utilitarianism

The biggest criticism of utilitarianism, then, is that often it is just too complicated to figure out. Not only that, but we have to calculate the best outcome for each and every action that involves making an ethical decision. However, some utilitarians have come up with a good solution to this problem by adopting rules of thumb based on precedent calculations. This is called 'rule' utilitarianism. The prior form, where the calculation is made in each situation, is called 'act' utilitarianism. Act utilitarianism looks at the consequences of each individual act, and calculates the utility each time the act is performed. Rule utilitarianism, on the other hand, looks at the consequences of applying a particular rule across a range of similar situations. So, while it is a bit cumbersome to be always deciding what is the best thing to do for each situation (act utilitarianism), it is often easier to use some rules of thumb. That is, we should adopt the rule that is going to have the best overall outcome for the greatest number of people involved across a period of time. John Stuart Mill made the case for rule utilitarianism in the following way:

> It is truly a whimsical supposition that, if mankind were agreed in considering utility to be the test of morality, they would remain without any agreement as to what is useful, and would take no measures for having their notions on the subject taught to the young, and enforced by law and opinion . . . to consider the rules of morality as improvable, is one thing; to pass over the intermediate generalisations entirely, and endeavour to test each individual action directly by the first principle, is another . . . The proposition that happiness is the end and aim of morality, does not mean that no road ought to be laid down to that goal . . . Nobody argues that the art of navigation is not founded on astronomy, because sailors cannot wait to calculate the Nautical Almanack. Being rational creatures, they go to sea with it ready calculated; and all rational creatures go out upon the sea of life with their minds made up on the common questions of right and wrong.
>
> (Mill 2014)

Examples of such rules of thumb include medical decisions about life support, where a terminally ill patient can be given lethally high doses of morphine when their pain registers at a certain subjective level. On a less dramatic scale, the government might have a policy where they will allocate funding to add facilities and services to a suburb when its rate of crime reaches a certain level.

Regardless of whether act or rule utilitarianism is employed, the resulting outcome is always directed toward the greater good. Nevertheless, act utilitarians argue that always following a rule without regard to particular circumstances is just rule worship. Sometimes rules are useful, but there might be situations where the rule should be overridden. They argue that rule utilitarians are too pedantic and that act utilitarians are more accurate in their calculations because they take particular circumstances into consideration, though they can still use 'rules of thumb' when convenient, as a short cut.

Rule utilitarians argue that act utilitarians justify violating individual rights, which should never be overridden. Also, as we saw earlier in this chapter, it takes far too much time to calculate each and every case or situation according to the utilitarian calculus. Recall, that so many factors are difficult to measure. So much of the outcome of a course of action cannot be predicted, and predictions will necessarily be based on certain assumptions that may or may not have a factual basis. Nevertheless, our government makes utilitarian predictions all the time, and uses them to allocate funding. For example, this year they may allocate $2m to eradicate child poverty—as our government did in 1985—when they said that no child will live in poverty by the year 2000. That prediction never eventuated—so you see how often they get it wrong! However, often governments (and people) need to make decisions based on the best available information. Otherwise nothing would ever get done.

What we can deduce from all this is that Utilitarianism is a very demanding theory. Even so, most people think in terms of utility—weighing up the pros and cons of a situation, or trying to decide what is best for one's family, or one's team, and are capable of sacrificing themselves accordingly. It is quite a useful way of thinking, if not necessarily accurate. That is why we use 'fuzzy logic'—that is, we make quick decisions based on information we cannot really identify. "We just know it" (or think we do). We use these kinds of utilitarian decision-making skills on a daily basis. It is when the decision encompasses an ethical dilemma that we find decision-making so difficult from this perspective.

Criticisms of utilitarianism

While utilitarianism is often employed when making ethical decisions in contemporary society, some philosophers have criticized it on a number of grounds. The first problem with utilitarianism is that it assumes we are responsible for the outcomes of our choices when this is not always the case (Williams 1973). Utilitarianism also sometimes asks us to act against our personal moral convictions and discounts our intentions and motivations. So, if it is my intention to create the greatest good for the greatest number, but for some unforeseeable reason my action does not have this consequence, then my actions are still perceived as unethical. Also, our social mores and personal convictions usually allow us to feel some compassion for a wrongdoer who did not mean it or is the victim of circumstance. Utilitarianism cannot adequately take these emotional factors into account.

In addition to the fact that calculations used by utilitarians are difficult to make, there are other difficulties. For example, who does the calculating and how? Who is the best person or group to judge what is good for the country, the world? A related problem lies with the scope of 'the greater good'—who is included? Our group, our community, nation, religion, race, or planet? Perhaps we should acknowledge the pleasure and pain of plants and rocks as well? This point remains unresolved by utilitarianism and causes major problems when attempting to use this ethical theory to guide moral judgments.

Regardless of these problems, we will find that utilitarianism often underpins the operation of the criminal justice system, and influences the actions of justice professionals. The justice system, and the laws and regulations it deals with, are social institutions, invariably put in place for the benefit of society. As such, decisions about what will produce the greatest good for the greatest number are a constant feature of the work of justice professionals.

Ethical egoism

The second kind of consequentialist theory we will discuss is ethical egoism. Egoists argue that the best way to act ethically is always to act out of self-interest. It is a consequentialist theory because to find out what is in our self-interest we need to look at possible outcomes and choose the one that best serves our interests. To the casual observer, it would be easy to think that our society is built first and foremost on self-interest—on the idea that people should 'look out for number one.' We are often described as a society of egoists, based on the shared belief that each person should live their lives self-interestedly, as they see fit, without too much concern for others. Self-interest is at the core of market capitalism, which exhorts us daily to nurture and take care of ourselves, to indulge and pamper ourselves. Indeed, Anne Manne suggests in her book, *The Life of I*, that our modern culture is turning us all into narcissists, or at least providing fertile breeding ground for narcissism (Manne 2014). Whether or not this is an accurate picture of Western society, it is interesting to consider the impact of such an ideal and what it means for our relationships with others. How does a society of purely self-interested individuals live together? More importantly, how *should* we live together as egoists? Consider the following ethical dilemma.

Josh's ethical dilemma

Josh is a first-year student studying ethics for the first time, and he is finding it all rather difficult and somewhat boring. There is an online exam in week six that he needs to study for, but he is having trouble concentrating. He knows that it is a multiple choice exam and so decides after some weeks to just wing it—he figures he knows about half the material and there is a good chance that he can get a few right by guessing. However, when Josh goes online to take the exam at the allotted time, he finds that the test has a software glitch. After answering the first couple of questions he discovers that if he clicks 'save' after each question and then hits the 'back' button, the correct answer pops up, allowing him to change his answer before submitting it. Josh realizes that he will get full marks for the test if he continues to follow this process for each question. He is overcome with joy and relief. The unit is fairly boring and he deserves a good mark! So Josh goes ahead happily, changing each wrong answer as he comes to it, and submitting a perfect exam at the end. Afterwards, he texts all his friends about the glitch so they can do the same, while marveling at his obvious genius.

Egoism is the paradigm case of an individual concerned only with his or her own self-interest. Egoists argue that they have no reason to abide by moral rules or standards unless it suits them. While this might seem similar to relativism or subjectivism, there is a clear difference. Egoist theory does have an ultimate standard of morality; namely, that each individual should always take account of his own self-interest when deciding what to do. This theory perfectly suits our hypothetical cheater, Josh. Josh acted purely in his own self-interest and, therefore, according to the egoist, did exactly what he was morally required to do.

Three types of egoism

There are two overarching types of egoism: psychological egoism and ethical egoism, the latter of which is divided into two sub-types. A psychological egoist would claim that humans always inevitably act in their own self-interest. Alternatively, ethical egoism asserts that the individual *should* make ethical decisions based on their own self-interest. Ethical egoism is a normative ethical theory because it "prescribes what we ought to do in a given situation" (Hayes 2006: 7). To the ethical egoist, selfishness is perceived as a virtue and those who act in an altruistic manner are considered to be foolhardy and unethical. Psychological egoism, on the other hand, is purely descriptive, purporting to tell us what, in fact, people are actually like. Sixteenth-century philosopher, Thomas Hobbes (1968) famously remarked that, before civil (that is, organized) society began individuals were of necessity pure egoists because they were forced to live lives that were "nasty, brutish and short." When individuals lack safety, food, and shelter, they must be self-interested in order to survive. However, as noted above, modern folk psychology tends to reflect this crude view of individuals even in our own civilized society, where food and shelter are abundant. The development of evolutionist theory also supports the "survival of the fittest" view, as does contemporary economics, which views society as an aggregate of rational, self-interested consumers.

However, even if psychological egoism were true—were people in fact purely self-interested—this does not necessarily commit us to claiming that people *ought* to be so. To make such an assumption is to commit what G. E. Moore (1903) calls the *naturalistic fallacy* (also known as the *is/ought problem*). In other words, just because something happens to be a fact of the world now, there is no logical requirement for that fact to become a basis for moral judgment. Thus, even if we can establish that people *are in fact* selfish, it does not necessarily follow that people should be selfish.

In the early twentieth century, Friedrich Nietzsche was one of the first philosophers to restore interest in egoism, after a long period of discrediting of the theory. Nietzsche (1973) argued that altruism is demeaning because altruists see others as more important than themselves. Such behavior belittles and devalues human beings. Acting selfishly is actually perceived to be a good thing and it is believed that if every individual looked out purely for his or her self-interests then the world would be a better place for everyone. Each person knows what is best for them and helping others only makes them dependent, which ultimately does no good.

Egoists are not always immediately apparent in society, although it is certain that about one percent of the population are psychopaths—a type of individual ethical egoist. Furthermore, most two year olds are also considered to be individual ethical egoists while many adolescents and adults are personal ethical egoists. In fact, our liberal democratic society and capitalist market are based upon the notion of individualism, which asserts that individuals should be free to pursue their own interests and goals. Hence, some still argue that egoism is a psychological truth. However, there are also a number of criticisms of ethical egoism.

This brings us to another distinction—between selfishness and self-interestedness. Selfishness refers to the individual who will only act to further his own ends, whether or not those ends are good for him. Self-interestedness encompasses all that is in a person's interests, and therefore may include many things that the individual does not like or want at this point in time, but which are good for him.

It is difficult to say which of these the egoist lives by. Consider someone who is the manager of a company. If the manager wants to be promoted then she will need to spend a lot of time helping others—clients, co-workers, her boss—to achieve their goals, so that she may be regarded as a good supervisor, manager, or producer, and therefore eligible for promotion. In this case help-ing others is purely in her own self-interest. On the other hand, someone might eat lots of fatty, sugary food, smoke two packets of cigarettes a day, and drink heavily, all of which she loves but none of which are in her best interests, at least long-term.

If we take the basis of egoism to be self-interest, then egoists could not be alcoholics, obese, or heavy smokers; indeed, they would need to be the most virtuous of individuals, always exercising, eating well, and going to bed early, or generally following what is good for them. But this does not seem to reflect the spirit of ethical egoism, which is more oriented toward self-centeredness than self-interest in the strict sense.

There are three main types of ethical egoism:

1   personal ethical egoism;
2   individual ethical egoism; and
3   universal ethical egoism.

Personal ethical egoism states that "I am going to act only in my own self-interest and everyone else can do what they want." Individual ethical egoism states that "everyone should act in my self-interest." Universal ethical egoism states that "each individual should act in their own self-interests." The first, personal ethical egoism, seems to reflect the view that underlies the common belief that people in our society are selfish. It suggests that people should be selfish because "if you don't look out for yourself, who will?" Individual ethi-cal egoism, on the other hand, suggests we adopt the kind of mind set usually attributed to toddlers and rebellious teens! To suggest that everyone should act in my self-interests is not only naive, it shows a reasonable lack of understanding of how our world works. Universal ethical egoism seems like a moderate view in comparison, and reflects the free market capitalist underpinnings of Western society. As Adam Smith (1892) once argued, the market and society in general work best if left to operate by the mechanisms of supply and demand. In other words, if we all act like good self-interested consumers, then the market and society will operate like clockwork to deliver the best outcomes for each of us.

There are several well-known criticisms of the latter view, and of egoism in general. The most compelling argues that egoism presumes we live in a world of strangers (Hinman 1994). If every individual is committed to acting self-ishly, then how can we experience love, friendship, and community? If one loves selfishly, the object of that love will not stay around very long. Similarly, friendship presupposes not only a certain amount of give and take, but also a generosity of spirit. We forgive our friends and children many things simply because we have a close and at least partly selfless connection with them.

It has also been argued that universal ethical egoism is flawed because it cannot be consistently universalized. If all individuals were to act in their own self-interests, then very few of our goals and projects would come to fruition. Indeed, it is in my best interests to act selfishly, and for everyone else to act altruistically!

Finally, egoism fails to take account of our common understanding of fair play. C. S. Lewis (1955) points out that fairness underlies all laws and social conventions, so much so that even small children see the point of it. The egoist, however, is committed to undermining fairness, or at the very least to ignoring it. If she is always to act in her own interests, then why should she be fair? Egoism cannot countenance any reference to fairness and this seems counterintuitive. Fairness lies at the very heart of our social and personal relations. Lewis asks us to think of the alternative:

> Think of a country where people were admired for running away from battle, or where a man felt proud of double-crossing all the people who had been kindest to him. You might just as well imagine a country where two and two make five.
>
> (1955: 3)

And this seems to ring true, at least for most people. Ethical egoism fails to account for this deep social and moral framework of fairness, which seems to invade our everyday existence. As Lewis points out, how many times have you heard a parent or teacher say to a child, "How would you like it if someone did that to you?" or children arguing in the playground: "Hey that's not fair, I was here first?" If we were to take egoism on board as a public morality, none of these statements would make sense (Lewis 1955).

Our commitment to fairness is not merely a recognition of displeasure at the other person's bad behavior. It is an acknowledgment that there is some standard which we expect others to know about. Is there, then, a "rule of fair play?" And if so, should we use it as our basis for moral judgment? Chapter 4 examines the view that there is indeed such a standard, though there might be varying views on how it is applied.

Review questions

1 What are the main principles of utilitarianism?
2 Why is utilitarianism a 'consequentialist' theory?
3 There are two kinds of utilitarianism—act and rule. Compare and contrast these different kinds of utilitarianism, and find some examples that illustrate these differences.
4 *Organ Transplant Scenario*: A homeless man goes into a hospital emergency room because he is very sick. He has no relatives, no home;

(continued)

(continued)

he has got nothing. A famous and well-loved politician comes along at the same time seeking treatment for a serious heart problem, and the doctors discover that he needs a heart transplant. According to utilitarianism, the doctor might be justified in using the homeless man's organs to save the politician because to do so would create so much more benefit for society, than keeping the homeless man alive. The homeless man is sick but they could save him if they wanted to. Some things a utilitarian might take into consideration are: Who is going to miss the homeless man? Is his life worth less? Is anyone's life worth less (e.g. soldiers)? What benefits would society obtain by keeping the politician alive? What is the downside—if there is one—of killing the homeless man?

5 What is the difference between egoism and relativism? Give some examples to illustrate.
6 It is often said that, "You've got to look out for number one!" In other words, if you want to succeed in life, you need to focus on yourself first and let others look out for themselves. Do you think this is a good philosophy to live by?
7 What do you think Nietzsche and C. S. Lewis would say to each other if they were debating egoism? Who do you agree with?
8 This chapter discusses three kinds of egoism—what are they and how do they differ?
9 What is the 'naturalistic fallacy'?
10 What are some criticisms of utilitarianism? Do you think the theory stands up well to criticism?

References

Bentham, Jeremy (1781). *An Introduction to the Principles and Morals of Legislation*. Available at http://www.utilitarianism.com/jeremy-bentham/ (accessed July 7, 2014).

Cohon, Rachel (2010). David Hume. *The Stanford Encyclopedia of Philosophy*. Available at: http://plato.stanford.edu/entries/hume-moral/ (accessed October 28, 2014).

Curtis, Michael (1998). The One Where Phoebe Hates PBS. *Friends*. Series 5, Episode 4.

Foot, Philippa (1967). The Problem of Abortion and the Doctrine of Double Effect. *Oxford Review*, No. 5. Available at http://philpapers.org/archive/FOOTPO-2.1.pdf (accessed August 29 2014).

Hayes, S. (2006). Ethical Theory in Context. In S. Hayes, N. Stobbs, and M. Lauchs (Eds.) *Social Ethics for Legal and Justice Professionals*. Sydney: Pearson Education, pp. 1–16.

Hinman, Lawrence (1994). *Ethics: A pluralistic approach to moral theory*, Fort Worth, TX: Harcourt Brace College Publishers.

Hinman, Lawrence. (2012). *Ethics: A Pluralistic Approach to Moral Theory*. Cengage Learning.

Hobbes, Thomas (1968). *Leviathan*. Edited by C. C. Macpherson. London: Penguin.

Hume, David (1739). *A Treatise on Human Nature: Being an attempt to introduce the experimental method of reasoning into moral subjects.* Available at http://ebooks.adelaide.edu.au/h/hume/david/h92t/ (accessed July 7, 2014).

Hurka, Thomas (2010). Moore's Moral Philosophy. *Stanford Encyclopedia of Philosophy.* Available at http://plato.stanford.edu/entries/moore-moral/ (accessed July 7, 2014).

Lewis, C. S. (1955). *Mere Christianity.* London: Collins.

Manne, Anne (2014). *The Life of I: the new culture of narcissism.* Sydney: Random House.

Mill, John Stuart (2014). *Utilitarianism.* Available at http://ebooks.adelaide.edu.au/m/mill/john_stuart/m645u/ (accessed July 7, 2014).

Moore, G. E. (1903). *Principia Ethica.* Available at http://plato.stanford.edu/entries/moore-moral/ (accessed July 7, 2014).

Nietzsche, Friedrich (1973). *Beyond Good and Evil.* Translated by R. J. Hollingdale. London: Penguin Classics.

Smith, Adam (1892). *An Inquiry in the Nature and Causes of the Wealth of Nations.* London: George Routledge and Sons.

Thomson, Judith Jarvis (1985). The Trolley Problem. *The Yale Law Journal,* 94(6): 1395–1415.

Williams, Bernard (1973). A Critique of Utilitarianism. In J. J. C. Smart and Bernard Williams, *Utilitarianism: For and Against.* Cambridge University Press.

Chapter 4

Non-consequentialism

Key terms: deontology; virtue ethics; categorical imperative; ends-in-themselves; duty; respect; dirty hands; Aristotle's virtues; the golden mean

Introduction

Imagine you are in Nazi Germany in World War Two, a Jewish family has escaped the authorities and is hiding in your basement. An SS officer comes to your door and asks you if you know the whereabouts of this Jewish family, as he has received reports that they are in the area. Obviously the officer wants to arrest the Jewish family to put them in a concentration camp or to submit them to some other form of humiliation, as was the usual procedure at the time. What do you do? Would you lie, continue to hide them, and risk persecution yourself? What do you say to the SS officer?

A utilitarian would weigh up the consequences, calculating the risk to his own family as well as that of the hidden family, his chances of lying well enough to convince the officer, and so on. An egoist would probably turn them in unless he thought he could get away with the lie—let us say he is protecting the family because they are close friends and he cherishes them. But let us imagine that we do not make decisions based on the best outcome; that instead, we rely on principles to guide our action, regardless of outcomes. Such principles might include a commitment to refrain from lying, cheating, stealing, and killing, no matter what. They are therefore what we call *absolute principles*. They are absolute because they require our ongoing commitment, even in situations that put us or others at risk. Now, imagine you are such a strongly principled person. What would you say to the SS officer?

In this chapter we will be exploring a group of theories that are non-consequentialist—that is, they are grounded in principles rather than outcomes. For a non-consequentialist, the end never justifies the means. In particular, we will be discussing two major non-consequentialist theories—deontology and virtue ethics. By comparing and contrasting these theories with consequentialism, we will come to understand the range and direction of ethical perspectives, which will provide firm grounding for ethical decision-making.

Deontology: the basics

Deontologists argue that we have a duty to treat others fairly and with respect. The term deontology derives from the Greek word *deon*, which means 'duty' or 'obligation.' Immanuel Kant (1964) argued that fairness and respect have priority over all other goals and ends. Contrary to the egoist's view, deontologists claim that individuals have an innate capacity and disposition to act apart from their wants, desires and interests. All human beings are moral agents—morally equal individuals with wants and goals of their own—and have the ability to recognize others as moral agents like themselves and to respect their need to pursue those goals and interests. Kant argued that because this is the case, we should always treat others as *ends-in-themselves*. For Kant (1964), duty is internally imposed by our own reason and conscience and people should act according to their duty, even when it results in adverse outcomes. This internally imposed sense of duty gives rise to a number of rules, which he called *categorical imperatives*.

Kant (1964) explains how our everyday behavior is guided by *maxims*. Maxims are general rules that guide actions; for example, 'always drive at the speed limit' or 'chocolate is bad for you.' They are subjective in the sense that they may differ from individual to individual, or situation to situation. Because such rules cannot provide absolute standards for ethical conduct, Kant argued that we need to act by rules that can be *universalized*—that is, rules that can apply to everyone all the time. He called such rules *categorical imperatives*, the main overarching one of which is:

> Always act in such a way that the maxim of your action can be willed as a universal law of humanity.
>
> (Kant 1964)

What Kant means is that we should only act if we know that it would be a good thing for everyone if they all acted the same way. For example, in the case of Josh, the cheater from Chapter 3, we would need to ask, "Would it be acceptable for everyone to cheat on a test when they had the chance?" If we can honestly answer "yes" to this question, then it would be morally acceptable for Josh to cheat. However, it is quite obvious that we cannot agree with this statement, for if we allowed everyone to cheat whenever they felt like it, there would be no educational standards by which to judge competence or knowledge and the entire education system, not to mention corporate and government recruitment systems, would fall apart, so according to deontologists, Josh acted unethically by cheating.

Another categorical imperative proposed by Kant has to do with *respect*:

> Always treat humanity, whether in yourself or in other people, as an end in itself and never as a mere means.
>
> (Kant 1964)

This imperative is quite important to Kant's theory, because it provides a framework for treating others with respect that precludes our using them merely for our own devices. Again, this rule acknowledges that we recognize others as equal moral agents like ourselves and should therefore treat them as we would want to be treated if put in their shoes. Respect, therefore, is also tied to *empathy*.

Kant argued that we are never justified in lying. His reasoning is based on causality, so that as long as individuals do the right thing—according to the rules or categorical imperatives—they are not responsible for adverse outcomes. From this view, even lying to save a life is never permissible. The following case study, made famous by Bernard Williams (1973), provides another example of an ethical dilemma in which the application of absolutist thinking may create adverse results.

Jim's dilemma

Jim finds himself in the central square of a small South American town. Tied up against the wall is a row of twenty Indians, most terrified, a few defiant, in front of them several armed men in uniform. A heavy man in a sweat-stained khaki shirt turns out to be the captain in charge and, after a good deal of questioning of Jim which establishes that he got there by accident while on a botanical expedition, explains that the Indians are a random group of the inhabitants who, after recent acts of protest against the government, are just about to be killed to remind other possible protesters of the advantages of not protesting. However, since Jim is an honored visitor from another land, the captain is happy to offer him a guest's privilege of killing one of the Indians himself. If Jim accepts, then as a special mark of the occasion, the other Indians will be let go. Of course, if Jim refuses, there is no special occasion, and Pedro here will do what he was about to do when Jim arrived, and kill them all. Jim, with some desperate recollection of schoolboy fiction, wonders whether if he got hold of a gun, he could hold the captain, Pedro, and the rest of the soldiers to threat, but it is quite clear from the setup that nothing of that kind is going to work: any attempt at that sort of thing will mean that all the Indians will be killed, and himself. The men against the wall, and the other villagers understand the situation and are obviously begging him to accept. What should he do?

(Source: Williams 1973)

If we exercise our moral imaginations, we can easily see what sorts of solutions to Jim's dilemma a utilitarian would come up with. Maximizing utility would require that Jim take up Pedro's offer of shooting one person to save the other prisoners. While there might be some debate about *whom* he should choose, it is clear that a utilitarian *would have to make that choice*. A deontologist, on the other hand, has no such dilemma. Indeed, Jim, the deontologist would be morally obligated to walk away from the situation. To see why this is so, we need to understand to what extent deontological principles—that is, maxims and categorical imperatives—are absolute.

For the deontologist, there are no 'grey areas.' Ethics is purely black and white, in the sense that the categorical imperatives hold for everyone, universally and for all time. But what does that mean for Jim? Surely respecting others as moral equals means that he should do his utmost to save as many people as possible. For deontologists, the value of a human life is reflected in the maxim requiring us to treat others as ends-in-themselves. It might be argued, then, that by walking away Jim is letting all the prisoners die, and that arguably amounts to killing them himself, since he could have done something to save them. There are many good reasons to equate letting die with killing. If Jim were walking by a pond and saw a child drowning, he would be regarded as morally reprehensible if he just kept walking and let the child die, in spite of the fact that he himself is a strong swimmer and the pond is not deep. A deontologist is compelled to save a life where there is no risk to themselves. However, deontologist Jim's situation is quite different. He can save some lives, but only at the expense of killing one prisoner. However, saving those lives would also cost Jim his principles. Williams (1973) argues that no one should ever be put into a position that requires them to go against their principles. If Jim walks away, then his principles are intact, and he has committed no moral breach. If he kills a prisoner, on the other hand, he has acted immorally. Williams (1973) further argues that Jim is *not responsible* for the deaths of the prisoners if he fails to act. Jim is just a bystander in the situation; he has not caused Pedro to take prisoners. Neither does he cause their deaths by failing to act.

This is an interesting case because, on the one hand, Jim is nobly upholding his principle (which would be something like "It is never right to kill a person"), and Williams argues that Jim has no cause for regret or guilt for the deaths because their deaths are not his responsibility. Before we continue further analysis of this viewpoint, we need to understand deontology in more depth.

Immanuel Kant

Born 1724 in Konigsberg, Germany, Kant led a religious life, doing good works, teaching at the university, and writing about ethics. He was very well respected, and never left his hometown during his life. He wrote several long and complex texts, which provide the objective basis for his deontological theory. That theory, including explanations of the categorical imperative, maxims and principles, is outlined in his *Groundwork for the Metaphysics of Morals*, a short and relatively readable book. Kant believed in an objective reality. He saw morality as something 'out there,' something real that we just need to discover. He believed that we, as moral agents, could discover the nature of morality through reason, and that reason could also help us determine the correct moral principles. He saw human beings as generally rational, capable of discerning these universal principles, and set about doing so. As mentioned earlier he came up with the principles of duty and respect. He argued quite vigorously that individuals have the capacity to act apart from their wants and desires, and that people are not naturally selfish. Rather, rational individuals have a *propensity* or *disposition* to put aside their own wants and desires in order to do the right thing.

As we saw earlier, the principle of respect requires us to respect all rational human beings as moral agents, and that people should be treated as 'ends-in-themselves,' worthy of dignity and respect, and not just as instruments for achieving our own ends.

These principles give rise to general rules, which he called maxims. Maxims that guide our actions, such as 'never lie to a friend' or 'never act in a way that would make your parents ashamed of you' are moral maxims. But it is the concept of a categorical imperative that drives Kant's theory. An imperative is something that you *must* do. The fact that it is *categorical* means that there are no excuses for not doing it. It is, therefore, absolutely essential that you follow these imperatives. Kant believed that the categorical imperative was a standard of rationality from which all moral requirements derive. They are rules that are binding on everybody all the time. For Kant, there is never a good reason to disobey a categorical imperative. Now, if we examine the first categorical imperative again, we can see how Williams' argument works.

Kant's categorical imperative

> Act only according to that maxim whereby you can at the same time will that it should become universal law.
>
> (Kant 1964)

In our modern language, this just means, 'always do only those actions that can be universalized,' or, 'if you cannot agree that everyone everywhere should be allowed to perform an act, then that act is unethical.'

To get back to Jim's dilemma, this means that Jim's refusal to kill one person to save the others is a result of his commitment to the categorical imperative. Jim's maxim "It's never all right to kill" is based on a universal rule that makes it impossible to universalize killing. However, this conclusion is the result of black-and-white thinking, because it fails to account for both circumstances, and the fact that such principles often conflict with each other, creating grey areas. For the deontologist, grey areas, as we saw, do not exist.

But what if there *are* grey areas in ethics? In his 1948 play, *Dirty Hands*, French philosopher and playwright Jean Paul Sartre presents us with another ethical dilemma that might help us understand the problem from another perspective. The play is set in a fictional country called Illyria, which is currently experiencing class struggle. The two main characters are Hugo and Hoederer. Hugo is a political idealist—a deontologist—who puts principles above all else. Hoederer is more pragmatic; he considers what needs to be done to achieve his goal (abolishing social classes) and believes that sometimes we must be pragmatic rather than principled for the great good. In a speech to Hugo, he accuses the former of being precious:

> How you cling to your purity, young man! How afraid you are to soil your hands! All right, stay pure! What good will it do? Why did you join us? Purity is an idea for a yogi or a monk . . . To do nothing, to remain motionless, arms at your side, wearing kid gloves. Well, I have dirty hands. Right up to the elbows. I've plunged them in filth and blood. But what do you hope? Do you think you can govern innocently?
>
> (Sartre 1948)

Hoederer taunts the younger Hugo for his ideals, arguing that his duty is to "get his hands dirty," to put aside his own principles for the sake of a greater good. Michael Walzer (1973) agrees with Hugo. However, he also argues that this does not necessarily mean that we should always forgo our principles in favor of utility. It is much more complicated than that. In his paper, "Political Action: The Problem of Dirty Hands," he states:

> My own answer is no, I don't think I could govern innocently; nor do most of us believe that those who govern us are innocent. . . . But this does not mean that it isn't possible to do the right thing while governing. It means that a particular act of government (in a political party or in the state) may be exactly the right thing to do in utilitarian terms and yet leave the man who does it guilty of a moral wrong.
>
> (Walzer 1973: 161)

Here, Walzer is arguing that sometimes we do need to get our hands dirty personally, if it is necessary to proper governing. The person who puts aside their moral principle for a greater good must find some way to come to terms with their violation, whether it be to accept the appropriate punishment with good grace, or to face a lifetime of repentance. In this way, they become 'clean' again—or as clean as a human *qua* human can possibly get (Walzer 1973). Jim's dilemma, then, is to choose whether he must be "cruel to be kind" (Walzer 1973), a dilemma which points up nicely the kinds of conflicts of principles we are faced with, both in politics and in our everyday lives. From Walzer's and Sartre's perspective, Jim needs to pull up his shirt sleeves and do the deed, because in the face of such death and destruction, he cannot afford the luxury of principles. Walzer also argues that simply refusing to act against principle will stop others from doing so, and that getting our hands dirty is braver and more courageous than upholding principles, because we must always pay the price.

> "We shall not abolish lying by refusing to tell lies," says Hoederer, "but by using every means at hand to abolish social classes." I suspect we shall not abolish lying at all, but we might see to it that fewer lies were told if we contrived to deny power and glory to the greatest liars. . . . If Hoederer succeeds in abolishing social classes, perhaps he will join the lucky few. Meanwhile, he lies, manipulates, and kills, and we must make sure he pays the price. We won't be able to do that, however, without getting our own hands dirty, and then we must find some way of paying the price ourselves.
>
> (Walzer 1973: 180)

While this might seem rather a harsh expectation of the average person, Stanley Benn (1986) came up with another solution to the dirty hands problem: the Rationalist Model. He suggested that when principles conflict, all we need do is trade them off to discover which one to follow and which must be sacrificed. He suggested that we all wear a number of 'hats' or roles, and that we can decide which principle to honor by choosing which role is most important or morally relevant at the time. Decision-making, therefore, is essentially a matter of trading off values and principles against each other. Benn's model uses the notion of roles and associated obligations to assist in determining how much weight to give to each value or principle. In chapter 3 of *A Theory of Freedom*, Benn gives the example of (ancient Roman historian) Livy's Brutus, a civic leader who must choose between saving his son from drowning or leading his people at a vital political forum (1986: 50ff.). Traditionally, the story of Brutus has been used by philosophers to demonstrate the paradigm of an ethical dilemma. However, Benn argues that the civic leader has *no dilemma* because he can make a rational decision based on his value rankings at the time. He can do this by identifying what roles are involved—his role as a leader and his role as a father—and by ranking their importance for this situation. See how he solves the problem in the box below.

Brutus' problem: save son or attend meeting?

Roles and weightings for this situation:

Table 4.1 Brutus' problem: save son or attend meeting? Table 1

Role	Weighting
Father	10
Civic leader	7

(continued)

(continued)

In this instance, Brutus chooses to save his son because he values his son (his role as father) more than his attendance at the forum (his role as civic leader) *in this situation*. In what circumstances might his decision change? See Table 4.2.

Table 4.2 Brutus' problem: save son or attend meeting? Table 2

Role	Situation	Weighting
Father	Save son from drowning	10
Civic Leader	Go to important town meeting	7
Father	Give son a lift home	4
Civic Leader	Lead troops to war	10
Father	Attend son's wedding	8
Civic Leader	Attend civic luncheon	5

Values:

The values involved in making this decision include the following:

- Value of human life—one or many;
- Value of personal relationships;
- Value of civic responsibility;
- Value of enjoyment.

(Benn 1986)

Of course, the question remains: how does one determine the numerical values to place on different people or experiences? Can ethical decision-making be reduced to a mathematical calculation? And even if it can, *should* it? How would Benn's neo-deontological method solve Jim's dilemma?

Criticisms of deontology

The problem of 'dirty hands' points up a key flaw in deontology—its inflexible, absolutist nature. Some philosophers criticize Kant's theory because it appears to defend a kind of *moral minimalism*—that is, sticking to a rule even when the situation seems to be more ethically complex than the rule would permit. For example, Kant argued that people should do their duty even when it is not heartfelt. In fact, Kant claimed that the person who does her duty when she least wants to is *more* virtuous than the person who does her duty willingly. Such action, claims Kant, is more virtuous because it denies one's desires in favor of doing the right thing.

Kant has also been criticized for denying the importance of emotions. He argued that emotions are unreliable and self-oriented and therefore cannot be trusted. However, many would argue that our emotions are irrevocably tied to our values and principles, and therefore must be taken into account when making ethical decisions. From this perspective, doing what you perceive as a duty simply because it is expected (rather than because you want to) is dishonest and even devious.

Thomas Nagel argues that Kant failed to account for the importance of unintended consequences in his theory. For Kant, an individual is not held accountable for any bad consequences that arise out of the performance of a duty. The duty must be followed, regardless of the outcomes. Nagel argues that this is too simple and "doesn't take account of the way external factors impinge upon us" (Nagel 1998: 352). Kant's rule that it is *never* morally permissible to lie, for example, denies the importance of context.

Suppose you live in a house in Nazi Germany and are hiding a Jewish family in your attic. According to Kant, when the SS comes knocking and asking if you are hiding any Jewish individuals, you are morally obliged to respond in the affirmative. How many of us would agree that telling the truth is more important than protecting a human life?

The last criticism of deontology canvassed here is its ability to deal with moral relativism. Moral relativism asserts that what is 'right,' 'good,' or 'desirable' differs according to cultural and social context. Therefore, what is 'good' in one country might be very different to what is considered as 'good' in another. If we accept this, then it is difficult to determine absolute rules about how to act ethically.

Despite these problems, deontology is an ethical perspective that one cannot escape from, particularly in the context of criminal justice. As we will see in later chapters, following the law and respecting due process requirements throughout the justice system, for example, express aspects of deontology, and these contribute enormously to producing just outcomes.

Virtue ethics

So far we have examined three major ethical theories: utilitarianism, egoism, and deontology. So far, they all seem to have some advantages, but also some grave flaws and inconsistencies. While each theory argues that morality resides in moral agents, they disagree on the principles or methods for arriving at moral rules. Nietzsche and Rand, both egoists, criticized both utilitarianism and deontology for trying to establish a universal objective standard, arguing that while moral agency does indeed reside with the individual, it was useless to try to discover any universal or objective principles. They argue that, since there are no such objective principles, each individual must dictate their own morality. Nietzsche went even further by arguing that the logical corollary is that the most powerful will rule out. However, as we have seen there are as many flaws in egoism—and especially in Nietzsche's version—as there are in the others. At this point, then, we might be wondering if anyone can come up with ethical standards that are relevant and yet not ad hoc. In fact, there is another answer to the problems raised by the Enlightenment philosophers and it was first proposed by Alasdair MacIntyre in his book, *After Virtue* (1984).

MacIntyre took ethical theorists to task for the same reason as Nietzsche, claiming that moral philosophy was in a very bad state indeed. He likened ethical theory to a science fiction novel, *A Canticle for Leibowitz*, in which science and scientific disciplines have been dismantled altogether. "The hypothesis which I wish to advance," he continues, "is that in the actual world which we inhabit the language of morality is in the same state of grave disorder as the language of natural science in the imaginary world which I described" (MacIntyre 1984: 2). MacIntyre argues that contemporary moral philosophy is impoverished because it accords all moral power to individuals absent any social context. This is irrational, he claims in the third edition of the book, amounting merely to a contest between

> rival and incompatible accounts, Utilitarians competing with Kantians and both with Contractarians, so that moral judgments. . . . Became essentially contestable, expressive of the attitudes and feelings of those who uttered them, yet still uttered as if there was some impersonal standard by which moral disagreements might be rationally resolved. And from the outset such disagreements concerned not only the justification, but also the content of morality.
>
> (MacIntyre 2007: Loc 57)

To remedy what he saw as a lack of moral content, MacIntyre suggested we move back toward a more *teleological* epistemology, or way of knowing. 'Teleology' refers to anything that is aligned with nature and seeks a goal or end (Kraut 1979). 'Epistemology' is the study of what we know—a theory of knowledge, for example comparing justified belief to mere opinion (Steup 2005). A teleological epistemology, then, is a theory of knowledge that takes values as the starting point for adopting principles. Prior to the Enlightenment, philosophy and other disciplines were very much teleological pursuits. Thinkers of the Enlightenment, however, sought to create a more rational basis for human life and thought, and it is this radical change that MacIntyre identifies as its fundamental mistake. He suggested that we should go back to thinkers such as Aristotle and his theory of virtue to understand how we can derive a meaningful content for morality and moral judgments (MacIntyre 2007). Aristotle was a philosopher in Ancient Greece around the fourth century BCE, a student of Plato, who wrote numerous texts about politics, morality, and how we should live. His theory of virtue challenged the idea that we should start from moral principles when deciding how civil society should be arranged and how members of civil society ought to live. His theory provides the starting point for virtue ethics.

Rather than proposing absolute rules, virtue ethics has developed as an ethical theory based on character or virtue. Rather than asking the question "What should I do?" the virtue ethicist asks, "What kind of person should I be?" Answering the second question provides a framework for answering the first. In theory, this combats one major problem with deontology. Since the virtue ethicist does not promote absolute rules, such as Kant's categorical imperative, it is more likely that virtue ethics will be acceptable to a greater number of people. However, we must also gain some understanding of the virtues that a virtue ethicist refers to when making ethical decisions.

As members of civil society we tend to put our trust in rules and expect people to abide by them, but we also put our trust in individual people such as judges and police officers and we expect such people to apply the rules with integrity. Judges, lawyers, and police officers (and social workers, teachers, doctors, and other professionals) are required to have strength of character in performing their duties. Aristotle argued that strength of character—or virtue—lies at the mean or mid-point between excess and deficiency. He calls this the *golden mean*, a balance between too much and too little.

Aristotle's notion of virtue

Aristotle (384 BCE–322 BCE) created a typology of human character that encompassed three different responses to the morality of virtue, reflecting three different ways of balancing our desires against our virtues: the *akratic* person, the *continent* person, and the *temperate* person (Aristotle 2004).

The *akratic* person has wild desires that they find difficult to keep under control. This kind of person lacks virtue because they are always acting on every whim, throwing duty and virtue to the wind (Aristotle 2004). Akratic individuals resemble the egoist in their attempts to always satisfy their immediate wants and desires. However, the egoist is not necessarily at the mercy of his desires—he has chosen to act selfishly. The akratic individual cannot act otherwise and therefore resembles more closely the neurotic obsessive-compulsive than the egoist.

The *temperate* individual is the complete opposite, always desiring what is good for them and what will most develop their character. This person has achieved the golden mean and therefore demonstrates the highest virtue (Aristotle 2004).

The *continent* person is one who has wild desires, but manages for the most part to keep them under control. This type describes the majority of individuals in our society, most of whom would love to give in to their desires—and might do so on occasion—but who have sufficient strength of character to override those desires most of the time, for the sake of duty (Aristotle 2004).

The aim of moral education is to teach us how to form the right desires. As children, our desires are controlled through rules, which are imposed upon us by parents, religions, and schools. At this stage our understanding of morality is negatively reinforced: "Don't lie or else!" This stage focuses upon the development of habits based on general rules designed to protect us and help us develop appropriate values. As we grow older we begin to internalize those habits and values and learn how to reason about morality. Ideally, by the time we reach adulthood, the primitive rules have been replaced by an holistic personal identity that is virtue-centered and modeled on ideals.

Aristotle's golden mean is not equivalent to mediocrity. Rather, it is balance and harmony of character. Aristotle (2004) also argued that we *can learn* to be virtuous simply by *acting as if* we are virtuous. The idea is that if we practice long and hard enough, we will eventually internalize the virtue and *become* virtuous, much as practicing anything will result in forming a habit. He proposed a list of virtues that he entreated individuals to develop. The box below outlines some of those virtues.

Aristotle's virtues

- Courage: the strength of character to continue in the face of our fears.
- Compassion: shows empathy for the suffering of others.
- Wisdom: the ability to know which goals are worth striving for.
- Cleverness: the ability to know the best way to achieve one's goals.
- Self-love: care, appreciation, and respect for self and others.
- Friendship: wishing good things for others, for their own sake, and being inclined to bring those good things about.
- Forgiveness: indispensable to human flourishing.

(Aristotle 2004)

Some of Aristotle's virtues might seem strange to us—*cleverness*, for example, or *self-love*. When we think of self-love, we think of the narcissistic person, who is self-centered and conceited. Similarly, cleverness is often taken to mean slyness or guile. In the context of Ancient Greece—Aristotle's milieu—these concepts took on very different meanings. As the box above shows, cleverness is more about being able to contrive appropriate strategies for achieving one's goals, while self-love is more akin to self-respect.

For Aristotle, virtues do not exist in isolation from each other—they work and develop synergistically. Wisdom without cleverness is all but useless, while it is difficult to conceive of friendship without self-respect (self-love), for how could we be a friend to others if we are not already a friend to ourselves.

> The same is true of honour and office; all these things he will sacrifice to his friend; for this is noble and laudible for himself. Rightly then is he thought to be good, since he chooses nobility before all else. But he may even give up actions to his friend; it may be nobler to become the cause

of his friend's acting than to act himself. In all the actions, therefore, that men are praised for, the good man is seen to assign to himself the greater share of what is noble. In this sense, then, as has been said, a man should be a lover of self; but in the sense in which most men are so, he ought not.

(Aristotle 2004: IX, 8)

MacIntyre (2007: 147) argues that "Aristotle takes himself not to be inventing an account of the virtues, but to be articulating an account that is implicit in the thought, utterance and action of an educated Athenian." As the political seat of Ancient Greece, Athens was a city of culture, education, and intellectual pursuit and Aristotle sought to articulate the virtues that characterized that state and its citizens. For Aristotle, every activity and thought aims at some goal, and those goals are best realized and expressed in civil society. Aristotle's virtues, then, describe the actual characteristics of the best and most worthy Athenians, as well as of Athenian society itself. It is this social aspect of his theory that sets it apart from the other theories—utilitarianism, egoism and deontology—each of which places the individual before the social. MacIntyre's own theory draws on Aristotle's view of the polis, proposing that we "work together in genuine political communities to acquire the virtues and fulfil their innately human purpose" (Clayton n.d.).

C. S. Lewis (1955) offers a similar view of virtue to Aristotle, although he called the virtues by different names. Cardinal virtues are those that everyone should aspire to and include temperance, justice, and fortitude. He also espoused theological virtues, which he said God calls all believers to embrace. These include the well-known virtues of forgiveness, humility, charity, hope, and faith. For both Lewis and Aristotle, however, regardless of which virtues we choose to list, it is clear that they must work in unison.

Aristotle argued that to be virtuous, the individual must strike a balance between all of these virtues because the virtues act holistically to create strength of character. Hence, an individual must possess all of the virtues in unison, and in doing so, the virtues moderate one another. For instance, wisdom turns our courage into practical action, while self-love prohibits our compassion from overwhelming us and making us into slaves. By attaining the golden mean, the individual finds balance and harmony of character.

MacIntyre (2007) takes Aristotle's theory as a marker for transforming contemporary civil society and argues that we develop virtue by engaging in *practices*, an element which he considers is missing in modern life. MacIntyre views practices as the vehicle by which, in the absence of a particular virtue or strength of character, we may be led to develop as a habit. Practices are not individual acts, such as kicking a football around, or playing noughts and crosses. Rather, a practice is "any coherent form of socially established cooperative activity," such as the *game* of football itself (MacIntyre 2007: 187). In the same way, building is not a practice, but engineering is. He uses the example of trying to teach a reluctant child to play chess to illustrate the benefits of such practices.

The virtuous chess player

Consider the example of a highly intelligent seven-year-old whom I wish to teach chess, although the child has no particular desire to learn the game. The child does however have a very strong desire for candy and little chance of obtaining it. I therefore tell the child that if the child will play chess with me once a week I will give the child 50 cents worth of candy; moreover I tell the child that I will always play in such a way that it will be difficult, but not impossible, for the child to win and that, if the child wins, the child will receive an extra 50 cents worth of candy. Thus motivated, the child plays and plays to win. Notice however that, as long as it is candy alone which provides the child with good reason for playing chess, the child has no reason not to cheat . . . , provided he or she can do so successfully. But so we may hope, there will come a time when the child will find in those goods specific to chess, in the achievement of a certain highly particular kind of analytic skill, strategic imagination and competitive intensity, a new set of reasons, reasons now not just for winning on a particular occasion, but for trying to excel in whatever way the game of chess demands. Now if the child cheats, he or she will be defeating not me, but himself or herself.

(MacIntyre 2007: 187)

Notwithstanding the improbability of any child in today's society doing anything for a mere 50 cents worth of candy, the point of this example is that, while we might begin by offering incentives to ourselves and others to achieve some goal, our best hope is that the continued practice of the actions that lead the goals to instill in us the desire to engage in the practice for its own sake. Thus, there are two kinds of goods attached to practices, the external or material good that attaches to its successful undertaking—money, power, candy—and the more enduring and fulfilling internal goods, which can only be achieved by engaging in the practice itself—"achievement of skill, strategic imagination and competitive intensity," for example.

To return to our case study of Josh the cheater (Chapter 3), how would the virtue ethicist view Josh's actions? Education is a practice similar to MacIntyre's example of chess, because it too has two goals—the external good of grades, diplomas, and hopefully, careers; and the internal goods of achievement of intellectual rigor, and skill, and participation in and camaraderie with a community of like-minded scholars. Josh seems a rather selfish individual who has no regard for the rules and standards associated with his university, or even for his fellow classmates. He does not think of the consequences of his actions in the broader sense, in terms of how it might impact on other students, on grades in the class, and on educational standards. Rather, he views only those consequences as they apply to him as grounds for his decision to cheat. Josh is focused only on the external goods of education—the achievement of high grades—while ignoring the equally if not more valuable internal goods of determination, academic skill, and integrity. One might say he is exhibiting Aristotle's 'cleverness' in pursuing his goals. But recall both Aristotle's and Lewis' claim that the virtues work in unison, not in isolation. If Josh does not display any of the other virtues, then he is not displaying strength of character. From a virtue ethics standpoint, Josh's actions were therefore unethical.

While it can be difficult to get one's head around virtue ethics, it is a useful ethical outlook to possess, especially for justice professionals. In many situations in which one must decide how to act, it might be the case that neither deontology nor consequentialism offers a clear answer. Virtue ethics can provide a fresh perspective on a problem, and suggest a clearer reason for acting in one particular way over another.

Review questions

1 Consider each of the following virtues: courage, compassion, self-love and forgiveness. For each and all virtues, identify at least three professions that ought to require that virtue. Were any of the professions you chose justice or legal-related professions? Should justice professionals express all these virtues?

2 How do one's circumstances affect one's ability to develop virtues? Do we all have the same opportunity for flourishing? Are some people more advantaged in developing their virtues?

3 What kind of virtues would you consider to be appropriate for our society today? How widespread are they and how difficult are they to develop and maintain?

4 What is Kant's categorical imperative? Give an example of a principle that conforms to that imperative.

5 According to Immanuel Kant, what should motivate moral action?

6 Deontological maxims such as "It's never right to kill" are categorical imperatives. Do you think we should respect categorical imperatives at all costs? If not, what are some instances in which it might be morally permissible to disobey an imperative?

7 What did you think of Jim's dilemma? Is Williams correct in arguing that, by walking away, Jim abjures all responsibility for the killing of the prisoners?

8 What was MacIntyre's criticism of contemporary moral philosophy?

9 What are the main underpinning concepts of deontology?

10 What are some important criticisms of deontology?

References

Aristotle (2004). *Nichomachean Ethics*. (Translated by J. A. K. Thomson. Revised by Jonathan Barnes.) London: Penguin Books.

Benn, Staney I. (1986). *A Theory of Freedom*. Cambridge: Cambridge University Press.

Clayton, Ted (n.d.) Political Philosophy of Alasdair MacIntyre. *Internet Encyclopedia of Philosophy*. Available at http://www.iep.utm.edu/p-macint/ (accessed July 24, 2014).

Kant, Immanuel (1964). *Groundwork of the Metaphysics of Morals* (Translated by H. J. Paton). New York: Harper and Row.

Kraut, Richard (1979). Two Conceptions of Happiness. *Philosophical Review*, 88: 167–197.

Lewis, C. S. (1955). *Mere Christianity*. London: Collins.

MacIntyre, Alasdair (1984). *After Virtue: a study in moral theory*. Second edition. Notre Dame: University of Notre Dame Press.

MacIntyre, Alasdair (2007). *After Virtue: a study in moral theory*. Third edition. Notre Dame: University of Notre Dame Press.

Nagel, Thomas (1998). Moral Luck. In L. P. Pojman (Ed.) *Ethical Theory: classical and contemporary readings*. Third Edition. Belmont, CA: Wadsworth Publishing Company.

Sartre, Jean Paul (1948). Dirty Hands (Les Mains Sales). In *No Exit and Three Other Plays* (ebook). Available at http://www.vanderbilt.edu/olli/class-materials/Jean-Paul_Sartre.pdf (accessed July 24, 2014).

Steup, Matthias (2005). Epistemology. *The Stanford Encyclopedia of Philosophy*. Available at http://plato.stanford.edu/entries/epistemology/ (accessed July 24, 2014).

Walzer, Michael (1973). Political Action: The Problem of Dirty Hands. *Philosophy & Public Affairs*, 2(2): 160–180.

Williams, Bernard (1973). A Critique of Utilitarianism. In J. J. C Smart and B. Williams *Utilitarianism: For and Against*. Cambridge: Cambridge University Press, pp. 77–135.

Chapter 5

Critical thinking and ethical decision-making

Keywords: paradigm; deductive logic; critical reasoning; argument mapping; soundness; validity

Introduction

Our survey of four of the major ethical theories, while not by any means exhaustive, hopefully has alerted you to some very different ways of thinking about ethics and ethical dilemmas. These theories, as outlined in the previous two chapters, provide frameworks for ethical decision-making processes. It is essential that we are able to fully justify an ethical decision and defend a particular course of action against critique, not only by using these theories, but also by supporting our position with facts and logical arguments. This chapter explores what constitutes critical thinking, how to assess the theories, and three methods of ethical decision-making. It describes and explains deductive logic and how to employ deductive logic to make an argument. It also provides a critique of the various methods employed by utilitarians, deontologists, egoists, and virtue ethicists, and provides some practical guidelines for making ethical decisions in everyday situations. We begin by discussing how to go about assessing the merits of the theories.

Assessing the perspectives

A theory cannot be proved to be true. A theory is an explanation for why something happens or how someone or something will act, but it is not generally something that can be proven by fact. At most we can demonstrate a particular theory to be the best theory; that is, the best explanation and therefore the most persuasive. Ethical theory works along similar lines to scientific theory, in process at least, if not in content. Up until the sixth century BCE or so, for example, it was widely believed that the world was flat. Pythagoras was the first scientist to theorize that the world is round, and in about 350 BCE Aristotle put together a proof in support of this view, which was subsequently further supported over the following century by Aristarchus and Eratosthenes, both of whom were able to measure the size of the Earth. However, people widely believed that the Earth was flat until 1522 CE when an expedition led by Portuguese explorer Ferdinand Magellan circumnavigated the globe. The idea that the world was flat 'worked' until someone actually sailed around the world and proved it wrong. Similarly, Darwin's theory of evolution changed the way people thought about the origins of the Earth and its various species. In science, if a particular theory makes the most sense based on the evidence available, it is adopted until a better theory is developed. Thus it is said that science works in 'paradigms.' Ethical theory (and all other theory for that matter) works in a similar manner—although there is much less agreement about which theory is most productive and explanatory, they are more or less minor variations on a main theme. In the case of our four theories in the preceding two chapters, their commonality lies in their ability to make sense of Western civil society. Virtue ethics, particularly MacIntyre's view, comes closest to challenging the paradigm, and in this chapter we will discuss how his theory might be adapted and extended to better serve the goal of ethical decision-making. Nevertheless, much like scientists, philosophers and ethicists are constantly debating with each other over whose theory is the best, and there are many challenges to the current paradigm that seek to create new theories to explain ethical issues and how to create the best response to ethical situations. While we cannot canvass all such efforts in this book, we can learn how to assess the reasonableness of any particular theory.

When considering the various perspectives presented in this book, therefore, it would be foolish to think that any of the views actually approach the truth of the matter or can be established beyond all doubt. We can judge them by how convincing or persuasive they are, *all things being equal*. There are several tests that can be used in judging whether a perspective is adequate or convincing.

Five tests of a good theory or world view

1 *Adequacy*: does the theory explain all the relevant questions and assumptions—or at least, does it explain it more completely than its rivals? Let us take virtue theory as our first example. When we apply virtue theory to a particular ethical situation, does it answer all the relevant questions? Virtue theory is useful because it does not require that we apply rigid universal principles to each and every ethical dilemma. Virtue ethics requires that I only have to think about what type of person I am and what that kind of person would do in this particular situation. However, this assumes that I can predict what my ideal person would do under the same circumstances. The test of adequacy asks whether it can explain more characteristics of a dilemma, and provide the most complete solution across a diverse range of dilemmas.

2 *External consistency*: does the theory conform to other well-established theories and bodies of knowledge? Recall the idea of ethical theories working

within a particular paradigm, which most people take to be authoritative. If the theory does not conform, the burden of proof lies with the theory that contradicts the established paradigm. The theories examined in this book lie within the paradigm of modern Western analytic philosophy. In analyzing their consistency, then, we must determine how well they sit within this paradigm. Many philosophers challenge this paradigm, inviting us to think 'outside the box.' The paradigm that is Western analytical philosophy assumes that we are all free and equal individuals, capable of making our own choices as rational individuals. A different paradigm, for example post-structuralism, suggests that societies are not constituted by free and equal individuals; rather they are constituted by power relations, technologies of practice, and constructions of identity. In terms of our test for external consistency, then, it is the role of the post-structuralist theorist to demonstrate why stepping outside the current paradigm will provide a better explanation and understanding of the world, ethics, and morality. They must produce a very convincing argument to persuade us to step out of our usual way of thinking. When we are evaluating the ethical theories in the foregoing chapters then, we are thinking within a paradigm that assumes that we can discover objective rules and guidelines for making ethical decisions.

Again, evolution is a good example here. Evolution is a theory that developed around scientific facts derived from biology, population genetics, and archaeology. Evolution is the current best-fit theory because it explains how species developed much more comprehensively and persuasively than any other theory. Most people believe in evolution—even many creationists believe in evolution because the fact that we have evolved over time from Neanderthal to who we are today, that the world has evolved, and that the various species developed through a number of eras, is fairly well established. Challenging evolution, then, would require some well-supported and persuasive evidence.

3 *Internal coherence*: are all aspects of the theory internally consistent? A theory or view is incoherent if its ideas, claims, and assumptions contradict one another, or if it cannot meet its own criterion for success. Think of a theory as a spider's web—spider webs are perfectly constructed such that all the parts conform to and connect with all the other parts. Similarly, our belief system is like a spider's web, a 'web of beliefs' so to speak (Benn 1986). So if we have one belief, it must conform with all our other beliefs. When we discover that we have a belief that contradicts another of our beliefs, then we must engage in an evaluation to determine which of the beliefs must be abandoned. While it is certainly the case that many people entertain conflicting beliefs, this is because they have not reflected on them, and therefore do not know that they are conflicting (Bonjour 1985). In general, however, our rational minds require that we create coherence in our thinking. A theory must also strive for coherence in this way, and a theory is incoherent if

one or more of its claims or assumptions contradict the others, or if it cannot meet its own criterion for success. A good example of internal inconsistency is a 2003 report on corruption in the public sector by the New South Wales Independent Commission on Corruption (ICAC 2003). In the preamble to the substantive report, it states that it has many good—that is, ethical and conscientious—employees who should be trusted to be ethical and that corruption only happens in a very small number of situations. The document then reports the statistics on corruption in the public sector for the previous year and suggests a series of 'lessons' for employees and managers. Lesson 1 states that everybody is capable of corruption and that we should trust no one. Clearly lesson 1 contradicts the statement about the trustworthiness of employees in the preamble—obviously it is not coherent on the one hand to say everyone is trustworthy, then on the other to say that everyone is capable of corruption. This example clearly fails the test of internal coherence.

4 *Fruitfulness*: Can the theory be successfully applied to new situations and to life in general? Can it provide solutions? A theory needs to be relatively simple to apply, providing reasons and assisting in finding solutions for your argument. An example to illustrate this test is Michael Sandel's theory of human nature. In the 1970s and 80s John Rawls, a highly regarded American philosopher, developed a sophisticated political theory in a book titled *A Theory of Justice* (1971). Rawls proposed that, based on our shared understandings of certain political phenomena, including the value of liberal democracy and the ability of citizens to make rational choices regarding their own lives, that the best way to order society was to maintain a free market, but with certain caveats. He proposed two principles: the first was equal freedom for all citizens, and the second was that citizens may benefit from the free market, so long as the least advantaged people also benefit. Rawls' theory was a watershed in the history of analytic philosophy at the time, because it attempted to articulate firm principles for ordering civil society from a (philosophical) liberal standpoint. However a few years later another American philosopher, Michael Sandel, wrote a book critiquing Rawls' theory. Sandel (1998) argued that, while Rawls' theory reflected certain shared understandings and values in our society, it was impoverished because it considered individuals as abstract rational beings devoid of social content. Rawls' theory did not explain how people are also constituted by their communities, kinship, and other groups to which they belong. In other words, many people considered Sandel's theory to be more fruitful because it offered a better understanding of human nature in the context of political theory.

5 *Drawing conclusions*: does the theory establish certain hypotheses beyond reasonable doubt? Recall that most people believed that the Earth was flat until it was proven empirically wrong by Magellan? Circumnavigating the globe

provided hard proof that the world was indeed round. That the world is round was proved beyond reasonable doubt. So unless our perceptions of space and time are somehow being manipulated in ways we do not know, the Earth is indeed round. 'Beyond reasonable doubt,' then, means making the most reasonable argument; one that is very difficult to refute without concrete proven evidence to the contrary.

Errors of reasoning

Even after we employ the foregoing tests of a good theory, however, there are also several errors in reasoning often encountered in ethical argument. These are the argument from authority, equivocation, against the person, and the naturalistic fallacy. These errors, which are to be avoided at all costs, are discussed below.

- *Argument from authority*: some people make the mistake of appealing to some authority in making an argument. For example, a Christian might appeal to the divine authority of God on the basis of faith. Alternatively, someone might appeal to the interpretation of a theory by someone whose expertise is outside the area of concern. If I were suddenly to decide to write a treatise on Quantum Physics based on a dream or vision that I had one evening, for example, and someone used my treatise to support their own views, they would be making an argument from authority, because they would be taking my treatise under faith (since I have not studied, nor do I have formal qualifications or training in physics). This is an error of theory—theories should not appeal to some divine entity or other faith-based authority. The theories discussed in this book derive from human reason alone and exist as part of a general body of thought and knowledge about ethics and morality. If a theory is not corroborated by others, and does not provide clear empirical evidence or thorough ethical argument, then it is an argument from authority.
- *Equivocation:* this describes the error of using a word in two or more different ways without explaining the differences in meaning. The word 'respect' is an example. There are two different meanings to the word 'respect.' On the one hand, you might respect someone because you admire that person; for example, you might respect a mentor, a famous politician, a movie star, or a sports person because of their achievements and talents. The other meaning of respect may be termed 'moral respect,' which is the respect you give other people because they are individuals like yourself, and they are by that very token deserving of respect. You respect other people's wishes, for example, if you respect them as a moral equal. If someone said "I don't want you to do that," you would be respecting their wishes by refraining because you understand that they are a moral person like yourself. Using 'respect' in both ways without explaining the

difference can be quite confusing. So, when making arguments you have to be very careful that you are defining and using words in the proper way.

- *Against the person*: this error entails rejecting the person advocating a particular view, rather than assessing the merits of their argument. This is an error that is often made in political debates about policy. It is quite common around election time, for example, to hear politicians criticize their opponent's character instead of looking at their actual policies. This applies equally for any argument. Dismissing an argument because the arguer has character flaws is not a good enough reason. Similarly, dismissing MacIntyre's arguments because he is a Catholic, or Kant's because he is German, for example, would be dismissing their arguments unfairly. A person's character does not solely determine the legitimacy of their arguments. While we might feel inclined to dismiss an ethical theory proposed by a serial killer, simply being a serial killer does not in and of itself prevent one from developing a sound and reasonable ethical theory.
- *Naturalistic fallacy*: This refers to deriving 'ought' from 'is.' For example, in the discussion on egoism in Chapter 3 we saw that psychological egoists argue that it is an empirical fact of life that people are selfish. However, just because something is a fact of the world does *not* mean that it is how the world *ought* to be. In other words, moral guidelines cannot be found in descriptive statements. Therefore, even if it can be empirically proven that people are in fact selfish, this does not imply that being selfish is a good thing, or that people *should* be selfish. Just because people act selfishly, does not mean that that is the best way for society to be organized, or the best way for people to behave. There must be some other, separate argument attached to the claim to make it plausible.

Deductive logic

Deductive logic is a form of reasoning used in ethics and philosophy to demonstrate the reasonableness of a position or view. It is a method in which, if the premises (basic statements of fact) are assumed to be true then the conclusion must follow (if x . . . then y).

Argument 1
Premise 1: Toto is a dog
Premise 2: All dogs are hairy

Conclusion: Toto is hairy.

Let us test this argument. Below is a photograph of Toto.

This is my dog, Toto. Premise 1 is correct because it is obvious that Toto is a dog. But is Premise 2 correct? See Figure 5.2 below.

As you can see, Premise 2 is not correct—*all* dogs are not hairy! Therefore, without access to her photograph, we cannot conclude that Toto is hairy.

Figure 5.1 Toto

Figure 5.2 Mexican hairless dog

Since Premise 2 is incorrect the argument, we must conclude, is clearly unsound.

We can use this kind of method to judge whether someone's argument is reasonable, or we can use it to construct our own reasonable argument.

C. S. Lewis (1955) gives us a more complex example of such an argument:

Argument 2

Premise 1: If morality has meaning, then it is objective
Premise 2: If morality is objective, then God exists
Premise 3: Morality has meaning

Conclusion: Therefore, God exists.

This method of deductive logic is not the only way to show the reasonableness of a position but it provides a strong basis for testing whether someone's view is valid and sound.

Soundness and validity

An argument is *valid* if the premises lead to the conclusion; it is *sound* if the premises are all indeed true. Whether or not you personally agree with the argument that C. S. Lewis provides here, the point is that in certain branches of philosophy these two tests are taken to be authoritative.

What you must remember, however, is that seeing is not necessarily proof of existence. In our contemporary society, we have to rely on more than simple representations or claims of truth—we have to look below the surface and consider all the assumptions. Photographs do not always represent real things, especially considering the high level of sophistication of graphics software today. Similarly, words do not always represent what they claim to represent. Recall our discussion in Chapter 1, where we compared two different news articles reporting on the same event. We also need to be rigorous in considering the perspective, evidence, and reliability of any information presented to us. When making an argument you have to determine how much evidence you need to prove a premise correct. This is easier if you are discussing facts.

As we saw above, the argument that Toto is hairy is unsound, but it is still valid because if the premises *were* true, the conclusion *would* follow. An invalid argument would be:

Argument 3

Premise 1: Toto is a chicken
Premise 2: All dogs are hairy

Conclusion: Therefore, Toto is hairy.

Argument 3 is invalid because the premises do not lead to the conclusion.

Deductive logic is not the only way to show the reasonableness of a position, but it does provide a strong and straightforward basis for testing whether someone's view is valid and sound. An argument is valid if the conclusion logically follows from the premise and it is sound if the premises are, in fact, true.

Making an argument

Now that we have seen how to structure and format an argument, we can move on to developing arguments of our own for various moral judgments. The theories discussed in Chapters 3 and 4 can provide the theoretical framework for an argument. Once we choose which theory most fits our own perspective, we can demonstrate how that theory commits us to a certain course of action. Let us take the very controversial issue of abortion as an example. Let us say you want to argue that abortion is never morally permissible. To begin, you must be able to employ your theoretical framework to demonstrate why abortion is immoral. Let us assume you are using deontology as your framework.

Arguing against abortion

Premise 1: Fetuses are human because they are potential persons
Premise 2: It is never right to kill a human being

Conclusion: Aborting a fetus is morally impermissible.

If we can demonstrate beyond reasonable doubt that fetuses are indeed potential persons, then our argument—from a deontological perspective—is valid and sound. However, it is never enough to simply make your case; you must also refute potential *objections* to your argument. For example, if the mother's life was in danger, you might have to consider whether allowing a fetus to live equals killing the mother—or at least letting her die. If we were less absolutist than Kant—like Benn, for example—we might address this problem by weighing up and trading off roles and values. This means deciding whether letting the mother die is equal to killing. If it is, then you must find some kind of trade off to decide who should die.

Of course, a utilitarian would argue that we should weigh up the value of the mother's life against that of the fetus, which is not an easy calculation to make. It would depend on many factors; for example, the mother's identity (prime minister? A criminal? A homeless person? A doctor?), her potential for living a valuable and fulfilling life, who she would be leaving behind and what impact her dying would have, and so on.

Once we have identified an objection, we need to address that objection with a *rejoinder*, or answer. In this case, the deontologist could argue that the mother's identity and life potential make no difference because all human beings are moral equals.

Another objection to the argument against abortion might be that a fetus is not a living being until it is born, so that means aborting it would not constitute killing. Michael Tooley (1972) made such a claim when he argued that both fetuses and young infants might be human beings, but they are not 'persons' because they lack certain qualities of personhood, such as a capacity for picturing a future and for fearing death. Tooley argues that it is precisely these qualities of personhood that attribute to persons the right to life. Judith Jarvis Thompson (1971), on the other hand, conceded that fetuses might be considered persons, but argues against their right to life by using an interesting example. She suggests we imagine waking one morning to find ourselves hooked up—against our will—to a famous violinist, who is unconscious. You have been kidnapped by the Music Lovers' Society because out of all the medical records, yours shows you as the best match for his condition. You are required to remain hooked up to the violinist for nine months so that he can heal. Thompson suggests that this example equates to becoming pregnant through rape or deceit.

These are just some of the arguments that have been forwarded both for and against abortion. It might seem almost impossible to make a compelling argument that resists all comers, but this is not necessarily the case. Ethical argument is about finding the most reasonable position, and if that results in plenty of healthy debate, then we are on the road toward some kind of eventual consensus.

The ethics essay

So, to reiterate: when you choose a perspective and use it to demonstrate how that perspective commits us to a certain course of action, then you are making an argument. In making an argument, you need to show that you know what the underlying assumptions are, what the facts are, and how they fit together to form the conclusion. But justifying a particular perspective is not just about demonstrating why your view makes sense. A good argument looks at all sides and tries to answer any objections up front. One way to do this is to construct your essay using the method outlined in the box below.

Essay topic: should police be allowed to use tasers?

Theoretical framework: Utilitarianism

A utilitarian considers only best outcomes for all stakeholders. The following is an example of an argument from a utilitarian perspective.

(continued)

(continued)

The argument:

Premise 1: Police work often involves dangerous and risky confrontations with suspected and known offenders

Premise 2: The use of tasers instead of guns will forestall the use of deadly force, which is safer for both police and offenders

Conclusion: Police should be allowed to use tasers.

Evidence for Premise 1: Provide focused empirical evidence, including statistics, interviews, news stories, and scholarly research to demonstrate how dangerous police work is. This premise will be fairly easy to demonstrate for most jurisdictions.

Objection 1: We will reasonably assume that there will be no objections to this premise if sufficient evidence is provided.

Evidence for Premise 2: Provide focused empirical evidence, including statistics, interviews, news stories, and scholarly research to demonstrate the advantages of using tasers in police work. This premise requires concrete evidence based on sound research.

Objection 1: There have been cases where the use of tasers has resulted in death, for example, in the elderly or ill (give some examples, or use a case study).

Answer to Objection 1: The death of a very few people who might be at risk of death by taser is outweighed by the greater level of safety for both police officers and the general public, especially those who confront police. Deaths by taser might be averted if police were more carefully trained to recognize at-risk offenders.

Objection 2: Police may see the taser as relatively harmless and be more prone to using it in situations where a lower level of force might be warranted.

Answer to Objection 2: Police are held accountable for their use of force and there should therefore be strong sanctions applied to officers who misuse the taser.

You can see here how the writer looks for objections to their argument and then tries to answer them up front. This is an important method of arguing in ethics because it helps to demonstrate your position beyond all reasonable doubt. In effect, you are saying "Don't just take my word for it—look at what others have to say about my view and how I can answer their charges against me." Arguing in this way makes your essay much stronger.

If you cannot think of any good objections to your argument, then you are probably not looking hard enough. Look in scholarly and other sources for views that oppose your own and then see what they have to say. Try to see your argument from their point of view and then answer their objections respectfully and honestly.

Argument mapping

One way of organizing your essay is to construct a conceptual map with all the components on it on a piece of paper. Then work with your premises, reasons (evidence), objections, and answers to objections until you have created the most sensible ordering that best helps the reader grasp what you have to say.

Ethical decision-making

Learning how to make a persuasive and coherent argument is just as important in the everyday context of the justice profession, and indeed, in everyday life, as it is in the formal context of study. As we saw in Chapters 3 and 4, there are several ethical decision-making models based on particular theories. In Chapter 3 we constructed a utilitarian argument, while in Chapter 4, we discussed Stanley I. Benn's method of trading off values and principles. Both required weighting and calculating, though they come from opposite ends of the ethics spectrum—Benn is a neo-deontologist, while Bentham of course is

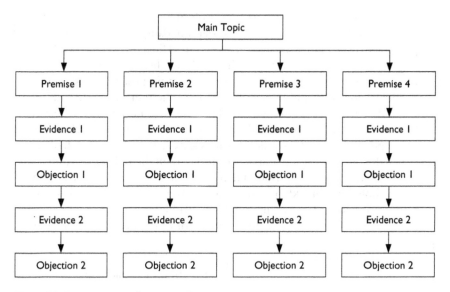

Figure 5.3 Basic argument/conceptual map

a utilitarian. Kant is more absolutist, arguing that we must adhere to strict universal principles, which cannot be 'measured' in quite the same way. Indeed, the entire concept of 'measuring' a principle in deontology (or in general) makes no sense. Nevertheless, his theory also provides clear, if somewhat rigid, guidelines for ethical decision-making. Aristotle focuses on human flourishing and virtue, arguing that we cultivate an ethical life by developing our characters as part of civil society. All four theories provide a framework for ethical decision-making from a particular perspective that claims to have universal ethical reign, as MacIntyre (1984) pointed out. So how do we, as individuals and as justice professionals, make a choice between these quite varying perspectives? MacIntyre suggests that we return to the *polis*, to civil and social life as a context for developing an ethical life, and focus on developing habits of virtue and character through practices that offer joy and fulfillment in the very doing of them—internal goods—rather than simply in the immediate rewards of engagement—external goods. This all sounds very nice, until we are faced with a serious ethical dilemma and are forced to make an authentic choice.

The fact that a particular ethical theory does not spell out a specific method for making decisions does not make that theory worthless. Nevertheless, it is less than clear how MacIntyre's virtue ethics can apply in practical terms. In order to find the method in MacIntyre's theory, it will help to think 'laterally.' To begin, we shall consider an ancient Chinese dilemma, traditionally called the Tale of the Two Pebbles.

The Tale of the Two Pebbles

A poor farmer owed money to a local old man and was having trouble paying it back. The farmer also had a beautiful daughter who the old man particularly fancied, so in exchange for canceling the debt, he offered to marry her. Of course both father and daughter were terribly upset by the offer, so to make it fairer, the old man proposed to pick up two pebbles—one black and one white—and put them in a bag. He said that if the daughter picked the white pebble, she would not have to marry him and her father's debt would be cleared. However, if she chose the black pebble, the debt would also be cleared, but she would have to marry the old man. If she refused to choose, then the old man threatened to throw her father in prison. Then he turned his back and picked up two pebbles and quickly put them into a bag. However, the daughter noticed that he had picked up two black pebbles.

What can she do? Expose the cheat? Sacrifice herself? Or let her father go to jail?

What would you do?

(My adaptation of an old Chinese fable)

This is an interesting tale because it highlights just how difficult some ethical dilemmas are, as well as the fact that in most circumstances, all things are *not* equal. In this case, the daughter has two dilemmas—the first is whether to expose the old man as a cheat; the second is whether to gamble her life away on the chance of saving her father from prison. Since she knows that if she plays the game she will be forced to marry the old man against her will, the second dilemma at least has some certainty attached. If she refuses to play, her father goes to prison. In the first dilemma, if she exposes the old man's cheating, her father will undoubtedly still go to prison and the old man will be very angry at his exposure. It is often the case in ethical dilemmas that we are given a choice between what we regard as two evils.

Kant's position on this dilemma seems clear cut—she is not responsible for the outcome, and therefore should not be required to act at all. The fact that this course of inaction will lead to serious consequences for her father is none of her business. However, what about her duty to her father? Could it be argued that she has a duty to protect him? Benn might suggest trading off her role as a devoted daughter with her role as a prospective wife, which would no doubt require that she play the game. Bentham would put all the variables into the utilitarian calculus and weigh up the best overall outcome—prison for her father or a marital prison for herself with the old man? She would have to weigh the hedons and dolors of each outcome, then multiply by their intensity to arrive at a solution. But she does not have time to conduct such a calculation.

Here is how the parable ends: The girl reaches into the bag and picks out a pebble, but 'accidentally' drops it onto the ground before either man can see its color. There were many such pebbles on the ground, so she says, "Oops, clumsy me. Never mind. The pebble left in the bag will show the color of the one I picked," knowing that the pebble in the bag was black. The old rich man did not dare reveal he cheated and therefore was forced to extinguish the debt without a bride in return.

Kant, of course, would be just as horrified by the girl's cheating as the old man's and would consider it morally reprehensible. Bentham, on the other hand, would condone the girl's cheating because the end would justify the means—if only he had time to think laterally, rather than doing all that calculating! In the end, the outcome was most advantageous for both the father and the daughter, and seems fitting considering the old man's tactics. Indeed, Bentham would argue that the girl is *morally required* to outwit the old man if she knows how. It is at this point where these ethical theories find it difficult to align with our everyday moral sensibilities, because cheating in order to achieve the best outcome just does not seem right.

The main insight of this parable, of course, is that there are (almost) always more variables (and possible solutions) in a situation than we have accounted for, and so sticking rigidly to one formula or principle might be counterproductive, if not outright foolish. Which solutions and variables we identify depends largely upon context, and how we deal with these variables is at least partly dependent upon the tradition or cultural context within which we live. This is not to concede relativism—rather, it is an acknowledgment of Sartre's challenge to get our hands dirty where necessary, even if it requires us to pay a price. We should align ourselves with certain moral and ethical standards for personal and professional conduct, and we should uphold those standards to the best of our ability. But when a dilemma of the 'two evils' kind presents itself, we can be forgiven for thinking laterally, and getting our hands dirty in pursuit of a higher cause.

In Part II of this book, particularly Chapter 10, we will examine the ways in which institutions and organizations formalize ethical decision-making through codes of conduct. Many such organizations provide clear guidelines about what behavior is deemed appropriate, what is unethical, and the sanctions attaching to breaches of the code. These are useful tools for understanding the standards of a particular organization or profession. Nevertheless, there might still be times when a dilemma arises that cannot be addressed by referring to the code of conduct. The foregoing discussion acknowledges this discrepancy and seeks to empower the reader to use their moral imagination to find the best solution all round.

Review questions

1 You are on a boat and nearby are two large rocks filled with persons waiting to be rescued; there are five people on one rock and four on the other. Assume that you cannot rescue both groups and that you are the only one able to rescue either group. The group of five includes a known rapist, a wealthy businessman, a doctor, and two children. The group of four includes the prime minister and three other politicians. Which group do you rescue?

2 What are the five tests of a good theory? Apply the tests to one theory from Chapters 3 and 4.

3 What do we mean by equivocation?

4 Choose a topic that has ethical currency and create an argument map showing how you would make your argument.

5 What is the purpose of deductive reasoning? What is its basic structure? Give an example of your own.

6 How do you use a rejoinder? Give an example.

7 Explain the difference between a sound argument and a valid argument.

8 Give an example of a paradigm.

9 What does internal coherence require of a theory? Which of the theories discussed in the previous chapters demonstrates a lack of internal coherence?

10 What is Sartre's challenge?

References

Benn, Staney I. (1986). *A Theory of Freedom*. Cambridge: Cambridge University Press.

Bonjour, Laurence (1985). *The Structure of Empirical Knowledge*. Cambridge, MA: Harvard University Press.

Independent Commission Against Corruption (ICAC) (2003). *Annual Report 2002–2003*. Sydney: Independent Commission Against Corruption.

Lewis, C. S. (1955). *Mere Christianity*. London: Collins.

MacIntyre, Alasdair (1984). *After Virtue: a study in moral theory*. Second edition. Notre Dame: University of Notre Dame Press.

Rawls, John (1971). *A Theory of Justice*. New York: Belnap Press.

Sandel, Michael (1998). *Liberalism and the Limits of Justice*. Cambridge: Cambridge University Press.

Thompson, Judith Jarvis (1971). A Defense of Abortion. *Philosophy and Public Affairs* 1(1): 47–66.

Tooley, Michael (1972). Abortion and Infanticide. *Philosophy and Public Affairs* 2(1): 37–65.

Part II

Ethics in public life

Part II examines what constitutes justice and the good society. It examines the importance of maintaining a distinction between our private morality and the morality we express in public or as professionals. It also explores how society ought to be organized to produce the maximum benefit to its members. This is truly a question of *social* ethics, and is essential for justice professionals to consider, given that their professional activities are conducted within the realm of the social.

Chapter 6

The good society

Key terms: public morality; public role; individualism; common good; liberal democracy; autonomy; tolerance; common good; institutions

Introduction

In Part I of this book, we examined the concepts of ethics and morality and examined a range of ethical theories as possible frameworks for examining ethical issues and dilemmas, and for making ethical arguments. We have examined utilitarianism, egoism, deontology, and virtue ethics, learned how to make an ethical argument, and discussed methods for ethical decision-making. What about *social ethics*?

The core question we consider in this chapter is: How is our ability to choose between right and wrong affected by the kind of society in which we live? The chapter will examine how issues of individual moral responsibility are related to social responsibilities, as well as various understandings about how society ought to be organized. The kinds of questions we will be addressing are:

1 What is the good society and how should a good society best be organized?
2 Can I simply apply my personal ethics to public life?
3 Is there such a thing as a 'public morality'?

The question of whether there is a common or public morality is much debated. Certainly our society seems to be based on certain social conventions and mores that suggest we hold a common set of values. However, there is some debate about what those values are and what they mean. In the early twenty-first century economic rationalism took a strong hold on society and this has led to some skepticism about the possibility of a public morality. The economic view suggests that liberal democracy revolves around the marketplace, where buying, selling, and trading of commodities is the modus operandi for all facets of life, including goods, occupations, services, and leisure. When the market runs smoothly, life proceeds on the basis of supply and demand, and there are no such things as moral problems. From this perspective, the market regulates everything; therefore we do not need ethics. Public life, like science and the market, is a self-regulating, value-free domain. This view ignores some important characteristics of public life. The following section reflects on those characteristics and asks what kind of society best supports a public morality.

Public and private morality

Let us concede that there is a public realm of morality and proceed to examine what that realm might look like. It has often been argued that the fulfilling of one's public duty often results in the identification of distinct and often con-flicting responsibilities. Views abound about what those distinctions are and how they ought to be addressed. For example, should one always pursue the public good or are there some aspects of life where we are morally permitted to respond according to our own personal morality? Further consideration suggests that, in some instances at least, our personal morality can and should take preference. This has been demonstrated in numerous instances through-out history—for example at the Nuremburg trials, where Nazis were tried for crimes against humanity during the Second World War, individual senior officers who were accused of malicious and senseless murdering of innocent people responded that they were 'just following orders.' Similarly, during the same trials Nazi doctors who were accused of torturing and killing disabled people in medical experiments offered the same excuse, claiming that they did not realize they were doing anything wrong. These doctors subjected severely disabled 'patients' to horrendous experiments involving poisons and poisonous gases, typhus and other vaccines, and mass sterilization experiments, during which they seemed "not to know" or to understand that they were tortur-ing actual human persons (Nuernberg Military Tribunals 1949). This 'psychic doubling' where we remove our personal morality and understanding from our professional role, is obviously problematic, not least because it is so pervasive. Can we legitimately claim innocence in such cases, even when the results are that we commit heinous crimes?

Private morality and the public interest

The idea of a public morality needs to be explored in the context of the pub-lic interest (Benn and Gaus 1983). Public officials, for example, are required always to act in favor of the public interest regardless of their privately held values and beliefs. When an official's private values conflict with their public duty, the official is required to set aside their private views and act for the pub-lic good. This assures us that, so far as possible, government decisions will be impartial and in the public interest. For example, officers of Centrelink—the Australian equivalent of the US Social Security Department—are not allowed to discriminate on the basis of race, ethnicity, sexuality, and so on, when assessing a client's need for payments. So even if a Centrelink officer personally finds openly homosexual men distasteful or immoral, she is not permitted to take that fact into account when assessing such a person's claim for payment. She must remain impartial, treating each individual with the same courtesy and consideration as any other.

This impartiality requirement also flows into some private and quasi-private organizations, especially those governed by regulatory laws and systems. Thus, professional associations—for example, the Australian Medical Association or trade unions—are not permitted by law to discriminate against individuals on the basis of race, gender, sexuality, or ethnic background. But the difference between public and private morality is not so clear cut as it seems, for it raises other issues such as the role of professional ethics, loyalty to one's employer, and the ethics of exclusivity. The following case study serves to illustrate.

The exclusive club

In New Orleans the existence of Mardi Gras clubs or *Krewes* is renowned. Each year Krewes compete against each other to see who can create the most lavish and eye-catching float in the parade. Many of the Krewes have a long history, dating back many hundreds of years and, until recently, many of them were exclusively male or white-only Krewes. One day an Africa-American man—let us call him Peter—applied to become a member of one of the more exclusive all-white clubs, The Krewe of X. His application was nominated and seconded, but in the end it was turned down, although no clear explanation was offered to Peter as to why he was denied membership. Peter sued Krewe X for racial discrimination, claiming that his application was refused because he was African-American. He argued that there were no non-white members in the Krewe of X and that this proved them to be racist. The attorney for Krewe X argued in their defense that since they were a private club, with no public role or responsibilities, they had a right to choose who could join and who could not. Indeed, he argued, the basis of a private club is its capacity to choose its members—otherwise it could not be called private in any real sense. Peter lost his case.

What do you think of the arguments presented above? What if it were also revealed that many of the members of Krewe X were high-profile professionals, business men, and politicians who often discussed business at the club, networking and presenting each other with business and professional opportunities not available to outsiders. Could such a club really claim it had no public role or responsibility? In fact, could it not be argued that these men kept the balance of social and political power in their grasp, due to their exclusivity? What do you think? Can an organization such as Krewe X really justify itself as a private club or does it have a public role that demands some level of impartiality, at least in terms of membership? Society is made up of many clubs, organizations, and institutions. How these impact on individuals is determined by the importance society as a whole places on the individual as opposed to the public good. Striking a balance between the two is a difficult, if not impossible task.

The distinctiveness of public roles

Whoever takes on a public or official role assumes the obligation to serve a special function. As we have seen, this implies a need for impartiality in the execution of an official role. Public officials serve the public interest, as we have seen, and this gives them an overriding reason to forgo their own interests, at least when they act in an official capacity. How far the commitment to impartiality extends is debatable—recall the case of the exclusive club above. A second case illustrates.

A case of discrimination?

This article makes reference to the Ontario Human Rights Commission, which ruled "that a Christian printer had illegally discriminated against a gay group by turning down a printing job for pro-gay literature, [they] said he had the right to his religious beliefs in his own home but he had to check them at the door when he left for work in the morning."

(Mark Steyn, *The Sunday Mail*, March 28, 2004)

What do you think?

This case is about a printer, but what about publishers? Should a publisher be able to state what kinds of literature it will publish? Some publishers specialize in a certain genre or orientation and therefore draw parameters around what topics fall within their specialty. No publisher is obliged to publish something they believe is either unmarketable or outside the scope of their market. But what if the gay group wanted to publish gay-friendly Christian literature? Surely there are many interpretations of Christian teaching and the gay group is offering just one of them. What if a Nazi group approached the printer wanting to print pro-Nazi material? Would the printer be obliged to publish such racist material?

Individualism versus community

It has been suggested that the language of individualistic achievement and self-fulfillment seems to make it difficult for people to sustain their commitments to others, either in intimate relationships or in the public sphere (Sandel 1982). There are two main, diametrically opposed schools of thought as to what the focus of social arrangements should be—the liberal and communitarian viewpoints. 'Liberal' in this sense refers to philosophical liberalism, as a stance informing politics, rather than a political stance itself, such as that typified by the Liberal Party in Australia. Philosophical liberals are, for this reason, sometimes referred to as 'small-l liberals' to denote the title as a descriptive label rather than a proper noun.

Philosophical liberals claim that all social problems can be solved by organizing society in such a way as to maximize the capacity for individuals to act autonomously, which is best achieved within a market economy, and regulated by a procedural state that is voted for democratically. Such a state, as you are no doubt aware, is called a *liberal democracy*.

Liberal democracy

Liberal democracy is characterized by representative democracy in which majority rule is qualified by respect for civil rights such as freedom of speech and assembly, freedom of religion, the right to private property and privacy, as well as equality before the law and due process under the rule of law. Such rights are guaranteed through various institutions and statutory laws in order to protect the interests of individuals and minorities against the "tyranny of the majority" (Adams 1788).

Ethical framework of liberal democracy

Liberal-democratic states are individualist by nature, in the sense that they promote the maximization of individual rights and personal autonomy as the foundation of a good society. Individual citizens are given sovereignty over their own affairs, and it is acknowledged that each knows best what are his or her wants and needs and how to satisfy them. Each individual is an equal moral agent in society with equal rights to the basic freedoms described above. However, the pursuit of rights is constrained to a certain extent by the common good and by observance of the Harm Principle. The Harm Principle states that an individual may have the freedom to pursue his or her interests without interference, *so long as he or she does not harm others* in the process (Gaus 1999). This minimal constraint is a necessary constraint to the emphasis on freedom. Were we all simply free to do whatever we wanted without regard for others, social chaos would ensue. The definition of harm has been the subject of some debate, but for our purposes we will define it as an action that sets back another's welfare interests (Gaus 1999: 159). In a liberal-democratic state, then, citizens are free to do as they wish so long as they adhere to the Harm Principle.

Familiar liberal-democratic notions such as rights, autonomy, and tolerance are valued almost worldwide as the foundation of a good society, and for good reason. A society might be rich and plentiful, but if its citizens are not given basic freedoms, then its social, political, and economic fabric will be thin indeed. The ideal of the autonomous individual who regulates his own life and is capable of achieving anything allows society to develop into a rich pluralistic blend of values, interests, and cultures. Privacy of moral conscience prevents the state from overly interfering in citizens' private lives and allows a greater range of personal behaviors to come under the domain of individual autonomy. The box below outlines the basic tenets of liberal democracy.

Key elements of liberal democracy

1 Civil liberties are key, including the right of all citizens to be governed equally;
2 Government intervention is restricted to provision of infrastructure and the protection of citizens' rights and property;
3 Free speech and freedom of belief and religion;
4 Equal opportunities and rewards based on merit;
5 Concern for the public interest and the common good.

(Adapted from australianpolitics.com 2006)

The common good

Individual freedom and autonomy may form the cornerstone of liberal democracy, but the liberal-democratic state is mandated to serve the common good. The common good is defined, at a minimum, as that which benefits society as a whole, as distinct from individual goods of particular members of the community. It can be defined more broadly as that which serves or benefits the public interest.

No substantive consensus is required as long as the common good protects liberty, autonomy, and diversity. Indeed, Saint Thomas Aquinas once stated that a ruler might be scandalously immoral in his personal life, but if he works for the common good, then he is a good ruler. This seems to have been borne out in contemporary politics, with events concerning the United States presidency of Bill Clinton being the paradigm case. While citizens were divided over the morality of Clinton's affair with his intern, he nevertheless continues to be held in high esteem for the work he did in advancing health and other welfare rights during his administration.

What is wrong with liberal democracy?

Criticisms of liberal democracy abound from both left and right of the political spectrum. It has been argued, for example, that liberal democracy is a state for the wealthy and privileged because it disadvantages those who cannot afford good health care, housing, or legal representation. What use are rights if one cannot afford, or is too debilitated, to exercise them? Philosophers such as Stanley Benn (1986) argued that the state has a moral obligation to provide the means by which individuals can realize their autonomy, and many Western nations do provide those means to a greater or lesser extent. Unemployment and other social security benefits, family payments, state schooling, and subsidized health and disability care are illustrations of how Sweden, Australia, and the United Kingdom, for example, provide for those who are disadvantaged. Many liberal-democratic nations, however, have failed to realize such a high level of welfare as a means for balancing out inequalities in the system.

Conflicting interests

A large cement company built a plant and began operating just outside Albany, New York in 1964. By 1970, the Atlantic Cement Company employed over 300 local people and had invested a small fortune into its development. However, the local residents complained because the plant gave off excessive amounts of pollution, not to mention causing annoying vibrations and noise in the surrounding environment. Eventually the local residents filed a suit against the company for its negative impact on their collective health and property. They asked the court to issue an injunction to stop the plant from operating until it had fixed the pollution and other issues. However, since the company was already doing the best it could do with the available technology, this meant that the plant would have to shut down for good. The court refused to close the plant and ruled that the company pay local residents the equivalent of the cost of selling their respective houses at fair market price as a one-off fee in compensation. It was argued that if the residents did not want to live there, they could buy elsewhere and rent out their homes if they wanted to.

Was the decision of the court fair in this case? If so, why? If not, why not?

(Adapted from Ladenson 2009)

The case study above highlights some real ethical issues faced by those working within the criminal justice system. Clearly, harm was being done to the residents living near the cement plant, but the judge decided that the cost of closing the plant would be onerous. So even though the court found in the residents' favor, they did not get the result they were looking for. This begs the question of how we can live in a society where injustice is allowed to continue, even where acknowledged, as long as it is offset by financial payment. In Chapter 7, we will consider the issue of distributive justice, which concerns the fair and ethical allocation of goods and resources in society. For the moment, however, it is important to note that sometimes justice comes up against economic imperative. Whether the two can be reconciled is a question that should and must be addressed if we are to continue living in a free and just society.

Liberal democracy has also been criticized for being excessively individualist. Its view of society as an aggregate of individuals reinforces this perception and suggests that Western society is lacking in community and social cohesion. As we saw in Chapter 4, Sandel (1993) argues that the liberal-democratic view of human nature as rational, autonomous, and individual is conceptually poor and unrealistic. He claims that individuals are richly constituted by their community and social groups, in the sense that their identities are products of those connections and therefore cannot be separated from them. For Sandel and others, society is more of an organic entity with rich social and communal underpinnings than a mere collection of individuals going about their own business. From this perspective, liberal democracy is poor in both spirit and practice and cannot provide an adequate foundation for the good society unless it embraces its communal nature.

The good society

Institutions

It is sometimes difficult to be a good person in the absence of a good society. If society, for example, favors economic rationalism as its modus operandi, then there will be many social injustices that the average person—even those not directly affected—might have difficulty in addressing. For example, homelessness in our society has been criminalized and this impacts on how the homeless are treated. Homeless people are seen as a problem in society—one that detracts from the overall experience of a great society by the rest of us—rather than the absence of housing (Schindeler 2010). Individual citizens might see or even feel the injustice of such action, but will be at a loss as to what to do about it. When society problematizes the homeless, they are removing social responsibility from their fate, and placing the onus on the individual as having the sole responsibility for his or her homelessness. Similarly, in a society where ethics is purported to be a moot point, acting ethically may have little impact on anyone other than the individual themselves. What is the point, for example, in always being truthful when everyone around you is more concerned with making more money, and buying more commodities, than they are with being truthful? Indeed, truth is often the first casualty on the road to wealth and glory.

To understand how this is so, we need to understand how much of our lives are lived in and through institutions and how better institutions are required if we are to lead better lives.

What is an institution?

Institutions are patterned ways of living together. They include anything from a handshake to marriage, to the taxation system and more. Indeed, health, education, sport and justice, and most other aspects of our lives, are overseen by institutions. Western society is built on complex intertwining and well-developed institutions and it is for this reason that it is often called The Great Society. In the 1995 film, *The American President*,[1] the President describes America as The Great Society. There is much political and social propaganda supporting the view that Western democracies, including the United States, Britain, Australia, and many European countries, are indeed 'great' societies because their citizens enjoy a higher standard of living and more 'freedoms' than less developed nations. However, a great society is not necessarily a 'good' society. We need to examine whether the quantitative achievements, such as Gross National Product, Balance of Payments, Bills of Rights and so on, are backed up by qualitative achievement. Time and again, the West fails to balance the equation. Rather than address issues such as homelessness, unemployment, and crime in ways that are socially just for all stakeholders, these issues are handled by building walled communities, houses with bars on windows, the legalized use of weapons, increased law enforcement, and the entrenchment of welfare for the rich and well-to-do in the form of subsidies, tax breaks, and so on. Again, there will be more discussion on distributive justice in the following chapter. The point here is that constructing a liberal democracy does not always guarantee the kind of social and criminal justice usually associated with a free and equal society. Homelessness, bars on windows, walled communities, and youth suicide are all endemic in our society. How much does society contribute to this and how much is the result of individual effort (or lack thereof)?

Ralph Waldo Emerson once stated that, "an institution is a lengthened shadow of one man" (Buell 2004). What he means is that institutions may regulate individual lives but it is individuals themselves who created them. Are we not therefore responsible for what happens as a consequence? The following section offers some responses to these criticisms from the contemporary literature.

Two major concepts

Current critics of liberal democracy tend to focus on two important concepts when addressing these problems—civil society and social capital (Cox 1995). Civil society describes a social order in which citizens participate and over which they take responsibility. Social capital provides the means for executing change.

Civil society

We, as citizens, must take some responsibility for changing what we do not like. However, in order for this to happen there must be processes in place to allow such change to come about. Society is based on trust, and this includes trust in the institutions that govern our daily lives. Centuries ago, civil society revolved around the town center, which usually included the church, town hall, and market, where people met, conducted business and politics, and participated in the community. Today we barely know our neighbors, let alone participate in community or political affairs. What impact has this had on civil society? Today we appear to live lives that separate us from each other and from our communities, which leads us to develop into self-regulated consumers, each within our own little nuclear existence.

The history of our culture is a story about who we are and how we came to be here, both as a society and as individuals. Some criticize liberal democracy for privileging some stories over others, and it is clear that there are cultures and histories in our society that have been suppressed and even denied. One need only look to the Stolen Generation of Indigenous children in Australia, or the Forgotten Generation of children migrated as orphans from the UK to Australia, both in the mid-twentieth century, and both only recently acknowledged and apologized for, to see how this can happen even today. What happens when our common story is replaced by a plurality of stories?

Trust in institutions also appears to be diminishing. Recently, US news network CNN reported that "trust in government is at an all time low" (cited in Wile 2014) and that "Just 13% of Americans say the government can be trusted to do what is right." The article goes on to quote CNN Polling Director Keating Holland, who stated, "It is hard to remember that there was ever a time when Americans routinely trusted the government" (*ibid.*). Recent Australian Broadcasting Corporation news reports seem to indicate that the same is happening in both Europe and Australia. A survey of five countries, conducted in 2011, for example, found that "78 per cent of people did not trust their governments to deal with the problems facing the country . . . [and] [e]ighty-nine per cent of people did not trust national politicians to act with honesty and integrity" (Berg 2012). In Australia, where the Coalition government has been implementing controversial conservative measures impacting on many low-income and disadvantaged groups, a Neilson Poll also shows that confidence in government is rapidly declining (Coorey 2014). But the government is not the only institution to be criticized. Recent years have revealed a deep distrust of the private sector as well, with managerial elites blithely leading companies into bankruptcy while drawing million dollar bonuses, as evidenced by the recent collapse of Enron in the US, and of OneTel in Australia in the first decade of this century. Consider the hypothetical below.

> ## Government subsidies
>
> Foster Friess, a wealthy manager of a multi-billion dollar mutual fund, loves music, but strongly believes that government agencies should not subsidize the arts. "Why should the single mother who makes $6 a hour as a clerk be subsidizing . . . my seats at the symphony through the local, state and federal taxes taken out of her paycheck?" asks Mr Friess. Recently, Mr Friess offered a donation of $40,000 to the Grand Teton Music Festival in Jackson Hole, Wyoming, which has an annual budget of $1.2 million, on the condition that the festival not accept a grant of $10,950 from the National Endowment for the Arts, an agency of the US Government.
>
> Assume you are on the Board of Directors of the Grand Teton Music Festival. Do you vote to accept or reject Mr Friess's offer?
>
> (Ladenson 2009)

With distrust in government and business comes a perceived need for more self-reliance. People feel they must rely on their own skills to get ahead and to gain control over their lives. What about those people who do not have skills (at least skills that can be sold through the employment marketplace) or the means of acquiring them?

Social capital

'Social capital' is the new buzz word in politics and replaces the concept previously known as the 'social fabric.' It turns the concept of social fabric into a commodity, like other forms of capital such as financial, physical, and human capital. In an economic-rationalist worldview, capital is the currency of success and advancement.

Social capital is described by the World Bank (2014) as

> the institutions, relationships, and norms that shape the quality and quantity of a society's social interactions. Increasing evidence shows that social cohesion is critical for societies to prosper economically and for development to be sustainable. Social capital is not just the sum of the institutions which underpin a society—it is the glue that holds them together.

The term 'social capital' was introduced by Bourdieu and Coleman in the 1980s, and has some characteristics of other forms of capital. For example, it is a resource one can build up and draw upon at a later date. It has been described as the 'raw material' of society and is created from the 'myriad everyday inter-actions between people' (Bullen and Onyx 1995; see also World Bank 2014).

> It is not located within the individual person or within the social structure, but in the space between people. It is not the property of the organization, the market, or the state, though all can engage in its production. Social capital is a 'bottom-up' phenomenon. It originates with people forming social connections and networks based on principles of mutual trust, mutual reciprocity, and norms of action.
>
> (Bullen and Onyx 1995)

Robert Putnam (1993), one of the most central proponents of the concept, outlines the potential of social capital in his analysis of the devolution of Italian government in the late twentieth century. Putnam noticed that while some governments failed miserably because they were inefficient and corrupt, others have seen a very high level of success. On this outcome, Bullen and Onyx note:

> Contrary to our expectation, we were unable to explain the differences on the basis of such obvious factors as party politics, affluence, or population movements ... The historical record strongly suggests that the successful communities became rich because they were civic, not the other way round. The social capital embodied in norms and networks of civic engagement seems to be a precondition for economic development as well as for effective government.
>
> (Bullen and Onyx 1995)

We increase social capital by working together voluntarily in democratic organi-zations. Accumulated social trust helps develop tolerance and the ability to deal with conflict. The social institutions that govern us must operate in ways that value diversity, belonging, debate, and questioning. If a social system isolates people, discourages informal and formal contact, or just fails to offer the time and space needed for social contact, then social capital comes under threat (Cox 1995). Shared ownership of public resources is also characteristic of these communities— a return to the notion of 'the commons.' That is, people in a community take collective responsibility for care and use of the commons in their midst.

However, as with all grand plans, even this ideal has its downside. Social cohe-sion has the potential to create insular communities which are too self-focused, regarding the outside as the 'Other.' We are members of multiple communities, and we must therefore learn how to reconcile those which might conflict.

Building an ethical community

Moral communities impose standards and traditions upon their citizens, leading to a danger of homogenization, domination, or separatism. Ethical communities, on the other hand, are capacity-building, involved communities that create ethical standards through cooperation and consultation. The resulting ethical standards are thereby owned by the group and a corresponding commitment is forged. Communitarians see a substantive role for citizens in making laws and setting standards.

Liberals see less of a role for the state and community in defining substantive issues. For liberals, the primary value is freedom, and the state's role is purely procedural, existing mainly to evaluate competing claims to property and resources, and to provide protection. Which of these views do you find more compelling?

Can society be organized around a definition of the good life, without this being seen as a depreciation of those who do not personally share this definition?

So, what then is the good society? It is clear that liberal democracy provides a solid foundation for rights and freedoms, but it has many problems that need to be overcome. The building of a good society requires a widening of democratic participation so that those who currently do not have a voice are no longer overlooked. It also involves higher-level accountability of institutions and the people who run them, as well as a right for citizens to participate in economic and political decisions that affect their lives. If people are interdependent and social-oriented, then we need, in addition, some deeper economic commitment to interdependent prosperity that will counter the vast imbalance of wealth. The good society is one in which the good life is not experienced only by those who can afford it.

Review questions

1 Australia has been strongly criticized, both internally and externally, for its responses to the plight of refugees, asylum seekers, and illegal immigrants. Using one of the theories studied in Chapters 3 and 4 (for example, deontology, utilitarianism, etc.), critically analyze whether a prosperous nation should have an open and flexible asylum seeker policy.

2 Western liberal democracies include the UK, the USA, Australia, New Zealand, France, Germany, Belgium and most of Europe and various other smaller pockets. What are some of the basic liberal-democratic characteristics shared by these countries?

3 Outline the main advantages and disadvantages of liberal democracy. Do you think the liberal-democratic state is representative of the good society?

4 At the beginning of this chapter it was suggested that people in our society agree on some common values. What common values do we share about how society ought to be organized?

(continued)

(continued)

5   Can I simply apply my personal ethics to public life? Why or why not? Give some examples to illustrate.
6   Is there a public morality? If so, on which theory, if any, is it based?
7   What is 'social capital'? Is social capital a crucial element of the good society?
8   It has been suggested that people do not trust institutions these days, particularly the government. What do you think of your government? Are they doing a good job? Discuss some issues with classmates or friends and see what others have to say. Conduct an informal survey of your area to gauge what people think about your government.
9   What do we mean by the term 'civil society'?
10   Liberal democracy has been criticized because it is based on an individualized view of human nature. What do you think?

Note

1   Aaron Sorkin (1995) *The American President* (film). Directed by Rob Reiner, for Universal Pictures. http://www.imdb.com/title/tt0112346/

References

Adams, John (1788). *A Defence of the Constitutions of Government of the United States of America*, Vol. 3. London, p. 291. Available at https://archive.org/details/defenceofconstit02aadam (accessed August 11, 2014).

Benn, S. I. (1986). *A Theory of Freedom*. Cambridge: Cambridge University Press.

Benn, S. I. and Gaus, G. F. (eds.) (1983). *Public and Private in Social Life*. London: Croom Helm.

Berg, Chris (2012). The Dramatic Collapse of Trust in Government. *The Drum*, January 25, 2012. Available at http://www.abc.net.au/news/2012-01-25/berg-the-dramatic-collapse-of-trust-in-government/3790244 (accessed August 11, 2014).

Buell, Lawrence (2004). *Emerson*. Harvard: Belknap Press.

Bullen, Paul and Onyx, Jenny (1995). Measuring Social Capital in Five Communities in NSW: Overview of a Study. Available at http://www.mapl.com.au/A2.htm (accessed August 29, 2014).

Coorey, Phillip (2014). Poll Reveals Tony Abbott's Trust and Competence Deficit. *The Financial Review*, July 21, 2014. Available at http://www.afr.com/p/national/poll_reveals_tony_abbott_trust_and_7OwhmWzNvTsNnjVDWCM6PN (accessed August 11, 2014).

Cox, Eva (1995). *A Truly Civil Society*. Sydney: ABC Books.

Gaus, Gerald F. (1999). *Social Philosophy*. Armonk, NY: M. E. Sharpe.

Ladenson, Robert F. (2009). Foreword. In P. Connolly, D. R. Keller, M. G. Leever, and B. Cox-White, *Ethics in Action: a case-based approach*. Malden, MA: Wiley-Blackwell, pp. xiii–xiv.

Nuernberg Military Tribunals (1949). *Trials of War Criminals Before the Nuernberg Military Tribunals Under Control Council Law No. 10*. Washington DC: Superintendant of Documents, U.S. Government Printing Office.

Putnam, Robert (1993). The Prosperous Community, Social Capital and Public Life. In Elinor Ostrum, and T. K. Ahn (Eds.) *Foundations of Social Capital*. Cheltenham, UK: Edward Elgar Publishers.

Sandel, Michael J. (1982). *Liberalism and the Limits of Justice*. Cambridge: Cambridge University Press.

Schindeler, Emily Martha (2010). A genealogy of the problematic of homelessness and *the homeless in Australia*. PhD thesis, Queensland University of Technology. Available at http://eprints.qut.edu.au/32068/ (accessed August 11, 2014).

Wile, Anthony (2014). 13% Trust Government—As Sirens Sound! *The Daily Bell*, August 9, 2014. Available at http://www.thedailybell.com/editorials/35545/Anthony-Wile-13-Trust-Government—as-Sirens-Sound/ (accessed August 11, 2014).

World Bank (2014). What is Social Capital? Available at http://web.worldbank.org/WBSITE/EXTERNAL/TOPICS/EXTSOCIALDEVELOPMENT/EXTTSOCIAL CAPITAL/0,,contentMDK:20185164~menuPK:418217~pagePK:148956~piPK:21661 8~theSitePK:401015,00.html (accessed August 11, 2014).

Chapter 7

The just society

Key terms: distributive justice; consumerism; contractarianism; utilitarianism; libertarianism; socialism; positive freedom; negative freedom

Introduction

In Michael Moore's 2007 video "Beat the Rich," he tells us that three of the richest people in the world are Bill Gates, Rob Walton (of the Walton family who own the Walmart Chain), and the Sultan of Brunei. Together, he says, they are worth US$181 billion, the equivalent of the Gross Domestic Product of 162 countries. At the time the video was made, Gates was worth US$97 billion, a net worth that equated to the net worth of the poorest 120 million Americans. Admittedly, the net worth of all three have risen considerably since then, which makes the statistics even more compelling, but even back then, Moore was rightly asking what these men had done to deserve so much wealth. "They must be pretty smart to get so rich," he says. So he devises a quiz show, pitting the rich of New York's Madison Avenue against blue-collar workers in Pittsburgh, Pennsylvania. The results were hilarious, but at the same time sobering. Moore stopped people in the street with his microphone and camera crew and asked them what he called 'tests of common knowledge.' The first question, "What is your zip code?" had the rich 'contestants' stumped, as did the price of upsizing at McDonalds, how to fix a toilet, how to change a bag on a vacuum cleaner and "What is the minimum wage?" The Pittsburgh contestants knew the answers to all these; however, they did not know the price of a bottle of Dom Perignon or a good year for merlot (pronounced "MAR-low" as one Madison Ave contestant pointed out). When asked about the best place for a winter vacation, the wealthy contestants suggested St Moritz, Aspen, St Martin, and Polynesia, while the blue-collar contestants suggested southern US states or closer places where they had family. The point of the exercise was not just to point out how little practical knowledge the wealthy have—obviously they do not need to know such things—but to highlight the huge discrepancy between the lives of the two groups of people. Indeed, their situations are so far apart as to bear absolutely no relation. Indeed, if you had transported the Pittsburgh-ians to Madison Avenue, they probably would have made up the core group of minimum-wage workers acting as maids, chauffeurs, doormen, and hairdressers to the rich.

Moore's video is funny, but his point is disturbing. That so many people at the wealthy end of the scale are so blissfully unaware of how most people actually live demands some explanation and justification. Recently it was made clear in news reports that the Walton family's wealth (at time of writing, $144 billion US dollars) was made on the backs of minimum-wage workers who had to be subsidized by welfare benefits, as well as employing charity tax laws to prevent being charged enormous estate and gift taxes (Midar 2013). Indeed, Quigley (2013) estimates that federal subsidies to US corporations cost the tax-payers over US$100 billion a year, while US$243 billion is spent in subsidies to the fast food industry. States Quigley (2013):

> There are thousands of smaller special breaks for corporations and businesses out there. There is a special subsidy for corporate jets, which cost taxpayers $3 billion a year. The tax deduction for second homes costs $8 billion a year. Fifty billionaires received taxpayer-funded farm subsidies in the past 20 years.

In the last chapter we discussed what constitutes 'the good life' and canvassed the relationship between private and public morality. This chapter examines the concept of the 'just society' and discusses some theories of distributive justice. Preston (2006: 29) states: "For a society or community to survive cohesively there must be some shared understanding and application of 'justice'." So, what does 'justice' mean within the Western context?

Justice is usually explained using terms such as equality, impartiality, fairness, reward and/or punishment (Preston 2006: 29). Generally speaking, there are four major categories of justice:

- *Procedural justice* (which highlights the importance of fair procedures within the legal context such as upholding the 'rule of law');
- *Retributive and restorative justice* (which articulate fair and just methods of punishment within the criminal justice system); and
- *Distributive justice* (which deals with the distribution of goods and services).

(Preston 2006: 30)

This chapter focuses on distributive justice and how it impacts our thinking about how to produce a just society. It compares various theoretical frameworks for considering justice, including contractarian, libertarian, utilitarian, and socialist perspectives. It asks, 'what is a just society?' and explores how we distribute wealth, what problems exist, and how we might do things differently.

What is justice?

> Too many people buy things they don't want, with money they don't have, to impress people they don't like.
>
> (Hamilton 2003)

Distributive justice and the market

There are varying viewpoints on how to achieve distributive justice. It is debatable, for example, whether goods and services should be distributed according to want, need, desert, equality, and so on. There are many ways of organizing economic systems in society, and we will discuss these later in this chapter. For now, we will examine how the economies of most liberal democracies work. In Western liberal democracies there are two quite separate but intertwining systems to manage the distribution of wealth: the *market* system and the *welfare* system. The ratio of one to the other varies according to the nation being discussed. The market system allocates goods according to individuals' (and groups' and organizations') buying and selling capacity. For example, my ability to purchase a car is limited by the amount of money I have access to, either through savings, gifts, or debt. The cost of a car depends upon its market value; that is, how much most people would be willing to pay for it. Similarly, how much I earn depends on the market value of my skills and how persuasive I am at selling them; that is, my ability to compete in the employment marketplace. This economic system, run as it is for the most part by markets, is known as capitalism because the market is based on the accumulation of capital. Eighteenth-century economist Adam Smith (1776) argued that if left to its own devices, the market acts like an 'invisible hand':

> It is not from the benevolence of the butcher, the brewer or the baker, that we expect our dinner, but from their regard to their own self interest. We address ourselves, not to their humanity but to their self-love, and never talk to them of our own necessities but of their advantages.

Smith argued that the individual benefits society the most when he acts in his own self-interest. Our self-interest generates a demand for goods and services that "compels others to deliver those goods and services in the most efficient manner so that they may be able to receive compensation from others and make a profit in doing so" (Gieseke 2010: 15). Smith's argument that the market was the most efficient mechanism for distributing goods and services is one that is widely adopted by economists today. However, there are several flaws with market capitalism for which the invisible hand theory fails to account. The first returns us to the issue of purchasing capacity and fairness in the market. As we saw, purchasing capacity depends upon the amount of money or credit we have or are able to obtain. However, this in turn depends on the market value of our employable skills, which are set according to supply and demand—not on education, merit, talent, or difficulty of the work, as one might think. Compare the CEO of a large corporation—let us say, Bill Gates, former CEO and now Chairman of the Board of Microsoft—to your standard university professor in the social sciences, for example. Gates dropped out of Harvard and started a software company backed by his well-heeled, upper-middle-class parents. The professor, on the other hand, came from a working-class family and was the first to enter college, from which he obtained at least three higher education qualifications over at least eight to ten years, but most probably longer. During his graduate study he was teaching part-time and perhaps being paid a small stipend or scholarship, finally landing a position as assistant professor in a small social science faculty in the mid-West. He worked several years before achieving tenure and was finally promoted to professor after about ten or fifteen years of long days spent teaching, researching, and writing scholarly articles and competitive grant applications. His salary at the pinnacle of his career, after he had written several important books, was around US$160,000, and he owned a house in a nice part of town and a fairly new mid-range car. There is little information accurately gauging Bill Gates' actual income, but his current net worth is around US$80 billion. Clearly Gates' entrepreneurial skills, together with his social and business connections and his family wealth, allowed him to quickly rise to the top. He has also used some very questionable tactics during his career, having been banned in college for stealing computer time, then later rigging his class schedules. During his career with Microsoft, the company has been the subject of continuing antitrust legislation over its business practices, many of which followed from decisions made by Gates.

By contrasting these two 'skill-sets,' it is not difficult to see that the way the market rewards some and not others is rather ad hoc, or at least tied to well-entrenched and marked differences in the distribution of wealth between those who work in education and those who engage in business. Clearly education level and hours of work are not indicative of financial success. It is also difficult to understand how Gates 'deserves' so much more wealth than the professor, although of course (economists and governments) will argue that 'money makes money' and that business, especially big business, creates jobs and 'keeps the economy going.' Nevertheless, there is certainly room for challenging and questioning the discrepancy.

Another problem with markets is the way they often develop monopolies—one of the issues that has, coincidentally, been the cause of complaint against Microsoft in recent years. Monopolies are created when one corporation gains a majority of the market share, eventually squeezing out all or most competitors because they are unable to compete. Yet another problem—related to monopolies, but usually involving a group of companies all engaged in selling the same commodity—is price fixing. The box below offers a good example of unfair practices around price fixing.

Price fixing in the UK

In 2007 several major supermarkets and food suppliers in the UK admitted to exchanging information with each other in secret to make consumers pay more for dairy products such as milk and cheese in a "£270m price-fixing conspiracy." Asda, Sainsbury's, Safeway, The Cheese Company, Robert Wiseman Dairies, and Dairy Crest accepted the UK Office of Fair Trading's judgment that they had conspired together and that their actions were against the interests of their customers. The companies attempted to defend their actions by publically stating that they were under pressure to help farmers who had been affected by outbreaks of foot and mouth disease. The Office of Fair Trading responded with the following statement: "I think it is reasonable to say we don't doubt the purpose initially was to pass money back to farmers but, in general, there is no evidence that farm gate price increased as a result of the initiative. We don't know what happened to the money."

In a free market, what is wrong with companies getting together to decide on a price for something? How might this be unfair to the consumer? What other problems might price fixing cause?

(Case adapted from Wikipedia 2014)

Price fixing in, and monopolizing of markets are 'good' business for companies aiming to increase their bottom line, but they are anathema to the consumer. Adam Smith would roll in his grave if he could observe markets as they are today. In the eighteenth century, markets were made up of individual traders, relatively small businesses and companies, and some larger factory operations, usually owned by one family—there were no multinational corporations, no financial trading markets, and no monopolies. In such a relatively humble market environment the invisible hand worked its magic well—supply and demand did indeed lead to the most efficient outcome (more or less) beneficial to all, considering the early state of industrialization. Over time, however, the nature of business and markets has changed dramatically, leaving open the issue of ethics in the market to further discussion.

Consumerism

Another factor that drives the contemporary market is consumerism. Today's consumer can literally buy almost anything, providing they have the money to do so. Advertising and media in general bombard us on a daily basis with goods, services, and experiences that we are told we want and must have. The pervasiveness of media and technology, especially through social media, allows us to compare our lifestyles with a range of others, encourages us to expand our list of wants and tells us that buying things brings value and meaning into our lives. In a society in which individual choice is magnified to the extent that many of us go into massive debt to accumulate the things we think we want, it is a rebellious soul who will refuse to do so. Even government economic policies encourage consumers to consume, providing tax cuts to citizens to 'stimulate the economy.' Indeed, GNP is largely determined by consumer spending.

> Gross National Product (GNP), a measure of a nation's wealth, is also directly affected by federal taxes. An easy way to see how taxes affect output is to look at the aggregate demand equation:

$$GNP = C + I + G + NX$$

> where:

> - C = consumption spending by individuals
> - I = investment spending (business spending on machinery, etc.)
> - G = government purchases
> - NX = net exports

> Consumer spending typically equals two-thirds of GNP. As you would expect, lowering taxes raises disposable income, allowing the consumer to spend additional sums, thereby increasing GNP.
>
> (Cloutier 2014)

As far back as the 1960s, Herbert Marcuse argued that the ideology of consumerism was creating a one-dimensional society in which there was no possibility of opposition to the dominant paradigm (Marcuse 1964: xi).

> "[A]dvanced industrial society" [has] created false needs, which integrated individuals into the existing system of production and consumption via mass media, advertising, industrial management, and contemporary modes of thought.

Consumerism, claims Marcuse, is a form of social control that employs the market to ensure people conform to the dominant ideology. The market gives consumers the impression of free choice, but the choices they are presented with are predetermined for them. Marcuse's criticism of capitalism has been much criticized, but it does highlight the ways in which our choices are controlled by media, advertising, and the government.

Another criticism of consumerism is its endless reproduction, such that no matter how much we have, it is never enough. We accumulate things to increase our happiness and satisfaction, but the diminishing marginal utility of wealth suggests that, at a certain point, having more will not bring us any more satisfaction or happiness. For example, if a minimum-wage worker loses $100, it could bring devastating results such as not being able to afford groceries or pay the rent. If billionaire Warren Buffet, on the other hand, were to lose $100, he probably would not even notice. The law of marginal utility states that as a person's income increases, any additional income will be perceived as less valuable (Wickstead 1910). But perhaps we should be asking another question: Just what is enough? Consider the image of a Guatemalan favela (or slum) below.

Can we really justify unlimited consumerism in our society when there are people in the world without access to clean water or sufficient food? Even in our own society, a significant percentage of people live below the poverty line, including many children. Clearly there is considerable inequality in access to wealth, which leads to other injustices, suggesting that not everything can be effectively and justly exchanged and regulated via the market.

To counter these failures of market, liberal democracies have instituted various forms of *welfare*, aimed at catching those who 'fall through the net' of market capitalism. For example, the provision of state-funded education and health care in many developed nations ensures that most people receive a minimum level of these goods. Nevertheless, those with more wealth at their disposal have many more significant opportunities or 'life chances.' Equality of opportunity is an empty freedom when there are many who do not have the wherewithal to take advantage of them. For example, state-funded education will give a child the basics, and sometimes even more, but when it comes to

Figure 7.1 Guatemalan favela

competing for entrance into the better colleges and universities, they will often be pipped at the post by those with privately funded education. Even if the child does manage to make it into an Ivy League university, she must receive a scholarship or find some other way to fund her study, or else go into massive debt for the foreseeable future.

So where does this leave us? If the market has failed, at least in terms of the most disadvantaged in our society, what guiding principles should we use to determine how goods should be distributed?

How *might* we create a just society?

Many 'theories of justice' have been put forward offering to provide such principles. This section will canvass some of the most prominent, many of which make a distinction between the concepts of 'positive' and 'negative' freedom.

Negative freedom refers to a state in which there are no constraints on an individual—he is free from restriction. This is the basic kind of freedom referred to in the US Constitution, and in the Bills of Rights adopted by other developed nations. Negative freedom means that I have the freedom to choose whatever I want; I am a slave to no one. Thus, I can choose to live, work, marry, and buy according to my personal tastes without constraint from others. This, however, has nothing to do with my actual capacity to make those choices. For example, I am free to buy a Hummer, but I might lack the funds to do so.

Positive freedom builds on negative freedom by providing the wherewithal to make certain choices. For example, I might be free to choose which school I go to, but if I cannot afford the fees, then my freedom is constrained by my financial position. State-funded education contributes to positive freedom because it allows all individuals to access education. Positive freedom is, therefore, the freedom to act, to do—it is opportunity to achieve autonomy in face of otherwise constraining circumstances. Other examples of provisions for positive freedom include state-funded health care, welfare payments, family allowances, and so on. These welfare payments and services increase an individual's autonomy by giving him more freedom of choice as well as the ability to exercise that choice. The following theories of justice employ negative and positive freedom to varying degrees.

Contractarian justice

Contractarianism is built around the theoretical concept of the 'social contract': a hypothetical document between those who govern and those who are governed (the 'contractors'), which stipulates the rules by which they are governed. In terms of contractarian distributive justice, the social contract would require fair allocation of goods and services.

The contractors agree upon the social contract during the 'state of nature': an imaginary situation before the advent of governmental rule. Thomas Hobbes

(1588–1679) and John Locke (1632–1704) developed classical contractarianism, however, John Rawls (1921–2002) expounded a contemporary version in his book, *A Theory of Justice* (1971).

Rawls' social contract differs from traditional contractarianism in two main ways. It includes:

- the 'veil of ignorance'; and
- the 'difference' principle.

Rawls' veil of ignorance exists within the 'original position' (Rawls' own version of the 'state of nature' in which contractors debate and agree on the social contract) and inhibits the ability of contractors to know their eventual position in society. That is, they are unaware of their status, skills, and other traits that might put them in an advantaged or disadvantaged position. Rawls argued that this would cause the contractors to agree on an altruistic contract, thereby ensuring the maximum benefit for the most disadvantaged groups in society. This last point is encapsulated in the 'maximin' or 'difference' principle, which asserts that the least well off should obtain the maximum benefit from the social allocation of goods and services. In this regard, Rawls attempted to address the problems of inequality caused by the libertarian and utilitarian versions of distributive justice. This theory, however, has also been criticized because the veil of ignorance is purely hypothetical and can never be practically applied. Furthermore, Preston (2006: 36) argues that it is too individualistic and "trusting of human rationality," taking "too little account of the realities of social conflict."

Utilitarian justice

As we discussed in Chapter 3, utilitarianism abides by the maxim "the greatest good for the greatest number" (Preston 2006: 33). Thus, the utilitarian perspective on distributive justice dictates that this maxim should provide the basis for the allocation of goods and services. The utilitarian perspective is useful, because it is difficult for a government to always satisfy every want and need of all members of society. Thus, the utilitarian perspective allows them to merely satisfy the majority. However, minorities may be ignored in this perspective. As Preston (2006: 33) states: "Narrowly applied . . . (utilitarianism) can support a crudely pragmatic economic rationalist approach which might reduce public services, thereby disadvantaging more vulnerable groups who presumably should be a focus of concern in terms of social justice or social inclusion."

However, at least one famous contemporary utilitarian, Peter Singer (2011), suggests that it is indefensible for some people to live in abundance while others suffer from poverty. Therefore, these obligations extend beyond our own society to take on global interests, such as helping the poor in undeveloped countries as well as in our own.

If we can prevent something bad without sacrificing anything of comparable significance, we ought to do it; absolute poverty is bad; there is some poverty we can prevent without sacrificing anything of comparable moral significance; therefore we ought to prevent some absolute poverty.

(Singer 2011)

However, if negative freedom comes second to the common good, then it *is* possible, even likely, that sometimes individual rights may be overridden. For example, Singer argues that euthanasia, abortion, and infanticide are morally justified in some instances. It has been argued by critics that this kind of thinking leads to a 'slippery slope' that has the potential for grave misuse. Bernard Williams, for example, argues that while Singer's arguments are "so damn logical," they nevertheless fail to take account of value, particularly with regard to human life (Specter 1999).

Libertarian justice

Libertarian distributive justice is based upon the presumption of the individual as a rational being. In this respect, their main purpose is to pursue their own goals in life, although they still have duties to others. Libertarians highlight the importance of a free market, believing that it provides the best distribution of goods and services. As Preston (2006: 31) states: "Libertarians agree that it is a good thing for the basic needs of all people to be met but they insist that the market, rather than governments, is more likely to ensure this." In turn, non-government charity organizations are preferred over government-sponsored welfare. However, there are obvious problems with this approach.

As Preston (2006: 31) points out, the United States of America, which is very close to a true libertarian economy, is a good example of the downfalls of libertarianism. In the United States, 50 million are unemployed, illiterate, socially alienated, and living in poverty amid crime (Preston 2006: 31). While North America is one of the most prosperous countries in the world, only a minority of its population enjoys any great benefit and, subsequently, the gap between rich and poor is constantly growing. The heavy reliance upon non-government charities to provide for these individuals is clearly not working: the free market has left them behind (Duncan 2005: 60). One alternative to this state of affairs is the socialist conception of distributive justice.

Socialist distributive justice

Rather than focusing upon the individual, the socialist conception of distributive justice focuses upon the community. In turn, the government plays a large role in overseeing the allocation of goods and services in a controlled economic environment. The government often controls banks, transport, health, and other key social goods so that fair, egalitarian allocation is ensured. In this respect, socialism is closely linked to communism, although communism deals with both the economy *and* political system while socialism focuses mainly upon the economic policy. While socialism avoids some of the problems of libertarian capitalism (such as the need to provide for the least well off in society), it has problems of its own.

The centralization of resources and power that is peculiar to socialism has, in the past, led to totalitarian regimes, where the authority invested in the government is abused for the gains of those few in power. The former Soviet Empire during the twentieth century is a good example of this. However, if there are clear problems with both the libertarian *and* socialist views of distributive justice, what is the basis for a 'just' society? Consider the case study below.

Does socialism work? A classroom experiment

An economics professor at a college in the United States failed an entire class of students because they said that socialism could work, and that in a system set up on socialist principles, no one would be either rich or poor. The professor challenged the class to an experiment, declaring that all grades would be averaged out, which is the socialist thing to do. After the first exam, the grades averaged out to a B. Naturally the students who had worked hard were quite upset, while the lazy students were quite excited! When the time came close for the next test, the lazy students did not bother to study at all, and the hard workers decided to study less so they too could get a free rise. The average grade was D. By the time the third test was over, everyone had received an F.

"As the tests proceeded, the scores never increased as bickering, blame and name-calling all resulted in hard feelings and no one would study for the benefit of anyone else" (Mitchell 2011). The final result was that all the students failed the class, and their professor was able to explain to them that people will make more of an effort the greater the reward they are likely to receive. Obviously, the flip side is that if the rewards are few, then no one will bother to try at all.

What do you think? Does this case study prove that socialism is indeed flawed? Can socialism work?

(Adapted from Dan Mitchell 2011)

Striking a balance

All of these conceptions of distributive justice have their advantages and associated disadvantages. One possible conclusion to the dilemma of which one contributes to the 'just society,' therefore, is to strike a balance between them all. In this respect, one attempts to cancel out the disadvantages of each theory by overlapping each of them. Most contemporary liberal democracies do this to some degree.

In Australia, we operate on an essentially free market system that is partially regulated and augmented by a welfare system. This structure derives from both the libertarian and socialist conceptions of distributive justice. The Australian welfare system works on a merit basis, attempting to provide for only the most needy in our society. This, in turn, works to advance Rawls' *maximin* principle. Last, because we have a democratic system of government, important decisions about social goods are generally resolved in favor of the majority. Hence, the utilitarian principle of the 'greatest good for the greatest number' is adhered to.

While it might appear as though we have diverted somewhat from considering the criminal justice system, taking a few moments to understand the way that ethical perspectives underpin our social systems is important. Inevitably, justice professionals work with a range of people, some of whom experience the full force of social disadvantage. Understanding how these situations come to be is an essential aspect of justice. Additionally, justice professionals are part of the system of social administration that, in many instances, perpetuates those very same situations of disadvantage, and thus must shoulder some of the responsibility for social injustice (and for changing this situation). Finally, justice professionals work in a broad variety of governmental and non-governmental offices, many of which seek to improve social justice in some form or another. Thus, understanding how this might be achieved, and some of the limitations of doing so, is an essential part of the professional development of justice professionals.

Review questions

1   What are some criticisms that may be leveled against liberal democracy in terms of distributive justice? How is the concept of freedom sometimes misused? How can a democratic society address inequality?
2   What are the principles of utilitarian justice?
3   Are we born with a sense of justice or is it taught to us?
4   What is the difference between procedural and distributive justice?
5   The libertarian theory of justice advocates a minimal role for government so that the market can naturally regulate society. What are the advantages and disadvantages of such a system? Is there any country in which this system rules?
6   What is the difference between socialism and communism?
7   What are the two principles on which Rawls bases his theory of justice? How does the Rawlsian system work?
8   What problems, if any, can you see with this system?
9   How does communitarianism attempt to overcome the problems identified in Rawlsian justice?
10   Do you think human nature is essentially individualist, or more communitarian? Or is it a combination—or even something quite different?

References

Cloutier, Richard (2014). Do Tax Cuts Stimulate the Economy? *Investopedia*. Available at http://www.investopedia.com/articles/07/tax_cuts.asp (accessed August 12, 2014).

Duncan, C. (2005). *Libertarianism*. Maryland: Rowman and Littlefield Publishers Inc.

Gieseke, Tim (2010). *EcoCommerce 101: Adding an ecological dimension to the economy*. Bascom Hill Publishing Group.

Hamilton, Clive (2003). *Growth Fetish*. Allen and Unwin.

Marcuse, Herbet (1964). One Dimensional Man: studies in the ideology of advanced industrial society (Ebook). Available at https://www.marxists.org/reference/archive/marcuse/works/one-dimensional-man/ (accessed August 12, 2014).

Midar, Zachary (2013). How Walmart's Waltons Maintain Their Billionaire Fortune. Bloomberg, 12 September 2013. Available at http://www.bloomberg.com/news/2013-09-12/how-wal-mart-s-waltons-maintain-their-billionaire-fortune-taxes.html (accessed August 11, 2014).

Mitchell, Dan (2011). Does Socialism Work? A Classroom Experiment. International Liberty. Available at http://danieljmitchell.wordpress.com/2011/11/16/does-socialism-work-a-classroom-experiment/ (accessed August 12, 2014).

Moore, Michael (2007). Beat the Rich. Available at: https://www.youtube.com/watch?v=gRwIZ36po3Y (accessed August 11, 2014).

Preston, N. (2006). The Just Society. In S. Hayes, N. Stobbs and M. Lauchs (Eds.) *Social Ethics for Legal and Justice Professionals*, pp. 29–42. Frenchs Forest, Sydney: Pearson Education Australia.

Quigley, Bill (2013). Ten Examples of Welfare for the Rich and Corporations. *The Huffington Post*, January 14, 2014. Available at http://www.huffingtonpost.com/bill-quigley/ten-examples-of-welfare-for-the-rich-and-corporations_b_4589188.html (accessed August 11, 2014).

Rawls, John (1971). *A Theory of Justice*. Cambridge: Belknap Press.

Singer, Peter (2011). *Practical Ethics*. Third edition. Cambridge: Cambridge University Press.

Smith, Adam (1776). *An Inquiry in to Nature and Causes of the Wealth of Nations*. London: Methuen and Co. Available online at http://www.econlib.org/library/Smith/smWN.html (accessed August 11, 2014).

Specter, Michael (1999). The Dangerous Philosopher. *The New Yorker*, September 6, 1999. Available at http://www.michaelspecter.com/1999/09/the-dangerous-philosopher/ (accessed August 12, 2014).

Wickstead, Philip Henry (1910). *The Common Sense of Political Economy*. London: Routledge and Kegan Paul. Available at https://mises.org/books/commonsense1.pdf (accessed August 12, 2014).

Chapter 8

Balancing law and justice

Key terms: due process; rule of law; objective vs subjective; violations of due process; law vs justice; natural rights; legal rights; moral rights; mercy and justice

Introduction

In the USA, some twenty-six states have adopted a 'Stand Your Ground' or 'Shoot First' law (Law Center to Prevent Gun Violence 2012). This law, which came into effect in 2005, gives people the right to shoot someone if they feel threatened. Prior to this law, individuals were only permitted to use a gun in self-defense, and only when someone invaded their home. The previous law was based on the assumption that, outside, the individuals would try to remove themselves from a potentially violent situation rather than shoot someone. Florida has the most open of the Stand Your Ground laws—in Florida killing can be justified if an individual believed they were being threatened. Since 2005, the number of justified homicides has tripled (Mahapatra 2013).

In the criminal justice system, the balance between enforcing the law and ensuring that its application is just and fair is generally very difficult. This chapter will discuss the various forms of justice that are sought in the application of the law, and will apply the ethical theories that we have discussed in the context of achieving justice in the legal system. This will provide an example of how ethical issues, theories, and decisions play out in this context.

Justice and the law

Law and justice are not the same thing. What is the difference between law and justice? Law is objective—the law requires that we abide by certain rules unconditionally. The law is a system of rules for arbitrating human relations, in the sense that it is the official framework through which disputes are resolved. Laws are, therefore, rigid imperatives that help maintain order in society.

Justice on the other hand is more flexible, open to interpretation, and arguably subjective. Justice revolves around the concept of standards governing how we conduct human relations. Such standards are often codified, but not always. Essentially, justice is about fairness, but even that does not explain it completely. We all have some idea about what is fair in our society, and we can all more or less decide if something is just or not. However, these things change over time, depending upon the particular moral priorities of a particular society. Laws change over time as well, depending on what the general public takes to be fair and just. One recent example is the campaign for marriage equality. Twenty or thirty years ago, no one believed that non-heterosexual people should get married. But attitudes change over time, as societies come to recognize flaws in their reasoning about rights and obligations. In recent times, there has been much awareness-raising about the rights of non-heterosexual people, and subsequently about marriage equality. LGBTI individuals are achieving a lot more acceptance, to the point where there has been a shift in public support for marriage equality—in Australia, a recent poll showed that eighty percent of the population supported it. With this kind of groundswell of support, marriage equality laws will be passed eventually, as they have in some states in the US, in the UK, France, New Zealand and many other countries. And that is how laws are made. Laws are grounded in real social debate—when an issue is recognized as a failure of civil rights, people start lobbying for change, first among their peers, friends, and communities, and then to parliament. When an issue is supported by the majority of citizens, a bill will be passed and a relevant law will be made.

However, it is important to remember that justice and law are not the same thing. Whereas law is objective, in the sense that it implements punishments and rules to resolve disputes, justice has more to do with how fair we are in applying those rules and punishments. Law is a system of rules. Justice is the concept of fairness; a system of rules for human relations. Justice is "the whole field of the principles laid down, the decisions reached in accordance with them, and the procedures whereby the principles are applied to individual cases" (Raphael 1964: 149).

Problems occur, however, when the rules or laws interfere with justice. Consider Case Study 1.

Case Study 1

In a civil dispute, one side has a very strong claim and would almost surely win in court. However, their lawyer missed the filing deadline, so the judge throws the case out of court. Is this fair?

Laws are created to maintain order, and sometimes a line has to be drawn to ensure the efficient application of the law. The deadline for filing documents to the court, for example, must be made and enacted; otherwise many court cases would be drawn out at huge cost in both time and money. But how do we know where to draw the line? Many decades ago, it was decided that the age of eighteen was a reasonable age to allow young people to drink alcohol and vote in Australia. However, there are many countries in which that age is twenty-one. The line is drawn based on prior experience, but quite often it is fairly ad hoc. If you have laws and you want to enforce them you need to decide to which groups they apply and to which groups they do not. In Case Study 1 the lawyer missed the deadline, so the judge threw the case out. These laws reflect the tradition of due process in our criminal justice system, which encourages the fair and equal treatment of all who are involved. However, what happens when the case is much more serious. Consider Case Study 2.

Case Study 2

Several years ago the *Houston Chronicle* reported that nine men on death row in Texas had been denied an appeal because their attorneys had failed to meet the deadlines for appeal. At the time of the report, six of the men had already been executed. Some of the failures were due to miscalculation of time on the attorneys' part, computer problems, and other such trivial mistakes.

James Marcus, an expert in capital case law who teaches in the Capital Punishment Clinic at the University of Texas School of Law, said missing the deadline for a federal writ of habeas corpus—thereby waiving all federal review—is the equivalent of "sleeping through the trial."

Apparently one of the attorneys missed two such deadlines in a row, and one of his clients had already been executed. The other did not even realize his appeal had not been lodged until he heard from the reporter. Apparently courts in Texas are particularly rigid about deadlines and the attorneys are all aware of that.

(Adapted from Death Penalty Information Center 2009)

It does not seem fair that someone may be put to death because a deadline was missed, yet at the same time it seems fair that if the lawyer misses a deadline, their case should not be considered.

In Case Study 1, where the person with a strong claim was not given professional support by the lawyer, they can make a claim for negligence, at least in some jurisdictions. In Queensland, lawyers can be sued for negligence through the Legal Practice Tribunal, which hears cases against lawyers concerning misconduct, negligence, and so on. However, in many other jurisdictions, a missed deadline allows no recourse and no one is held accountable.

So there is much tension between justice and law. The following examines some of those tensions and the connections between them. In doing so, we will examine the role of due process, and the consequences in terms of mercy.

Are there times when we should show mercy before the law? And should judges show mercy? Law is an imperfect system, with many possibilities for failures that weaken the system's ability to resolve disputes or control conflict in a fair and objective way. These failures include:

- a failure to achieve rules;
- a failure to publicize rules;
- the retroactive application of law;
- the existence of contradictory rules;
- frequent changes in rules; and
- a lack of consistency between rules and their administration.

"Some argue that because of the legal system's inability to determine what is just, justice derives not from the application of legal rules but from deciding each case on its merits without regard to rule or precedent" (Pollock 2006: 93).

So, does the peculiarity of each case make legal precedent useless? It may depend on the kind of case. For example, achieving justice in property or interest cases, or in contracts, might be a lot simpler than achieving justice in human conflict cases.

Due process

Although we assume law is necessary for maintaining order, it is not necessarily useful in determining what is just. However, rules that specify procedures for determining cases do attempt to achieve justice. Due process exemplifies this kind of 'procedural justice,' and can be considered an expression of deontological ethics. After all, due process effectively refers to the obligations owed to alleged offenders as well as to victims, so as to ensure that the operation of the justice system is ethical.

Due process endeavors to regulate the criminal justice system according to established procedures that presume an alleged offender is innocent until proven guilty. It requires many processes that must be adhered to by the judges, police, lawyers, and the court. And if these laws are not adhered to then a case might get thrown out of court. In short, due process:

- is a legal and moral right;
- requires careful inquiry and investigation before punishment or forfeiture of right; and
- is a sequence of steps taken by the state to minimize error.

In countries such as Australia, the USA, and the UK, due process is achieved via a neutral hearing body, trial by a jury of peers, cross-examination, presentation of evidence, and legal representation. The intended outcome is that an adherence to due process should result in more just deprivations and punishments.

Due process is a legal and a moral right, which means we have a duty to make sure that everyone who goes before the criminal justice system is processed with equal care, according to the rules. As stated above, this requires careful enquiry and investigation, before punishment or forfeiture of rights.

One way in which due process is upheld is through the 'exclusionary rule.' The 'exclusionary rule' states that evidence obtained by illegal means cannot be allowed in court. Can this be perceived as a legal protective device created by the court or a natural right? Many people argue that the exclusionary rule allows criminals to go free. However, the rule of law exists to protect victims and offenders alike and violations of due process undermine the legal system in a way that can become insidious.

As this example shows, attempting to achieve justice in the application of the law is fraught with tensions—does one concern oneself with outcomes or with doing one's duty? Clearly, this is not always an easy question to answer.

Violations of due process

There are many possible violations of due process, and some of the violations do routinely occur, particularly in corrupt police departments, etc. Overall, however, the system more or less works. The kinds of violations that we hear about the most include such issues as *coerced confessions*, where an alleged offender is badgered or deprived of sleep, to the point where they might confess to something they did not do, or that they had not intended to confess to. *Tainted evidence* is evidence that has been obtained outside the agreed process, such as in a search of premises without a warrant (where a warrant is required), the stealing of evidence, or tricking someone into giving you evidence. Further violations include improper police or court room procedures; for example, forcing a young person into the back seat of a police vehicle without informing them of their rights. Most young people, in particular, would not know what their rights are. In Queensland, once you step into a police vehicle, police are entitled to take you to a police station for questioning. However, a person has a right not to get into a police vehicle without being arrested; a fact that should be made known to the person at the time of questioning.

Thus, injustice does not arise because an offender does not deserve to be punished; rather, it occurs because the state, having relied on an unfair or improper process, does not have the right to punish. Even if someone is guilty, process violations and inadequacies can allow the person to go free. It might seem unfair to allow guilty people to go free, but the intention of the laws surrounding due process is to protect the innocent from unjust accusation and punishment. Due process is a deontological concept because it demands that we follow the correct process regardless of the consequence. It is the process that makes the outcome fair.

One problem with procedural justice in Australia is that it is only recognized and available to certain groups. Asylum seekers do not have any rights in Australia, so procedural justice is only recognized for Australian citizens and legal residents or visitors with a valid visa. Asylum seekers are not legal visitors unless they come to the country for some other reason on a valid visa, and then seek asylum. For example, during the Sydney Olympic Games in 2000, a group of athletes from Nigeria legally came into the country to compete but, once legally in the country, were able to request asylum. They already had rights because they had legal entry to Australia. Often asylum seekers are incarcerated without due process. Do you think that is fair? The problem of gaining legal access to Australia is exacerbated by discriminatory immigration processes that tend to favor visitors from developed countries. This is contrary to the policies for asylum seekers developed by the United Nations and endorsed by many countries, making Australia one of the harshest countries in their dealings with refugees.

Another potential failure of due process is the holding of those suspected of terrorist ties. Since the bombing of the World Trade Center in New York in 2001, many developed nations have enacted anti-terrorist legislation that allows suspect individuals to be held without evidence, sometimes indefinitely. Consider the case of Dr Mohamed Haneef below.

The case of Mohamed Haneef

On July 2, 2007, Dr Mohamed Haneef, a medical doctor who was originally from India, was arrested at Brisbane airport for suspected terrorist activity. He was imprisoned for twelve days, then charged with providing information to a terrorist organization. However, there was not enough evidence to sustain the charge and it was dropped. Meanwhile, Dr Haneef's visa had been cancelled "on character grounds." When he was released he therefore had to return to India before being able to renew his visa.

Dr Haneef's arrest was the first to be made on the basis of new anti-terrorist legislation which had been introduced earlier that year. This case revealed several important issues with the legislation:

- Problems with the operation and application of sections 3W, section 15AA and Part 1C of the Crimes Act—most notably the 'dead time' provisions;
- Problems with the Criminal Code terrorist organization offence provisions; and
- Problems with section 501 of the Migration Act and the intersection between migration law and criminal law (Law Council of Australia 2008).

(continued)

(continued)

A year later, the Attorney-General announced an inquiry into Dr Haneef's treatment, which resulted in a number of legislative and procedural changes.

(Adapted from Law Council of Australia 2008)

Dr Haneef was picked up and held on suspicion of links to terrorists because he gave his UK sim card to a friend, who passed it on to someone who was allegedly involved in terrorist activity in the UK. He was detained for twenty-four days and then deported because his visa had been revoked. Such anti-terrorist legislation is grounded in consequentialism, which advocates that it is morally permissible to detain one person to potentially protect a larger number of people. Proponents of the legislation make the argument that, even if you only catch one out of every ten suspects, many hundreds and possibly thousands will have been saved, since we often cannot be certain whether suspected terrorist activity will lead to actual terrorism. Many years ago, I had a friend who worked as a public servant. One day he was taking his usual morning train to work, and when he alighted at his station, turned as usual into the underground tunnel that leads downtown. Before he knew what was happening, he was surrounded by police, who threw him up against a wall and hand-cuffed him, before dragging him into a police car, which took him to the station for questioning. Apparently he looked very similar to a suspected drug dealer! Now this was many, many years ago when there were no anti-terrorist laws, so when they realized their mistake, the police apologized and let my friend go. Under the current legislation, they could have held him for twenty-four days . . . just because he looked like someone else.

The issue for law enforcement agencies, then, is how *much* 'evidence' must be gathered before someone can be arrested on suspicion? Surely due process requires much more rigorous investigation than is currently the norm?

On the other hand, one of my ex-law enforcement friends once told me that a huge intelligence operation indicated an imminent bomb threat in Sydney CBD. Such was the strength of the evidence that they eventually arrested the would-be terrorists before they could do any damage. The point is that if you knew there was an imminent bomb threat in downtown Sydney, you would want to prevent it, so you are going to be looking for anyone who appears suspicious. This begs the question of how many suspects were detained before they found the right one?

In sum, a violation of due process is effectively a failure of the justice system to act ethically. Such a violation will often mean that alleged offenders will be set free, regardless of whether they are guilty or not. Nevertheless, there might be certain sorts of crimes where it can be justified that due process be overridden for public safety reasons or, more broadly, for the common good.

Natural vs legal rights

A major concern of an ethical criminal justice system is ensuring that punishments, such as the deprivation of liberty, are meted out only to those who deserve it, and only if the way that this is determined is fair and just. Is the right to be free from governmental deprivation of liberty without some finding of guilt a natural right or a legal right? Here are some basic differences between natural and legal rights:

- A natural right exists for all people for all time; it is not contingent upon laws, customs, or beliefs as they exist in any particular cultural milieu.
- A legal right exists only so long as the majority approve of it or it is enshrined in law. A legal right can be written in or out of existence depending upon perceived threat.

Natural rights arise out of our person—that is, our moral agency—and are *inalienable*, in the sense that they cannot be sold, traded, or removed. John Locke argued that property is a natural right, particularly a person's own self, but that when one mixes ones labor with something, it also becomes one's property.

> [E]very man has a *property* in his own *person*. This nobody has any right to but himself. The labour of his body and the *work* of his hands, we may say, are properly his. Whatsoever then he removes out of the state that nature hath provided, and left it in, he hath mixed his labour with, and joined to it something that is his own, and thereby makes it his *property*. It being by him removed from the common state nature placed it in, it hath by this *labour* something annexed to it that excludes the common right of other men. For this *labour* being the unquestionable property of the labourer, no man but he can have a right to what that is once joined to.
>
> (Locke 1690: 3057)

Locke argued that everybody is born with certain inalienable rights, regardless of nationality or station in life. It is this notion of inalienable rights that the American founding fathers used in drafting the American Declaration of Independence (1776) and the Bill of Rights (1791). Natural rights are also strongly evident in the writings of Thomas Jefferson and Samuel Adams. Thomas Paine also drew upon natural rights to justify revolution. Other classic expressions of natural rights include the English Bill of Rights (1689) and the French Declaration of the Rights of Man and the Citizen (1789). They also underpin the United Nations Universal Declaration of Human Rights (1948) (Hittinger 1988).

Legal rights, on the other hand, are more transient and can change over time. While the previous paragraph demonstrates how natural rights are often enshrined in law, the reversal of such laws will never diminish the power of natural rights. Thus, legal rights are often related to natural rights, but they are more subjective in that they arise by agreement within specific legal codes. They can, therefore, be overridden by law. In reference to the example above of anti-terrorism laws, one might argue that such laws are actually violating the natural rights of individuals, even—or maybe especially—where they are not written into law. Australia has no Bill of Rights as such, although certain rights are built into legislation, which makes them relatively easy to override. The rights written into the first ten amendments of the US Constitution, however, are a different matter. Arguably one could charge anti-terrorist laws in the US as unconstitutional. The US Patriot Act 2001 allows for roving wire taps, searches of business records, and surveillance of suspects, all of which appear to violate the right to privacy. Although they were only meant to be a temporary measure after the 9/11 attacks, these provisions were extended in 2011 by President Barack Obama using the sunset clause, and as such are still fully enforceable (RT 2011).

In the following section, we examine other ways in which the law might not achieve a just outcome.

Mercy and Justice

As the law does not always appear to produce a just outcome, how can we bring law and justice closer together? One way that many people suggest is through introducing *mercy* into the law—by asking judges or police officers to be merciful, for example. While having mercy on offenders may sound desirable as a way of reducing injustice, we must ask whether it is *ethical*.

One of the problems with allowing judges to have mercy on offenders is the level of personal discretion (and bias) it introduces into the application of the law. It gives judges a lot of power to alter the application of the law, when in fact such power should not be in their hands as it can lead to unequal and unpredictable outcomes. In fact, they do not have the power to offer mercy—only those affected by a particular action (such as victims) do. While judges are allowed some discretion in some cases as to the severity of punishments they mete out, there are guidelines to assist this, and the guidelines are decided on by legislators acting as representatives of the people—they are not arbitrary. So, this becomes something other than mercy—it is equity, as it introduces an equitable calculation into the operation of the law (see Lauchs 2006).

This is an important distinction to make, and means that we really must reflect on what we do to draw law and justice closer together. Methods that might appear sensible, such as offering mercy, may actually increase injustice and be unethical in themselves. Consider Case Study 3 below.

Case Study 3

Robert was married with a small child when he was in a motorcycle accident which paralyzed him from the neck down. He had always been active, and being incapacitated made him depressed. He was also in a lot of pain, and he begged his doctors and family to put him out of his misery. After a few days, his brother visited the hospital and asked him if he was sure he wanted to die. When Robert responded in the affirmative, his brother pulled out a gun and shot him dead. He was tried for murder but the court found him not responsible by virtue of temporary insanity.

Was what Robert's brother did moral? Do you think he should have been brought to trial at all? Do you think he should have been acquitted? Would you do the same for a loved one if you were asked?

(Brain Mass 2014)

How can we ensure that the application of law is more just? In the criminal justice system, judges do not really have the discretion to show mercy. There are clear rules about what sentences have to be apportioned to certain crimes. They do have some discretion over the length of sentence, so long as it falls between the minimum and maximum sentence outlined in law.

Case Study 3 above is instructive because of the way in which Robert's brother was acquitted. Since the law will not allow judges to be merciful, the only alternative to jailing Robert's brother was to declare him temporarily insane. A deontologist would argue, on the one hand, that the value of a life can never be trumped by pain and suffering. On the other hand, Robert's brother showed incredible mercy to someone who was in terrible pain, and without dignity. Perhaps the value of a life can be regarded as severely diminished if its bearer cannot stand to live it. If the person is going to die anyway, then assisted suicide may be deontologically sound. But the deontologist would also wear the consequences of that decision. We have laws for a reason, and while engaging in assisted suicide might be merciful, the legal consequences may have to be accepted. Robert's brother did accept the consequence by allowing himself to be arrested and put on trial. Perhaps the judge was showing mercy in declaring him temporarily insane.

Lauchs (2006) argues that when judges act this way, they are being equitable rather than merciful. Judges are performing a duty in sentencing; they cannot be lenient unless legislated power allows them to be. Nevertheless, they can be lenient within the law so as to achieve a more equitable outcome. Equity, he states, has a similar meaning to 'justice'—"the quality of being equal or fair; fairness, impartiality; even handed dealings." But it also has an additional meaning:

The recourse to general principles of justice . . . to correct or supplement provisions of the law. Equity in a statute: the construction of a statute according to its reason and spirit, so as to make it apply to cases for which it does not expressly provide.

(Lauch 2006: 99)

Equity achieves justice by "avoiding a literal reading of the law" (Lauchs 2006: 99). So even when judges use their discretion to be lenient it can only be within the law, and not in spite of it. The use of equity allows the use of reason to help achieve justice according to the spirit of the law. When adopting this guideline, then, judges are being equitable, rather than merciful. Nevertheless, acting equitably does allow the "incorporation into consideration of circumstances which reasonably obligate leniency" (Lauchs 2006: 99).

Review questions

1 What is the difference between 'blind justice' and equity?
2 Should judges be free to by-pass the law under certain circumstances? If yes, what would those circumstances be?
3 What is the difference between equity and mercy?
4 What safeguards does our criminal justice system have in place to ensure that justice will be done?
5 What sort of situations in daily life would qualify as in need of showing mercy?
6 Is a public campaign to change a harsh law an act of public justice or mercy? Give an example.
7 English judges in the eighteenth century used to reduce the charges of potential convicts so that they would qualify for transportation to Australia rather than face execution. Was this a case of mercy? Ought the judges to have done this?
8 What is the difference between natural rights and legal rights? Give an example.
9 What are some violations of due process?

References

Brain Mass (2014). Ethics and Values Case Study—Mercy Killing, Euthanasia. Available at https://brainmass.com/philosophy/ethics-morals/86151 (accessed August 12, 2014).
Death Penalty Information Center (2009). Attorneys' Late Filings Forfeit Final Capital Appeals. Available at http://www.deathpenaltyinfo.org/attorneys-late-filings-forfeit-final-capital-appeals (accessed August 12, 2014).
Hittinger, R. (1988). A Critique of the New Natural Law Theory. Notre Dame: University of Notre Dame Press.

Lauchs, M. (2006). Justice and Equity v. Mercy. In S. Hayes, N. Stobbs and M. Lauchs (Eds.) *Social Ethics for Legal and Justice Professionals*, pp. 29–42. Sydney: Pearson Education Australia.

Law Center to Prevent Gun Violence (2012). Stand Your Ground Policy Summary. Law Center to Prevent Gun Violence. Available at http://smartgunlaws.org/stand-your-ground-policy-summary/ (accessed August 12, 2014).

Law Council of Australia (2008). Mohamed Haneef Case. Available at http://www.lawcouncil.asn.au/lawcouncil/index.php/10-divisions/145-mohamed-haneef-case (accessed August 12, 2014).

Locke, John (1690). *Second Treatise of Government*. Chapter 5, Sec. 27. Available at http://www.ucs.louisiana.edu/~ras2777/judpol/lockerights.htm (accessed October 28, 2014).

Mahapatra, Lisa (2013). Stand Your Ground: 26 States Have "Shoot First" Laws. *International Business Times*, July 18, 2013. Available at http://www.ibtimes.com/stand-your-ground-26-us-states-have-shoot-first-laws-1351127 (accessed August 12, 2014).

Pollock, Jocelyn (2006). *Ethical Dilemmas and Decisions in Criminal Justice*. Fifth edition. Melbourne: Wadsworth Publishing.

RT (2011). US Patriot Act is Unconstitutional. *RT: Question More*, February 8, 2011. Available at http://rt.com/usa/usa-patriot-act-unconstitutional/ (accessed August 12, 2014).

Chapter 9

Ethics, law, and morality

Key terms: legal paternalism; legal moralism; adversarial system; inquisatorial system; due process; social construction of morality; the harm principle

Introduction

Recently in Australia, there has been some controversy about schools allowing same-sex couples to attend high school 'formals'; that is, the formal dance held at the end of an academic year—what are called 'proms' in the US and Canada, and increasingly more often in the UK. In 2010, for example, Henrietta Cook reported in Australian media that a young woman named Hannah Williams was not permitted to attend the senior formal with her female partner, Savannah Supski. The school maintained that the reason was because her girlfriend was only fifteen. However, it was clear that other girls had been allowed to bring fifteen-year-old male partners. As a result, both girls changed to a less discriminating and more tolerant school. Understandably, Hannah was extremely upset by the whole affair and described how she tried to tackle the situation by "trying to fix things. I had meetings with principals; looked through the Equal Opportunity Act; all my friends put posters up around the school and the teachers ripped them down. There was an easy solution; they just needed to let me go with my girlfriend" (Cook 2010).

Why are same-sex couples being banned from school formals? Is it more than a moral objection to the idea of homosexuality? Admittedly, the school in question was a private all-girls school, but it did not operate under the auspices of any religious organization, so any religious objection was a moot point. The fact that many of Hannah's friends were supportive suggests that there was little in the way of objection from families at the school. The fact that, in an era when rights of LGBTI individuals are finally being recognized, and equal marriage rights have already been recognized and enacted in many states, two young girls still cannot openly express their relationship in public, suggests that public morality still has considerable hold on our private lives. This chapter seeks to unpack this tension between public and private, especially with respect to 'crimes against morality.'

To begin, it compares and contrasts the adversarial and inquisitorial systems as a starting point for examining the relationship between law and morality. Moving from the procedures of the law and the way in which ethical perspectives are enshrined within them, this chapter considers the purposes of the law, and the ways in which the law expresses particular forms of morality. It also examines the historical influence of morality on the law and on society in general. In doing so, it explores the relationship between crime and morality, with a specific focus on crimes *against* morality. While we have already seen in Chapter 8 how laws have a general moral basis, aiming to sanction behaviors condemned as 'wrong' or 'bad' and proscribed by a society, there is a specific group of offences in modern democratic nations labeled 'crimes against morality.' Included within this group are offences related to prostitution, pornography, and homosexuality. What do these crimes have in common? Most clearly they tend to have a sexual basis and are often argued to do sexual harm, in both a moral and/or psychological sense, as well as physically. Conversely in some cases they are argued to be victimless crimes, especially when the acts occur between consenting adults. Finally, they are considered essentially private acts but they often occur, and are regulated, in the public domain. Most importantly, each of these crimes against morality has only relatively recently (i.e. in the past 150 years) become identified and regulated by the state as a criminal offence.

In previous chapters, we have considered the application of ethical theories to public morality and our system of law. Chapter 8, in particular, explores some of the ways that deontological and consequentialist ethics are embodied within our legal and criminal justice systems. This chapter considers the ways in which egoism and virtue ethics also feature here. It focuses on morality and the law, which has important implications for a discussion of virtue ethics and how the law seeks to shape different kinds of individuals. We will return to this below; however, to begin, we will discuss the differences between the adversarial and inquisitorial judicial systems and their respective implications for justice and fairness. In this way we seek to understand how morality impacts on the law.

What is the adversarial system?

An adversary is an individual who opposes another in a conflict. The term 'adversarial' is derived from 'adversary' and denotes a judicial system whereby two parties (either the accused and the prosecution in a criminal trial, or the plaintiff and defendant in a civil trial) compete in a court of law. In a criminal trial, each party is attempting to "win over the confidence of the jury" (Stobbs 2006: 59).

We can think about the adversarial system from the perspective of ethical egoism, which can help us note its advantages and disadvantages. Although based on the rule of law, which is strongly deontological, the adversarial system encourages people to be self-interested—ultimately, the case an individual makes must be designed to favorably influence or persuade the court. This can be understood as an ethical way of doing things: it means that people are encouraged to defend themselves as much as possible against the coercive power of the state, and that specific safeguards protecting individuals are enshrined in the operation of the law. However, there are numerous problems that can arise from this focus on self-interest, some of which may reproduce entrenched social disadvantage. Some of these problems are discussed below.

During a trial, it is generally up to each party what evidence or witnesses are brought before the jury (although there are some minimal guidelines). Thus, evidence is largely chosen as a matter of strategy rather than in the interests of fairness. In this regard, some argue that the adversarial system is less concerned with discovering the 'truth' of a matter, and more about "aggressively furthering the interests of the client" and deciding a 'winner' and a 'loser' (Stobbs 2006: 59–60). This system is said to place many (especially 'minority' groups, usually non-white, youth, and people from low socio-economic backgrounds) at a serious disadvantage.

In the USA, Australia, the UK, Canada, and New Zealand, everyone has the right to legal counsel in court. However, lawyers are often very expensive to employ and not everyone has access to the best or most competent lawyers. Those who cannot afford legal counsel may have the opportunity of either asking for legal aid representation (a group of government-funded lawyers) or they can self-represent. While various criticisms have been leveled at the quality and availability of legal aid, self-representation is often much worse, especially for the individual who does not have an adequate understanding of the court process. Having to face a magistrate or judge on one's own is often very intimidating and most individuals who self-represent end up pleading guilty to avoid a lengthy and daunting trial (Stobbs 2006: 61). In turn, the fairness and justice of the process is seriously undermined and there is little doubt that some who plead guilty could avoid conviction with proper investigation and instruction. In addition to this, the jury system is also raised as another problem inherent in the adversarial justice system.

Trial by jury is recognized as a right in most liberal democracies. Criminal juries in Queensland consist of twelve members who are chosen at random from the electoral role (Stobbs 2006: 63). In other jurisdictions the number may range from six upwards. The main criticism of trial by jury is that there is no assurance that jurors know anything about the legal system or the criminal law and, thus, are not well enough equipped to make serious decisions on legal matters. Even though the judge must explain and summarize the evidence for the jury at the close of proceedings, there is no way to ensure that the jury members fully understand the evidence that has been put to them. In particular, eyewitness evidence is often understood by jurors to be a 'silver bullet' when in fact it is often flawed. Because jurors are human and make mistakes, not to mention letting personal bias intrude on their judgment, the wrong people are sometimes convicted of crimes they did not commit.

Are juries racially biased?

Economists Shamena Anwar, Patrick Bayer and Randi Hjalmarsson analyzed the verdicts given by juries in Florida between the years 2000 and 2010 and discovered that "(i) juries formed from all-white jury pools convict black defendants significantly (16 percentage points) more often than white defendants and (ii) this gap in conviction rates is entirely eliminated when the jury pool includes at least one black member." Elsewhere, John Roman analyzed the data on "justifiable homicide" determinations. These are decisions about whether a homicide is justified and they are made by police or prosecutors before a case is heard by a jury; in his research Roman found that the murders of black people by white perpetrators were twice as likely to be found "justified" than the murders of white people by white perpetrators. They were three times more likely to be found "justified" in those states that are described as stand-your-ground states.

(Adapted from *The Economist* 2013)

Given these criticisms of the adversarial legal system, alternative options have been suggested. One such alternative is the inquisitorial system, which is currently used in most European, Central American, and some African states.

The inquisitorial system

In contrast to the adversarial system, the inquisitorial system follows legal codes very closely rather than allowing the interpretation and development of the common law. Furthermore, in the inquisitorial system the judge takes an inquisitorial role, personally investigating the evidence at hand. The judge also oversees the police investigation of the case, decides whether there is enough evidence for a trial to proceed and also which evidence or witnesses should be allowed to appear during the trial (Stobbs 2006: 67). Alternatively, in the adversarial system the judge is required to remain completely objective and detached from the investigative process.

Because the judge adopts the investigative role, the problem of poor legal representation (say, through legal aid) or self-representation is largely removed. Thus, in the inquisitorial system, the outcome does not depend on the quality of the lawyers who have been hired; rather, it relies on the evidence presented by police and the integrity of the presiding judge. However, some argue that this role leads the judge to be too subjective and undermines the presumption that all individuals are innocent until proven guilty. Nevertheless, while the judge participates in the investigation of the case, they are still required to present the evidence in an unbiased and impartial manner. In fact, there is considerable evidence that this process has the opposite effect of encouraging fewer cases to be followed through to trial in the inquisitorial system (Stobbs 2006: 68). In this regard, the inquisitorial system may be much more cost-effective than the adversarial system. Also, "lack of legal representation is rarely a problem" because cases are less labor intensive and run more efficiently (Stobbs 2006: 68).

However, while there are a number of advantages to the inquisitorial system, some also argue that it places too much trust in judges who are fallible humans. It also pays to consider, in line with what was discussed in Chapter 8 regarding due process, whether the inquisitorial system of justice is ethical. Does it give fair consideration to the due process rights of the accused? Do its other benefits outweigh the potential for subjectivity here? These are not easy questions to answer.

Both the adversarial and inquisitorial systems have their advantages and disadvantages. Perhaps the answer, therefore, is to combine both systems in an attempt to cancel out the disadvantages in each. This has been achieved in Italy, where the adversarial and inquisitorial systems operate simultaneously. Either way, as Stobbs (2006: 68) argues, "It would be simplistic and unhelpful to suggest . . . that the adversarial system is unfair and needs to be amended. What is needed is specific suggestions for reform," which address the specific disadvantages of this system.

Law and morality

Moving from the procedures of the law and the way in which ethical perspectives are enshrined within them, we will now consider one of the purposes of the law, and the role of virtue ethics here. We discuss the way that the law expresses particular forms of morality, and the way that this can be understood in terms of virtue ethics. We also consider here the historical influence of morality on the law and on society in general.

Morality does not necessarily coincide with the law, but it contributes to it. An act may be legal but nevertheless considered to be immoral in a particular society. For example, the use of pornography might be considered by many to be immoral. Nevertheless, the sale and distribution of non-violent, non-child-related, sexually explicit material is legal (or regulated) in many jurisdictions. Many laws are informed by, and even created by, morality (Carpenter and Hayes 2009).

The social construction of morality

It has been argued by philosophers that law is informed by the particular moral values and beliefs that exist at a particular time (e.g. Cane 2003). While law goes somewhat beyond morality in some instances, and not quite as far as morality in others, it is clear that what is legislated and how it is legislated are shaped by the particular social mores of the time. For example, in the early to middle part of the twentieth century, wives and children were considered to be chattels—that is, the property of the men who governed them, such as husbands and fathers. Thus, husbands and fathers were free to discipline wives and children (to a certain 'reasonable' extent at least) with violence, or to treat them in any way (within reason) they deemed suitable. However, the women's liberation movement of the 1960s and 70s impacted on society's collective views about the relationships between husbands and wives and parents and children, so much so that laws governing these relationships began to change. Today, many countries now have laws prohibiting violence against and abuse of domestic partners and children. Another example would be the age of consent, which increased from twelve in mid-eighteenth-century England, to sixteen in 1885, and still stands at sixteen today. This same piece of legislation also outlawed prostitution and homosexuality. This was mostly to do with social mores concerning childhood and sexuality, with lobbyists at the time expressing fears of young women being sold into slavery and prostitution (Quinn and Taliaferro 1999).

If law is informed by morality, then we need to understand how morality has developed over time before we can understand how laws have developed.

Law and society

Whether an action is moral or immoral is a different question from whether there should be laws and government sanctions regarding the behavior. Citizens might agree that a particular behavior is immoral, yet at the same time not believe that the government should have the right to restrict an individual's choice on the matter. Examples include abortion, prostitution, recreational drugs.

Some of the justifications underpinning such laws include (Feinberg 1990):

- the harm principle—preventing harm to others;
- the offence principle—preventing offence to others;
- legal paternalism—protecting an individual from themselves;
- legal moralism—prohibiting immoral conduct; and
- benefit to others—when prohibition provides some benefit to others.

The kinds of justifications we will be exploring in this chapter are the harm principle, legal paternalism and legal moralism.

The harm principle

As we saw in Chapter 7, the harm principle, first articulated by John Stuart Mill, provides the basis for many laws in our society, as well as the underlying rationale for liberal democracy. It is also the foundation for the United Nations Declaration of Human Rights. Mill (1869: 68) defines the harm principle as follows:

> The sole end for which mankind are warranted, individually or collectively, in interfering with the liberty of action of any of their number, is self-protection. That the purpose for which power can be rightfully exercised over any member of a civilised community against his will, is to prevent harm to others.

The harm principle allows us to exercise our free will so long as we do not harm others. But Mill is careful to point out that this principle does not apply to oneself. He argued that one cannot do harm to oneself because one is the author of one's own action. "Over himself," Mill writes, "over his own mind, the individual is sovereign" (Mill 1869: 68). This notion of harm is tied very closely to the notion of consent, in the sense that one does not 'harm' another if they consent to an act. Their consent is an act of self-sovereignty on their part.

Nevertheless, in our society, laws are enacted to protect us from ourselves. These kinds of laws are *paternalistic*, and will be discussed in the following section.

Legal paternalism

Legal paternalists argue that we need laws to protect us from inadvertently (or even knowingly) inflicting harm upon ourselves. Some examples of such laws in our society include:

- seat belt laws;
- motorcycle helmet laws;
- regulation of alcohol consumption; and
- regulation of tobacco products.

Each of these laws is enacted to prevent us from harm. It has also been argued that the following laws are also designed to prevent us from harming ourselves, although as we shall see below, that is certainly up for debate:

- laws prohibiting and regulating drug use;
- laws prohibiting and regulating the distribution of pornography;
- laws prohibiting and regulating prostitution.

Libertarians argue that individuals know what is best for them and that, as long as we are not hurting anyone else, we should be able to do what we want. However, the paternalist argues in response that all citizens have value for society; therefore, society must protect the citizen from themselves whether they like it or not. The paternalist argues that there are *no* harmful or potentially harmful behaviors that do not *also* impact negatively on (i.e. 'harm') others. For example, speeding drivers might crash into others and drug users and gamblers might commit crimes to support their habit or they might cause much grief to their families; pornography and prostitution both degrade (and therefore harm) women and possibly children; riding a motorcycle without a helmet can lead to very serious injury, which increases the burden on the public health system.

Criticisms of paternalism

Paternalism *may* be justified for the good of society, but only with certain restrictions. For example, if a person's decision-making ability is impaired (through lack of knowledge or drug use) we might be justified in making a law to protect them. Impairment of one's decision-making ability impacts on an individual's ability to give their informed consent to participate in a behavior/ act. Child labor laws and laws against under-age drinking are instances of this. There is a presumption that children are not rational enough to understand the dangers associated with certain behaviors. Hence the institution of age limits for certain activities such as drinking alcohol, voting, and driving a car.

However, it is easy to see how this kind of thinking might lead us down a 'slippery slope,' such that, eventually, more and more behaviors come under the purview of the state, to the detriment of individual freedom. It has been argued, therefore, that regulation of dangerous behaviors is always preferable to absolute bans, ensuring that any restrictions are as limited as possible. The following examples show how this might be done:

- Drink driving laws define the point of legal intoxication as the level where one's driving ability is impaired.
- Laws prohibit children from buying cigarettes, but adults are able to buy them because research shows that smoking prohibits growth and children might not be rational enough to make an informed decision about whether or not to smoke (assuming adults *are* rational enough . . . !)

Supposedly, adults have reached a level of maturity that gives them the capacity to understand the dangers associated with smoking, drinking alcohol, etc. It has been argued that paternalistic laws should therefore seek only to prevent a serious and irreversible error: e.g., a death from drink driving, stunting children's growth from smoking, etc. Such rules aim to create a balance between individual liberty and government control, and are supported by both conservative and liberal discourses.

Autonomy

Liberal discourses on 'autonomy' argue against overregulation and prohibition of 'victimless' crimes. Such discourses appeal to the need for individuals to decide their own fate, arguing that individuals have a right to autonomy, or that individuals are only able to develop their autonomy if given free rein in how they choose to live their lives. This view draws heavily on the notions of personal sovereignty, which is the sphere of influence a person has over their own life.

Arguably, it might be possible to autonomously forfeit one's liberty, if one clearly gives one's informed consent—voluntary slavery is a case in point, although there is much debate in the philosophical literature that argues that voluntary slavery is either an oxymoron or a paradox.

Legal moralism

The law serves to regulate citizens, but it also acts as the moral agent of society, especially in areas where there is no moral agreement. For example, recreational drug use, gambling, abortion, child pornography, suicide, and euthanasia are all regulated or prohibited by law because they are regarded as inherently immoral or just 'wrong.' The laws may be based on principles of harm or paternalism, but they also serve to reinforce society's definitions of moral behavior.

Case Study: Prostitution

A recent government inquiry into prostitution in Australia articulates the moral nature of many community concerns and their relationship to the law. The idea that the removal of criminal sanctions would convey to the community an inaccurate social belief, by giving "a veneer of respectability to an occupation which is based on promiscuity and is socially unacceptable" was often noted (CJC 1991: 81). While perhaps not the dominant position, the perception that the retention of criminal sanctions is a part of a "community obligation to state its moral convictions and practices as a clear guide to its members" (CJC 1991: 91) relies on the belief that the criminal law is a "direct reflection of Christian morality and that the criminal law must be used to restore religious, moral and social values" (CJC 1991: 91). This understanding of a relationship between the criminal law and morality is historically accurate; however, whether it has ever been the dominant force is open to debate and tends to ignore the complexity of change.

(Carpenter and Hayes 2007)

Apart from the United States, many countries have decriminalized or legalized prostitution over the past couple of decades due to more relaxed attitudes towards sex work and the public health issues involved in prohibiting it. The problem arises when we consider laws against behaviors that arguably do not hurt anyone, but are nevertheless seen as socially abhorrent. The above case of prostitution is a case in point. Consensual sexual behavior between adults arguably harms no one, yet in many countries there are state and/or federal laws prohibiting sex work. Clearly, the only harm being prevented by such laws is the 'harm' caused by the threat to personal moral beliefs and values, or to community standards of morality. The danger of such laws is that they condone personal discrimination, which can, once again, lead to the 'slippery slope' argument. Such laws also create public health issues—if sex work is illegal then workers are prone to disease due to lack of adequate health care, and extortion by pimps and drug peddlers.

Even in countries where such legislation does not exist we find other forms of morality enshrined in the law. For example, most Western nations discriminate against sex between adult immediate relatives in both legislation and policy. Two further case studies are instructive.

Case Study: Incest

Father, daughter plead guilty to incest

A 61-year-old man and his 39-year-old daughter have pleaded guilty to two counts of incest . . . [they] were charged after authorities were notified about the birth of their children . . . Their first child died from a heart condition soon after birth and their second child was born last year.

(ABC News 2008)

The above quote is from a 2008 article by ABC News Media Australia, which reported that the couple, who had been estranged since the woman was a young girl, had met again in 2000, when they started a relationship. Their lawyer claimed they were literally strangers when they met for the first time as adults, and that it was therefore not a clear-cut case of incest. Nevertheless, the Crown Prosecutor condemned their behavior as illegal, and expressed concern that they had a biological child together. Judge Steven Millstead ruled that they could remain together as a family unit so as not to cause hardship, but that they were not to engage in a sexual relationship.

The law prevents closely related parties from engaging in sexual acts and marriage, but in the case of consenting adults, the rationale is unclear. In past eras, the taboo against incest was biologically based on the risk of deformities in offspring of people directly related by kinship. It was also morally based, however—for example, the Old Testament and other revered religious texts strongly prohibit it. But the taboo against incest is more than just legal, religious, or biological. When I put it to my students to explain to me why it was so wrong for the two people in the case study above to be in an intimate relationship—apart from the biological risks to children—the most common response was a resounding "Ewwww!" Indeed, the very idea of incest makes people uncomfortable because it tests their ingrained moral sensibilities and even their moral imagination—even (or especially) when putting ourselves in the couple's shoes, the immediate visceral response is one of distaste or disgust. Clearly the incest taboo is one of those conventional moral taboos that is very, very deeply ingrained, and perhaps, I suggest, grounded in strongly held archetypes of the family—the mother as nurturer and father as protector. In any case, incest is probably not one of those moral conventions that will change any time soon!

But let us examine another case that is not so easily decided.

Case Study: Pornography

In 2008, an exhibition of photographic work in a prestigious gallery in Sydney, Australia, was raided by police and subsequently closed from public viewing. According to media reports of the time, the exhibition was closed because it consisted of images "of naked children as young as twelve in a variety of poses." The New South Wales Minister of Community Services sanctioned the raid on the premises, stating that the photographs were "highly inappropriate . . . I can't see any reason why images of naked children need to be created or displayed in that way . . . as a community, it's our responsibility to protect the innocence of childhood and these images step over the line."

[. . .]

What is most interesting about this case of alleged child pornography is that the photographer in question, Bill Hensen, is a respected artist whose industrial landscapes and soulful images of androgynous young people have been acclaimed throughout the world for thirty years. . . . To the art world, Hensen was a shining light, a "photographer of the human condition and an experimenter of remarkable skill and conviction."

(Hayes et al. 2012: 11–12)

The case of Hensen, above, excited much debate in the press and in politics at the time. Child protection advocates were very outspoken about what they saw as obscene, and yet, in other circles—for decades—Hensen had been regarded as an artist, and the exhibition in question contained some images that had previously be lauded. Pornography is defined as "Printed or visual material containing the explicit description or display of sexual organs or activity, intended to stimulate sexual excitement" (*Oxford Dictionary* 2014). Under this definition, an image depicting "sexual organs" is obscene if it is "intended to stimulate sexual excitement." While a few of the images exhibited by Hensen depicted breasts and, occasionally, male genitals in shadow, they could not in any sense be regarded as 'explicit'; nor were they "intended to stimulate sexual excitement" and it is this latter that makes the difference. I argue elsewhere that the naked human body—even children—has been the subject of artists for millennia, but that it is only in our age that we consider that people will necessarily be sexually stimulated simply by looking at it—or at least in danger of it. This probably has to do with the rising moral panic about pedophiles more than anything, and is clearly indicative of the ways in which moral conventions still rule our lives and the law in spite of much progress.

Conclusion: ethical theory and legal moralism

So, what does all of this have to do with ethics? Well, clearly, determining what kinds of laws we ought to follow as a society, particularly when the activities that they attempt to regulate do not clearly harm other people, is an important ethical question. Legal regulation obviously has serious impacts on the lives of people, and also speaks to questions of what constitutes a good and just society (which we have previously explored).

We can, however, also consider this from the perspective of virtue ethics. Laws that seek to prevent us from harming ourselves or others (such as bicycle helmet laws, speed limits, smoking restrictions, and so on) can be considered as attempts by the law to shape the kind of people that we are, and to temper the possible excesses of human behavior. If we were all to act selfishly, then at some stage our behavior would clearly have negative impacts on others. Thus, there need to be some restrictions in place to regulate what we do.

Our previous discussions of virtue ethics can help us think about this. It is possible to consider the law as attempting to produce *temperate* individuals, or at the very least, *continent* persons (those who manage to keep wild desires under control, due to the threat of legal regulation). In these cases, the law seeks to regulate those it considers to be *akratic*. Whether it is through the threat of legal sanction, or through attempts to govern the moralities that it sees as desirable, laws relating to the regulation and expression of morality have a clear link to virtue ethics, and can be usefully discussed and critiqued along those lines.

Review questions

1 What is a victimless crime? Give an example?
2 What is the moral foundation for criminalizing prostitution?
3 What do you think about two closely related consenting adults being in an intimate relationship? Did you immediately appeal to the 'ewww factor'?
4 This chapter considered pornography, incest, and prostitution as laws based on 'crimes against morality' rather than laws made to protect us from (non-moral) harm. Can you think of any others?
5 Should marijuana and/or other forms of recreational but currently illegal drugs be decriminalized?
6 What is the harm principle? How might it relate to prostitution?
7 What is the difference between legal paternalism and legal moralism?
8 Which paternalistic laws do you think are justified (if any) and why?
9 What do we mean by the 'social construction of morality'?
10 Outline the fundamental differences between the adversarial and inquisitorial justice systems.

References

ABC News (2008). Father, Daughter Plead Guilty to Incest. Available at http://www.abc.net.au/news/stories/2008/03/04/2179412.htm (accessed August 21, 2014).

Cane, P. (2003). Theory and Values in Public Law. In Paul Craig and Richard Rawlings (Eds.) *Law and Administration in Europe. Essays in honour of Carol Harlow*. Oxford: Oxford University Press, pp. 3–21.

Carpenter, Belinda and Hayes, Sharon (2007). Crimes against Morality. In H. Hayes and T. Prenzler (Eds.) *Introduction to Crime and Criminology*. Sydney: Pearson Education Australia.

CJC (1991). *Regulating Morality? An inquiry into prostitution in Queensland*. Brisbane: Criminal Justice Commission.

Cook, Henrietta (2010). Girls Interrupted: Same Sex Couple Banned From Ball. *Sydney Morning Herald*, November 10, 2010. Available at http://www.smh.com.au/national/education/girls-interrupted-samesex-couple-banned-from-ball-20101109-17m29.html (accessed August 21, 2014).

Feinberg, Joel (1990). *The Moral Limits of the Criminal Law Volume 4: Harmless Wrongdoing*. Oxford: Oxford University Press.

Hayes, Sharon, Carpenter, Belinda, and Dwyer, Angela (2012). *Sex, Crime and Morality*. London: Routledge.

Lauchs, M. (2006). Justice and Mercy v. Equity. In S. Hayes, N. Stobbs, and M. Lauchs (Eds.) *Social Ethics for Legal and Justice Professionals*. Sydney: Pearson Education Australia, pp. 29–42.

Mill, John Stuart (1869). *On Liberty*. Library of Economics and Liberty. Available at http://www.econlib.org/library/Mill/mlLbty1.html (accessed October 28, 2014).

Oxford Dictionary (2014). Available at http://www.oxforddictionaries.com (accessed October 28, 2014).

Quinn, P. L. and Taliaferro, C. (1999). Introduction. In P. L. Quinn and C. Taliaferro, *A Companion to the Philosophy of Religion*. Oxford: Blackwell Publishing.

Stobbs, N. (2006). The Adversarial Court System—Is it Fair? In S. Hayes, N. Stobbs, and M. Lauchs (Eds.) *Social Ethics for Legal and Justice Professionals*. Sydney: Pearson Education Australia, pp. 59–70.

Ethics in the criminal justice system

Part III examines ethical issues specific to a range of justice professions and institutions, including public officials, lawyers, policing, and punishment.

Part III

Ethics in the criminal justice system

Chapter 10

Public sector ethics and corruption

Key terms: accountability; misconduct; corruption; public sector ethics; public interest; role ethics; code of conduct; whistleblower

Introduction

On July 8, 2013, Jonathan Owen reported in *The Independent* that Britain has become so corrupt that one in twenty people had admitted to bribing a public official (Owen 2013). He also reported that two-thirds of citizens in the UK believed that corruption had increased over the previous two years. The report was based on the 2013 annual corruption index published by Transparency International (TI), a survey involving 114,000 people in 107 countries. Sections of government most susceptible to corruption were the courts, permits and licenses, and land services. "It reveals," stated Owen (2013), "a crisis of trust in Britain's political system, with 90 per cent of Britons believing the country to be run by 'a few big entities acting in their own best interests'." But Britain is not the only nation feeling the creeping tide of corruption. According to TI's Corruption Perceptions Index 2013, while Canada and Australia both scored 81 out of a possible 100 (100 = no corruption), the US ranked even lower than Britain's 78 with a rank of 73 (Transparency International 2013). But in spite of Australia's higher score, TI revealed that in 2013, two New South Wales state ministers were stood down and charged with 'corrupt behavior' involving several businessmen, while two federal ministers were charged with misuse of funds. Moreover, subsidiaries of the Reserve Bank have been "implicated in bribery of foreign officials" and earlier, a "Queensland Minister of the Crown" had been jailed for accepting bribes from a businessman (Transparency International Australia 2013). So it seems that even higher-ranking nations are subject to ongoing endemic corruption among their public officials.

While the problem of corruption has been recognized in these countries for some decades now, it seems little has changed. This chapter explores why this might be so. Public officials, elected and non-elected, have a duty to act in the public interest and for the public good. This chapter defines the public good, and examines issues in public sector ethics, including bribery, fraud, conflicts of interest, and other kinds of 'official misconduct' and the cultural characteristics of organizations that foster corruption. The public sector performs a vital role in the implementation of an elected government's policies and the delivery of a wide range of services to the community. In doing so they are entrusted with the responsibility for public spending and wield considerable power in doing so. These powers include the power to detain and sentence, to collect and store private and confidential information, and even which school our children can attend. Abuse of any of these powers might involve corruption, but also involve a significant breach of public trust. This chapter explores the notions of public trust and public good, how corruption occurs, and strategies for its prevention. It also examines whistleblower legislation and application and the development of codes of conduct.

What is corruption?

There have been many attempts at defining exactly what is corruption. Transparency International (n.d.) describes it as "the abuse of entrusted power for private gain." The *Macquarie Dictionary* (2003) describes corruption as "the perversion of integrity" or "dishonest proceedings," while the *Oxford Dictionary* (2014) defines it as "dishonest or fraudulent conduct by those in power, typically involving bribery." Boyd (2006: 71) argues that "corruption is like beauty—its perception is all in the eye of the beholder," with public perceptions of corruption tending to focus on what is regarded as 'improper behavior.' Definitions outlined in legislation are usually more detailed. The Queensland Crime and Misconduct Act 2001, for example, defines corruption as official misconduct, which includes

> serious misconduct relating to the performance of an officer's duties or that is dishonest or lacks impartiality, or involves a breach of trust, or is a misuse of officially obtained information. The conduct must be serious enough to be a criminal offence or to justify dismissal.
>
> (Boyd 2006: 72)

In the United Kingdom, legislation is more focused, as described in the Bribery Act 2011, which sanctions all forms of bribery, while legislation in the US dates back to the mid-1970s with the Foreign Practices Act 1977, which was intended to address bribery of foreign officials. This was later amended to be the International Anti-Bribery Act 1998. Most contemporary legislation addresses the anti-bribery conventions developed by the Organization for Economic Cooperation and Development (OECD) (OECD 1997).

Many countries also enshrine anti-corruption sanction in the criminal law; for example, extortion, false claims, stealing, misappropriation of property, forgery, election fraud, and revenue evasion are all the subject of respective Criminal Codes in developed nations. Nevertheless, corruption is culturally defined—what is considered corrupt in one country, might not be considered so in another. In some developing countries, for example, bribery of officials is an everyday occurrence that is taken for granted (Boyd 2006). It is for this reason that organizations such as the OECD and TI work towards increased global awareness of such issues.

Credit card misuse

Investigations of an alleged misuse of corporate credit cards by senior officers of a medium-sized local authority, indicated credit cards were issued by the council to the mayor and seven high-ranking officials, with no financial limits on the individual accounts, with no clearly defined policy on the use of credit cards and the users were expected to be 'on their honor' to advise of any private usage. The council's finance committee occasionally queried the amount of an expense but rarely questioned the purpose of the expenditure. No vouchers submitted to the accounts section had any notation regarding the expenditure. Expenditures charged by the credit card holders and paid by the council included lunches in five star hotels, and drinks and dinners in restaurants with topless waitresses. As the accounts had been legitimately approved for payment by the finance committee no criminal charges applied, and as there was no code of conduct at that time, no disciplinary action occurred.

(Adapted from Crime and Misconduct Commission 2005)

The failures of the finance committee and the council officers themselves to act with integrity when using public funds, highlights the need for checks and balances in the public sector. These might include codes of conduct with detailed guidelines for a range of behaviors, line accountability where several people are responsible for 'signing off' on expenses and other purchases, and transparency in reporting by making accounts available for public scrutiny. Strategies for corruption prevention will be discussed later in this chapter. First, however, we need to define what it means to act in the public interest.

Causes of corruption

Grabosky and Larmour (2000) argue that the occurrence of corruption can be explained through Routine Activities Theory, which claims that a crime occurs when the following three elements come together:

1 a motivated offender;
2 an accessible target;
3 the absence of capable guardians.

In the case of public sector corruption, they replace the third criteria with "lack of internal controls" (Grabosky and Larmour 2000). Where someone is motivated to commit a crime—or engage in corrupt acts—often they will engage in 'neutralization'; that is, they will neutralize certain values that would normally prevent them from offending, such as moral values, commitment to abide by the law, and so on. They might convince themselves why they ought to be corrupt—they deserve better conditions, for example, or they work too hard, they are not rewarded well enough, and so on. This neutralizes the offence, allowing them to engage without guilt (Boyd 2006). Corruption occurs, then, because of greed and a lack of sufficient oversight. Public officers who are entrusted with a great amount of discretion are particularly prone to engage in corruption. Police officers, for example, enjoy a relatively high level of autonomy and discretion, particularly when patrolling. Arguably, judges and lawyers also exercise a fair amount of discretion. Wherever people are required to act on their honor, there is always opportunity for corruption.

The public interest and role ethics

In Chapter 8 we examined the difference between public and private morality and how they impact on justice. In this section we consider the distinction between private and public interests in a similar fashion. Private interests are governed by private morality, whereas public interest is governed by public morality. That means that whatever your private interests are—political, cultural, religious, taste, beliefs, and so on—they are governed by private morality in so much as they are governed by you and you alone, so long of course that you stay within the law. The public interest is another matter entirely. When a private individual takes on a public role they consent to act in the public interest, irrespective of their private interests. The public interest relates to the public good—or the common good, as we referred to it in previous chapters. But while the public or common good described what is best for society as a whole, the public interest describes our duty to act in order to fulfill the public good. Public officials are, therefore, required to put their personal interests aside when they step into their public role. When public and private interests conflict in the performance of their duty, an official is required to report the 'conflict of interest.' An example of a conflict of interest is when a local government official charged with deciding among tenders is faced with a tender by a close relative. Because he has an interest in the outcome of the tender—his relative will benefit—he must disclose his conflict of interest to his line manager or other superior, who will allocate the task to someone else. Even if the officer would have treated his relative's tender like any other, the conflict of interests gives the *appearance* of possible corruption, which could lead to a lack of confidence in government.

Preston (2006) suggests that role ethics provides the foundation for ethics in the public sector because it responds to the obligations that attach to one's public role.

According to role ethics, the test of professional or public ethics is not that of satisfying one's personal conscience, but of acting in ways that are consistent with the duties entrusted to one in a public or professional role.

(Preston 2006: 171)

The public role is therefore reminiscent of virtue ethics, in the sense that it describes the kind of person we should be when adopting and acting in that role; that is, one that acts in the public interest. The public interest, then, is just that which will advance the public good. The public good is defined by law and parliament (as the representative of the public) as those goods that make for a better life for everyone. Acting in the public interest ensures that the best possible means are employed for achieving the public good. Public officials are, therefore, required to declare any conflicts of loyalty between their private interests and the public interest. Preston (2006) argues that it is difficult to define the public interest because it is difficult to define 'the public.' Does it include all citizens in society, for example, or just some? Not every decision taken by a public official will affect all citizens, but I think it is fairly obvious to conclude that 'the public' refers to those stakeholders who will be affected, both directly and indirectly, by the decision being made.

However, Preston (2006: 171) points out that a public official is responsible, not only to his or her CEO and minister, but also to "a more profound obligation to support the system of government and its democratic purposes." It is problematic to regard one's public role as simply responsible to the government of the day. Preston points to the Nuremberg trials as evidence that sometimes acting according to the requirements of one's role is not in the public interest at all. Clive Ponting, a British public servant who leaked secret information about an attack on an Argentine ship in the Falklands War, for example, defended his action on the basis that he owed his duty to the parliament—the representative of the people—rather than to his government (Preston 2006).

The role of a public official requires that they adhere to certain rules of conduct that ensure their actions are taken with their official responsibilities and obligations in mind, but this does not mean that an official should not sometimes act against orders for the betterment of the public good.

Codes of ethics and codes of conduct

In basic terms, public officials must be accountable, responsible, and transparent. These and other attributes are often outlined in codes of conduct and codes of ethics. A code of ethics describes the values, commitments, and general obligations owed by a particular public entity to the public. A code of conduct, on the other hand, is grounded in an organization's code of ethics, but more practically describes the rules of behavior expected of public officials within that organization. An example of a code of ethics can be seen in the British report handed down by a committee into public sector ethics led by Lord Nolan in 1995, which cited "Seven Principles of Public Life": selflessness, integrity, objectivity, accountability, openness, honesty, and leadership (Preston 2006: 172). These 'principles' are really the values underlying public life, since they do not provide any guide for action. They do tell us what kinds of values ought to be attached to a public role, however. Codes of ethics may be enshrined in legislation. In Queensland, for example, the Public Sector Ethics Act 1994 outlines the following values: respect for law and government, respect for persons, integrity, diligence, economy, and efficiency.

Ideally, a code of conduct would draw on these values, while providing practical guidelines. The box below shows an example code of conduct provided by Apprenticeships Queensland to companies employing apprentices.

Example code of conduct

(Insert name of company) commits to encouraging a safe, supportive and productive work environment. This can only happen when everyone cooperates and agrees to suitable standards of conduct. The following are acts that the company considers unacceptable. Any employee found engaging in these acts will be subject to disciplinary action which may include reprimand, warning, suspension or dismissal:

- Being absent from work without a valid reason
- Wilfully damaging, destroying or stealing property belonging to fellow employees or the company
- Fighting or engaging in horseplay or disorderly conduct
- Refusing to follow or failing to carry out the reasonable instructions of a supervisor
- Ignoring work duties or wasting time during working hours
- Coming to work under the influence of alcohol or any drug, or bringing alcoholic beverages or drugs on to company property
- Intentionally giving any false or misleading information to obtain a leave of absence
- Using threatening or abusive language towards a fellow employee
- Smoking contrary to established policy or violating any fire protection regulation
- Wilfully or habitually violating health and safety regulations
- Failing to wear clothing conforming to standards set by the company
- Being late or taking unexcused absences from work
- Not taking proper care of, neglecting or abusing company equipment or tools
- Using company equipment in an unauthorised manner
- Possessing firearms or weapons of any kind on company property

(Apprenticeships Info 2014)

What values are being reflected in each of these directives? While this is a code designed for both businesses and public sector employers, it is fairly representative of the kind of content provided in a code of conduct.

Accountability

Accountability is the foundation of public sector ethics and a key preventive element in dealing with corruption. There are two types of accountability: inward and outward. Inward accountability refers to a public official's duty to obey their personal conscience, while outward accountability requires officials to be able, if challenged, to defend their actions as being in conformity with moral standards and/or a code of conduct. As mentioned above, one cannot rely solely on one's public role to guide behavior, since there might be times when your line manager or organization requests you perform a corrupt act (or to turn a blind eye to one). Personal conscience is not a luxury, even in the public sector—it is a legal requirement. The box below describes three scenarios where officials are not held accountable.

Scenario 1
Ken is an administrative officer with the Department of Justice. To make some extra money he types up resumés and assignments for university students. Some days he just eats at his desk and types up these documents.

Scenario 2
Brenda is a Magistrate's Court Clerk. She also does volunteer work for a women's shelter. The shelter is writing to a large number of people asking for donations. Brenda uses the photocopier at her work to copy 2,000 of the letters for posting.

Scenario 3
Heidi is an administrative officer working for a university. She has worked there for six years, and although she has been absent from work for forty-two days due to illness, she has never recorded her sick leave. As she has responsibility for monitoring leave in her unit, it is unlikely anyone will ever become aware of this.

Discuss which values are being dishonored in each of these scenarios. What would you do if you worked with one of these people and knew what was happening?

Why have codes at all?

Research demonstrates that there is not a strong correlation between personal moral development and ethics in the workplace (ICAC 1997). Rather than acting according to their personal values, employees tend to behave in the ways expected by managers and peers. As Adams et al. (2001: 201) remark: "Regardless of the individual's ability to make moral judgments, in the organisational setting there are strong pressures to conform to the expectations of managers and peers." Are codes of conduct effective in preventing corruption? While their intention is honorable, at least one study has shown that most people do not remember their code of conduct at a later period of time. In the study of the effect of a code of conduct in the Queensland Public Service, a group of employees were asked what they recalled. The fact that honesty and respect were two of the values outlined in the code was remembered by 49.6%; 6.2% recalled that stealing is prohibited; 5.3% remembered dress requirements; and 4.9% knew the penalties. Of the employees, 10.9% recalled nothing at all. Nevertheless, it has been suggested that just having a code sends a message to employees that the organization will not tolerate corruption or misconduct. Not having a code also sends a message, obviously, but the opposite one!

The following section outlines examples of some of the requirements of a code of conduct—the example outlines those in the code of conduct for Queensland public sector employees (based on the Public Sector Ethics Act 1994)—and explores some more scenarios to stimulate discussion about how they should apply.

Obligation 1: Respect for the law and system of government

s.7 Respect for the law and system of government

1   A public official should—
    a   uphold the laws of the State and Commonwealth; and
    b   carry out official public sector decisions and policies faithfully and impartially.

2   Subsection (1)(b) does not detract from a public official's duty to act independently of government if the official's independence is required by legislation or government policy, or is a customary feature of the official's work.

Scenario 4

Deena is a senior policy advisor working for the Department of Fair Trading. She recently advised the government, as part of her role, that the laws relating to the regulation of gym memberships in Queensland needed to be tightened, as her investigations found that many people were entering into contracts without fully understanding the financial commitment they were making. When the government decided against amending the legislation in this area, Jane became very angry and gave an interview to a local radio station in which she described the government's actions as "callous and short-sighted."

Obligation 2: Respect for persons

s.8 Respect for persons

1 A public official should treat members of the public and other public officials—
   a honestly and fairly; and
   b with proper regard for their rights and obligations.

2 A public official should act responsively in performing official duties.

Scenario 5

Butch is a councilor on the Brisbane City Council and chairman of the Neighborhood Security Committee. A number of representatives from Brisbane's Vietnamese community have approached him with concerns about lack of proper street lighting in several suburbs, and other security concerns. Butch is not particularly interested in helping them, since the Vietnamese vote is not crucial to his re-election chances, and he also believes that Australia takes in too many migrants. He is a politician and elected on such platforms.

Obligation 3: Integrity

s.9 Integrity

1 In recognition that public office involves a public trust, a public official should seek—
   a to maintain and enhance public confidence in the integrity of public administration; and
   b to advance the common good of the community the official serves.

2 Having regard to the obligation mentioned in subsection (1), a public official—
   a should not improperly use his or her official powers or position, or allow them to be improperly used; and .
   b should ensure that any conflict that may arise between the official's personal interests and official duties is resolved in favor of the public interest; and
   c should disclose fraud, corruption, and maladministration of which the official becomes aware.

Scenario 6

Sam works for the Commission for Children and Young People. His job is to investigate the backgrounds of people applying for approval to work with children. Sam is also an activities coordinator for the local Police

(continued)

(continued)

Citizens Youth Club. The club has applied for approval of eight of its volunteer workers to provide coaching services for their gymnastics team. Although Sam takes his role very seriously and would treat this application in the same way as any other, he wonders whether there would be anything unethical about him investigating his own club's application.

Obligation 4: Diligence

s.10 Diligence

1 In performing his or her official duties, a public official should—
  a exercise proper diligence, care and attention; and
  b seek to achieve high standards of public administration.

s.87 Grounds for discipline

2 The employing authority may discipline an officer if the authority is reasonably satisfied that the officer has—
  c performed the officer's duties carelessly, incompetently or inefficiently

Scenario 7

Alice is a security officer employed by the Queensland government. Her job involves providing physical security for state government buildings and offices. She also has part-time work as a singer in a jazz band. Her singing career involves a lot of late nights, and she often finds herself tired and unable to concentrate fully while doing her security work.

Obligation 5: Economy and efficiency

s.11 Economy and efficiency

In performing his or her official duties, a public official should ensure that public resources are not wasted, abused, or used improperly or extravagantly.

Scenario 8

Sally is a researcher working for the Legal Aid Office. A friend from the Nottingham office often sends her emails containing jokes and rude images, which she forwards on to several other friends working in the same building.

Devising a corruption prevention strategy

The Queensland Crime and Misconduct Commission (2005) suggests agencies implement a ten-step 'integrated' strategy for corruption control. The strategy should be integrated, it argues, because strategies that focus on one element or initiative tend to fail. For example, some organizations rely solely on financial control mechanisms, but even where they are coupled with a code of conduct, they will not work unless accompanied by education, and the development of reporting, disclosure, and investigation policies (Boyd 2006).

> Agencies committed to developing an integrated corruption prevention strategy are more successful in changing their organizational culture to reflect ethical values and discourage incidents of fraud and corruption.
>
> (Boyd 2006: 79)

The box below outlines the CMC's recommendations.

An integrated corruption prevention strategy

1 Agency-wide integrated policy
2 Risk assessment
3 Internal controls
4 Internal reporting
5 External reporting
6 Public interest disclosures
7 Investigations
8 Code of conduct
9 Staff education and awareness
10 Client and community awareness.

(CMC 2005)

Reporting corruption: whistleblowers

In order for corruption and misconduct to be properly addressed, there needs to be some process in placing for reporting it. Sometimes legislation will place a direct obligation on a CEO or minister to report corruption that comes to light, for example, the Queensland Crime and Misconduct Act 2001. Whether such action is legislated or not, all employees have a moral obligation to report corruption of which they become aware—that is, to make a 'public interest disclosure.' However, history shows there is considerable resistance to reporting fellow employees who are suspected of misconduct. It is for this reason that whistleblower protections have been put into place in many jurisdictions. The first whistleblower protection law was enacted in the US by the Continental Congress in 1778 (US Government 1908). Today, whistleblowing in the United States is governed by an array of legislation, including the Whistleblower Protection Act 2007. A similar situation exists in the UK. However, both countries have established bodies to deal with whistleblower protection. In the US it is the *National Whistleblower's Center*, while UK citizens can look to *Whistleblowers UK* and *Public Concern at Work*. In 2013, The UK Government initiated a Whistleblowing Commission to explore whether there were aspects of whistleblowing not adequately protected by law and whether there ought to be further provisions. In Canada, The Office of the Public Sector Integrity Commissioner is the go-to point for reporting corruption, although there are no actual whistleblower protections legislated at the time of writing. Over fifty other countries have adopted protections as part of anti-corruption, freedom of information, or employment laws (Banisar 2011).

Reasons that whistleblowers might need protection include workplace reprisals, bullying, being stood down, being overlooked for promotion, and possibly being brought to suit for defamation. In Queensland, a person who suffers detriment from reprisals is entitled to damages from the offending party.

Moral courage

Boyd (2006) argues that while our society respects and honors acts of physical courage, they very rarely celebrate courageous acts of exposure and whistleblowing. "Moral courage," he claims, "involves maintaining an ethical stance and caring enough about your values that you uphold them in the face of personal risks. Many high profile corporate failures represent not only significant corrupt behaviour but also major failures of moral courage" (Boyd 2006: 92). Legislation, codes of ethics and conduct, government commissions, and education can only do so much. In the end, promoting integrity, accountability, and transparency requires good leadership and moral courage. As President-elect John F. Kennedy remarked in his address delivered to the General Court of the Commonwealth of Massachusetts just prior to his inauguration:

> Today the eyes of all people are truly upon us and our governments at every level, national, state and local, must be as a city upon a hill— constructed and inhabited by people aware of their great trust and their great responsibilities . . . When at some future date the high court of history sits in judgment on each one of us, recording whether in our brief span of service we fulfilled our responsibilities.

> (Cited in Boyd 2006: 93)

Review questions

1 It is suggested the corruption is culturally defined. Can you identify some differences in ethical standards between different cultures; for example, your group of friends compared to your sporting club?
2 What is the difference between public interest and public good? Give an example.
3 What are some of the values found in organizational codes of ethics?
4 Conduct a search of the internet to find a code of conduct used by your local government or other organization. How well does it fit the values and obligations described in this chapter?
5 What are the elements of a good corruption prevention strategy?
6 Do a search of the internet to identify some well-known whistle-blowers. How were they treated? Do you feel they were protected sufficiently from reprisals?
7 What do you understand by the term 'moral courage'? What factors might facilitate or inhibit a justice professional displaying it?
8 What is a conflict of interest? Find some examples and discuss how they should be addressed.
9 What do we mean by 'role ethics'? What is the purpose of seeing public sector ethics in this way?
10 How does a code of ethics differ from a code of conduct? Give examples of each.

References

Adams, Janet S., Tashchian, Armen, and Shore, Ted H. (2001). Codes of Ethics as Signals for Ethical Behavior. *Journal of Business Ethics*, 29: 199–211.

Apprenticeships Info (2014) in 'Training' on Queensland Government website. Available at http://training.qld.gov.au/resources/employers/pdf/example-code-conduct.pdf (accessed September 9, 2014).

Banisar, David (2011). Whistleblowing: International Standards and Developments. In I. Sandoval (Ed.) *Corruption and Transparency: debating the frontiers between state, market and society*. Washington, DC: World Bank-Institute for Social Research, UNAM.

Boyd, John (2006). Corruption and Public Sector Ethics. In S. Hayes, N. Stobbs, and M. Lauchs (Eds.) *Social Ethics for Legal and Justice Professionals*. Sydney: Pearson Education.

Crime and Misconduct Commission (CMC) (2005). *Fraud and Corruption Control: Guidelines for Best Practice*. Brisbane: CMC.

Criminal Justice Commission (CJC) (1991). *Complaints Against Local Government Authorities in Queensland—Six Case Studies*. Brisbane: CJC.

Grabosky, P. and Larmour, P. (2000). Public Sector Corruption and its Control. *Trends and Issues in Crime and Criminal Justice*, No. 143.

Independent Commission Against Corruption New South Wales (ICAC) (1997). *Corruption Matters*, November, No. 7. Sydney: ICAC.

Macquarie Dictionary (2003). Available at https://www.macquariedictionary.com.au/ (accessed October 28, 2014).

OECD (1997). Convention on Combating Bribery of Foreign Public Officials in International Business Transactions. Organization for Economic Cooperation and Development. Available at http://www.oecd.org/corruption/oecdantibriberyconvention.htm (accessed August 13, 2014).

Oxford Dictionary (2014). Available at http://www.oxforddictionaries.com (accessed October 28, 2014).

Owen, Jonathan (2013). Britain's Bribery Boom: One in 20 Has Bribed a Public Official as Corruption Rises. *The Independent*, July 8, 2013. Available at http://www.independent.co.uk/news/uk/home-news/britains-bribery-boom-one-in-20-has-bribed-a-public-official-as-corruption-rises-8696181.html (accessed August 13, 2014).

Preston, N. (2006). *Understanding Ethics*. Third edition. Sydney: The Federation Press.

Transparency International (2013). Corruptions Perceptions Index 2013. Available at http://www.transparency.org/cpi2013/results (accessed August 13, 2014).

Transparency International (n.d.). FAQS on Corruption. Available at http://www.transparency.org/whoweare/organisation/faqs_on_corruption/2/ (accessed August 13, 2014).

Transparency International Australia (2013). Corruption and the Australian Election. *TI Australia News*, September 2013, No. 75. Available at http://transparency.org.au/wp-content/uploads/2013/09/13-Sept-TIA-Newsletter-A4.pdf (accessed August 13, 2014).

United States Government (1908). *Journals of the Continental Congress 1774–1789*. Government Printing Office.

Chapter 11

Regulating the legal profession

Key terms: law as profession; duties to the court; duties to clients; confidentiality; conflicts of interest; oversight; pro bono

Introduction

This chapter explores issues in legal ethics and the legal profession. Traditionally, legal professionals have been subject to higher standards of conduct than most other professionals, for example, by being subject to stringent admission requirements such as requiring full disclosure of any criminal history, including even minor traffic offences (Thomas 2006). Nevertheless, the legal profession is fraught with ethical dilemmas. Issues such as client confidentiality, duties owed to the court, duties owed to clients, conflicts of duty, and negligence continue to make headlines around the world. This chapter will explore some real-life case studies as a way of problematizing ethics in the legal profession, to demonstrate the often unclear and hazardously fuzzy ways in which unethical behavior is detected and uncovered. A study by Bruce Green (2000) found that lawyers and potential lawyers are more likely to perceive real stories of unethical behavior as moral tales, even when the facts are incomplete, because they are able to put themselves into the story and imagine what the consequences would feel like. Fictional or hypothetical stories, in contrast, made little impact on their moral imagination. Thus, news stories, court cases, and complaints will provide excellent illustration of the issues faced by those in the legal profession.

In 2005, I was appointed as a lay member of the Queensland Legal Practice Tribunal (now the Queensland Civil and Administrative Tribunal), a newly created mechanism for hearing cases of serious misconduct in the legal profession. The first case on which I sat, with Mr Justice Moynihan as chair, and Mr K. Horsley as the other legal member, concerned complaints against a senior partner of Baker Johnson, a firm well known for winning personal injury suits. Michael Baker was reknowned for his extensive community and charity work, but also for his larger than life personality, including a very colorful vocabulary. Eighteen charges were made against Baker, including wrongful charging of professional fees where no fees were due, and using "crude, insulting and offensive language in communications with and in the presence of" both clients and employees of his firm (Foote 2006). The wrongful charging of fees concerned a no-win-no-fee policy for personal injury cases dealt with by the firm. He was also charged with failing to maintain reasonable standards of competence and diligence, resulting in his staff permitting proceedings to be instituted and pursued against a client. In a subsequent report for the Queensland Law Society on 'Solicitors' Professional Responsibilities to Their Clients,' Foote described the latter case as an example of unprofessional conduct.

> Charges 2 and 7 concerned a personal injury matter conducted by the firm on a "no-win-no-fee" basis. The matter settled on a basis whereby Mr Baker recommended the client settle for a certain sum and the firm (under the terms of the retainer) became entitled to charge costs.
>
> However, the costs exceeded the settlement sum with the effect that the client recovered nothing and in fact owed the firm money.
>
> The firm then attempted to sue the client in the Magistrate's Court but failed. The firm unsuccessfully appealed to the District Court, McGill DCJ deciding that, if the client recovered nothing, then it was not a "win" for the client and the firm breached its fiduciary duty to the client by placing its own interest ahead of the client.
>
> The court of appeal upheld the findings of Moynihan SJA that the firm charged fees in circumstances where the retainer did not permit it and the decision to sue the client for fees was "unmeritorious" and taken with Mr Baker's knowledge and endorsement.
>
> (Foote 2006)

The Tribunal found Baker guilty of five charges of professional misconduct and three charges of unprofessional conduct, and ordered him to be struck off; a decision that was later upheld by the Court of Appeals. The difference between professional misconduct and unprofessional conduct will be discussed further below. The main point here is that, in spite of previous attempts by clients to have their complaints heard, it was not until the Tribunal was established that they were able to see justice done. Previously, clients only had recourse to the Law Society and the Bar in lodging complaints, a process that was criticized as amounting to "Caesar judging Caesar" (Foote 2006). In the Law Society report, Foote (2006) remarked that the purpose of the Legal Services Commission, which oversees the Tribunal, was to not only seek justice for clients against negligent and unprofessional lawyers, and to make examples of them, but also to work with the Society and Queensland lawyers to raise awareness of ethical standards in the profession in order to prevent such complaints being made. The following sections explore the law as a profession and the duties owed to both clients and the court, with a view to unpacking the nature of misconduct and unprofessional behavior.

The law as profession

Traditionally, the word 'profession' was reserved for only three occupations—medicine, the church, and the law (Thomas 2006). The etymology of the word means to "testify on behalf of" or "to stand for something," in the sense of demonstrating a commitment to serve (Preston 2006). A profession is, therefore, more of a vocation than simply a career, comprising more than just technical competence and specialist knowledge, but also an "intrinsic commitment to public good and willingness to provide services gratuitously beyond the call of duty" (Preston 2006: 173). Indeed, Preston (2006: 173) considers this type of public commitment to be indicative of the taking on of "civil responsibility." Contemporary interpretations, however, tend to focus on more measureable qualities, such as tertiary qualifications, professional preparation, and membership of a professional association with an accompanying code of ethics, all of which suggest a measure of social status (Preston 2006). Professions also carry with them the recognition of a high level of trust in dealing with clients, something that has often been the butt of jokes within the legal profession. One does not often hear public affirmations of the trustworthiness and ethics of lawyers. George Bernard Shaw even suggested that professions were "a conspiracy against the laity" (Thomas 2006: 43), and this kind of attitude is no more obvious than in the profession of law.

In spite of the denigration of and humor surrounding members of the legal profession, they are subject to much more stringent standards of conduct than many other occupations. For example,

> while the provisions of the *Criminal Law (Rehabilitation of Offenders) Act 1986 (QLD)* generally mean that a person need not disclose the fact of criminal conviction once ten years has elapsed from the end of any sentence imposed for the offence, applications for admission as a legal practitioner in Queensland are required to disclose "contraventions of any law, whether committed in Queensland or elsewhere."
>
> (Thomas 2006)

This means that even minor traffic offences and parking infringements must be included in applications for admission—certainly a strict criteria by any standards. Admission to legal practice is usually controlled by legislation. For example, in Queensland, the *Legal Services Act 2007* provides a penalty of two years' incarceration for failing to provide accurate details on the application to admission. Often, regulations and principles governing the legal profession mirror those that apply to the public service (outlined in Chapter 10). In England, for example, the legal profession is regulated by the Legal Services Act 2007 and the Solicitors Act 1974. In 2011, The Solicitors Regulation Authority (SRA) enacted "10 Mandatory Principles" governing the legal profession in England. These principles and other regulations are outlined in the SRA Handbook (2011). The principles are reproduced in the box below.

SRA Principles

These are mandatory Principles, which apply to all.
You must:

1 uphold the rule of law and the proper administration of justice;
2 act with integrity;
3 not allow your independence to be compromised;
4 act in the best interests of each client;
5 provide a proper standard of service to your clients;
6 behave in a way that maintains the trust the public places in you and in the provision of legal services;
7 comply with your legal and regulatory obligations and deal with your regulators and ombudsmen in an open, timely and co-operative manner;
8 run your business or carry out your role in the business effectively and in accordance with proper governance and sound financial and risk management principles;
9 run your business or carry out your role in the business in a way that encourages equality of opportunity and respect for diversity; and
10 protect client money and assets.

(Solicitors Regulation Authority 2011)

It has been argued that legal services have become compromised by the recent corporatization of the legal industry in developed nations, with national law firms taking on the bulk of services to the community (Thomas 2006). This has led to a move away from the traditional concept of the legal professional as a small business model, and a move towards regulating in terms of consumer protection rather than traditional ethical principles. Certainly the ten principles described in the SRA Handbook above suggest that is the case, with its focus on clients. The SRA itself states that legal practitioners must be 'outcomes-focused':

> Outcomes-focused regulation concentrates on providing positive outcomes which when achieved will benefit and protect clients and the public. The SRA Code of Conduct (the Code) sets out our outcomes-focused conduct requirements so that you can consider how best to achieve the right outcomes for your clients taking into account the way that your firm works and its client base. The Code is underpinned by effective, risk-based supervision and enforcement.

(SRA 2011)

In both England and Australia, the profession has traditionally been divided into solicitors and barristers, with separate acts governing each. In Australia, barristers usually act as specialist advocates for clients in court and are hired by solicitors, who deal directly with clients and attend to day-to-day legal matters. However, recent changes in Queensland and other Australian jurisdictions mean that all lawyers are now admitted as 'legal practitioners' with no formal distinction between the two. Nevertheless, in practice the distinction still often remains (Thomas 2006). The legal profession in England has a much broader range of legal practitioners: as well as barristers and solicitors, there are also registered foreign lawyers, patent attorneys, trade mark attorneys, licensed conveyancers, commissioners for oaths, immigration advisers, and claims management services (Legal Services Act 2007).

The legal profession in the US is a fused model, where lawyers, who are referred to as 'attorneys,' include all those who practice law. In Canada, the term 'lawyer' refers only to those who have been admitted to the bar, and who are properly referred to as barristers or solicitors depending upon speciality.

Duties of the legal profession

The title of this section suggests that we are talking about a deontological issue, and that may indeed be the case. Lawyers are subject to a set of rules that they must follow regardless of the consequences for themselves or clients. Legal practitioners have certain obligations that they must fulfill, and they owe certain duties, most importantly to the law, the court, their clients, and the public. Breaches of these duties occur when legal practitioners fail to act according to duty, and instead rely on utilitarian or egoist motives. The reasons for a deontological framework will become clear as we progress through this chapter.

As we saw in the box above, legal practitioners in England are subject to stringent rules, with an expectation of uncompromising ethical conduct at all times. In Australia, the standard of conduct for legal practitioners is set out in the *Australian Solicitors' Conduct Rules* (Law Council 2011). Similar principles can be found in most other common and civil law countries. Legal practitioners are often faced by multiple obligations—to clients, the courts, the profession, and the public—and with so many interests to serve, are often faced with conflicting decisions. Clear ethical guidelines ensure at least some accountability and transparency in decision-making is maintained. The following sections discuss some common duties and obligations and how they might be breached.

Duties to the court

While the legal profession has become more commercialized in recent years, its duties to the court have remained the same. Commercialization has therefore imposed more potential conflicts on practitioners than ever before. Warren (2011) argues that the emphasis on acting in the clients' interests has resulted in an overburdening of written and verbal evidence, argument, and process. She cites the case of *Thomas v. SMP* heard in the Supreme Court of Australia, in which Pembroke J was faced with a 500-page affidavit, most of which was irrelevant. After reading 3,000 paragraphs, the judge stopped, claiming that the affidavit was inappropriate, not just because of its content but because, in submitting it to the court, the practitioner had failed in his duty to the court, which in some cases requires the "restraining of the enthusiasm of the client" where matters are irrelevant (Warren 2011: 2). In a speech to the Judicial College of Australia, Chief Justice Keane remarked:

> [I]n the traditional conception, the courts are an arm of government charged with the quelling of controversies . . . the courts, in exercising the judicial power of the state, are not "providing legal services." The parties to litigation are not acting as consumers of legal services: they are being governed, whether they like it or not.
>
> (Cited in Warren 2011: 3–4)

With that in mind, a legal practitioner's duty to the court must always outweigh his or her duty to the client—they are first and foremost 'officers of the court' (Thomas 2006: 45). Moreover, due to the adversarial nature of courts in many countries, trust in legal practitioners is of the utmost importance. Apart from avoiding irrelevant documentation and argument so as to avoid wasting the court's time, practitioners also have a duty of disclosure; that is, they must disclose all evidence to the court, regardless of whether it is in their client's interests. Evidence that is relevant but adverse to a client's interest must be presented to the court along with all other documentation. If a client admits to guilt but refuses to plead guilty, for example, counsel must not hold back any damning evidence, even if the client requests they do so. In such cases, the practitioner can withdraw from the case, but only if there is enough time for the client to find another suitable lawyer. If that is not possible, the lawyer "may have to run what is called a frozen defence" (Thomas 2006: 46), requiring the prosecution to prove its case without making any admissions of guilt or innocence.

Practitioners also have a duty not to mislead the court. The case study below is instructive.

Misleading evidence

In *Legal Services Commission v. Hackett [2006]* a barrister misrepresented communications in a matter in which he had a personal interest, by omitting some documents provided by a body corporate manager. The case involved whether a corporate vote had been irregular, and the communications provided by the manager were contradictory. The barrister chose those documents that supported his case and omitted those that did not. He later blamed his behavior on an oversight, claiming he had not intended to mislead the court. The court fined him $5,000.

(Adapted from Queensland Law Society 2014)

While this offence might seem minor, the ability to illegally skew a case in one's favor should not be taken lightly. In another case in the same court, *Legal Services Commission v. Karl Storm Jameson [2006]*, one of the litigants (a solicitor) fabricated evidence and as a result was struck off the role of solicitors (Queensland Law Society 2014). The cautionary tale from observing these two cases is that practitioners cannot rely on the leniency of the court, regardless of how minor the infraction might be.

In addition to making misleading statements and offering false—or omitting—evidence, there have been cases where evidence has been destroyed or 'warehoused' offshore where it is out of reach of the process of discovery, for example in the case of *British American Tobacco Australia Services Limited v. Cowall* (Thomas 2006). This goes against the legal practitioner's duty of disclosure to the court.

Finally, barristers and other lawyers who represent clients in court have a duty to advise the court of any and all relevant legislation pertaining to the case. This means providing legislation that is adverse to the client as well as that used in defending their case. Even after the trial is over, if a barrister becomes aware of a piece of legislation before the judge's decision has been handed down, they must make it known to the judge (Thomas 2006).

Duties to the client

Lawyers have a duty of care to their clients, much the same as do doctors and other professionals, and can be sued for negligence in most jurisdictions, except under certain circumstances. In Queensland, the *Solicitor's Rule* states that solicitors "must act honestly and fairly, and with competence and diligence, in the service of a client." Similarly, the *Barrister's Rule* states that, "the role of barristers as professional advocates in the administration of justice requires them to act honestly, fairly, skilfully, diligently and fearlessly" (cited in Thomas 2006: 47). To these we might add the duty to maintain confidentiality in all dealings with clients and to avoid conflicts of interest (Auditore n.d.). The American Bar Association's (ABA) *Model Rules of Professional Conduct* (2013) provide much more in-depth explanations about specific duties owed not only to current clients, but to former clients, but in essence, amount to the same thing. In the UK, the *SRA Handbook* (2011), of course, provides similar advice for lawyers in England and Wales.

Confidentiality

Lawyer's communications with their clients about their case are covered by legal professional privilege. This means that legal practitioners are obligated to keep any and all communications with their clients in confidence. This allows the client to be open and honest and to provide as much information as they can in order for their legal counsel to best represent their case. Unfortunately this sometimes means that information that could be valuable in uncovering the truth of a matter may be withheld. Generally, it is considered that "the balance of factors in favour of keeping information confidential outweighs the public interest in allowing it to be released" (Thomas 2006: 51). In England and Wales legal privilege is recognized in the common law and is seen as a 'fundamental principle of justice.'

Generally, legal practitioners are not required to reveal confidential disclosures in court; however, in the US, attorneys may reveal such confidences to prevent death, to prevent substantial injury to the property of another, or to prevent a client from committing a crime or fraud (ABA 2013). In England and Wales, the Proceeds of Crime Act (2002) allows that practitioners who suspect their clients of money laundering are required to report them to the law enforcement authorities without notifying their clients. Nevertheless, the Court of Appeal found in *Bowman v. Fels [2005]* that this does not override legal professional privilege. Clients, however, can waive their privilege if they so choose, but because the privilege is wholly client-based, the legal practitioner has no right of waiver.

The Lake Pleasant murders

In 1973, Frank Armani and Francis Belge were appointed to defend Robert Garrow, the accused murderer in the Lake Pleasant murder case. During his interviews with Garrow, Armani and Belge learned of the location of at least two additional victims murdered by Garrow, even as the families of these victims still searched for their daughters. As a result, the two attorneys were torn between their concern for the two victims' families and their attorney–client obligation to Garrow. In spite of finding the burial site and photographing it, Armani remained silent, even after the father of one of the victims approached him and asked him specifically whether he knew anything. Eventually, Garrow admitted to the murders under cross-examination in court and was sentenced to life in prison. It was only after the trial that Armani and Belge admitted that they knew about the murders and the location of the victims. As a result, and in spite of being upheld as models of ethical conduct by his fellow legal practitioners, they were publicly vilified and their law practice ruined.

(Case discussed in Goldfarb 2009)

The most interesting aspect of this case is how the ethical conduct exhibited by Armani and Belge was not considered as ethical by the community, the parents of the victims, and the public at large. These two lawyers acted in perfect synchronicity with their legal responsibilities—they presented the best case possible for their client, and kept his confidences—and yet the public believed they had a 'higher' duty to disclose. The fact is that, had they disclosed, they could have been disciplined by the court and/or their professional association, including possibly being struck off. The fact that they located the graves to be sure of their client's guilt, and then took photographs as possible evidence, suggests that the two men had perhaps intended to reveal the information should it not have been revealed in court during the trial. Armani and Belge knew what their duty was and, I suggest, were prepared to accept the consequences in that case. Luckily they did not have to disclose, as their client did it for them. Little did they know how immense would be the public backlash. To put it in perspective, here is what one legal academic at Syracuse University had to say about the case: "Mr. Armani made an immeasurable personal sacrifice during his representation of Robert Garrow and in the face of inconceivable opposition, strengthened our legal system by personifying what it means to be a lawyer" (Wilson 2010).

Conflicts of interest

As we saw in Chapter 10, public servants are required to avoid conflicts of interest in the performance of their public duties. Similarly, lawyers are required to put their clients' interests before their own. However, there are times when conflicts might arise between duties owed to current clients and past clients, and duties owed to potential or future clients.

A tale of the accused

Two young men are accused of killing another man in a street fight. Because the issues in each trial relate to exactly the same set of circumstances, they are tried together. A renowned barrister, with considerable experience in trials of this nature, is approached to appear for both men accused of the murder. Both young men claim that they were at a cinema 10 miles away when the killing occurred.

Should the barrister act as defence counsel for both men? Would it make any difference if both admit to being involved in the fight, but one accuses the other of pulling the knife?

(Thomas 2006: 50)

Generally, lawyers are not allowed to act for both parties in a dispute or transaction. However, in the case above, both potential clients are on the same side and taking the same stance of not guilty, so the case is much more complicated. Nevertheless, the lawyer in question should probably consider the impact on his representing both of at least one of his clients being guilty—that would indeed be a conflict of duty, because he would then be representing one person whose eye-witness testimony might lead to a guilty verdict for the other.

Similarly, lawyers are prevented from acting for someone in a case where they have previously acted for the other party (Thomas 2006). The reason for this is that while acting for the other party they might have had access to information that could assist their current client. Unfortunately, as legal services become increasingly corporatized, it is highly likely that one or both parties in a case will have been represented by someone employed by the firm. The solution, states Thomas (2006), is the construction of "Chinese walls," which means a series of mechanisms which isolate people with confidential information from the particular case or cases being represented and their relevant files.

Trust accounts

In Australia, barristers are prevented from dealing with clients' money, a role which is dealt with solely by and through solicitors. Solicitors charged with handling clients' money in the course of their dealings must open separate trust accounts, which are operated separately from the firm's own accounts. Although the solicitor is legal owner of the account, it must be operated under strict rules protected by legislation. In New South Wales, for example, under the Legal Profession Act 2004 solicitors must:

- Disburse trust money only as directed by the person on whose behalf it is held
- Deposit trust money to a general trust account maintained with an approved authorised deposit-taking institution in New South Wales, such as a bank, building society or credit union
- Keep accurate records of their trust accounts and make them available for inspection by external examiners appointed by the Law Society.

(Law Society of NSW n.d.)

According to Pfeiffer (2014), there are three ways in which lawyers might misuse trust funds. They might 'borrow' money from a trust fund, either by taking funds out before it is earned or by borrowing with the intention of paying it back. Or they might steal from the account, of course. Second they might not keep trust money separate from company funds. For example, if legal fees are $2,000 and court costs are $400, and a client writes a check for $2,400, the lawyer might deposit the entire funds into the business account. They might also fail to remove their costs from the trust account when they are due, which is also an ethical violation. The final mistake lawyers make is failing to accurately record client transactions; for example, by failing to keep a separate ledger for each account. Misappropriation of trust funds usually results in the solicitor being struck off, but failure to keep adequate accounts may also lead to disciplinary proceedings.

Oversight of the legal profession

Lawyers in every country have national bar associations that oversee their conduct, as well as regulating admission to the profession, as we saw above. In the US, this of course is the ABA, and in Canada, the Canadian Bar Association, which is supplemented by law societies for each state. In the UK the General Council of the Bar regulates barristers, while the Law Society represents solicitors in England and Wales. Similarly the Australian Bar Association represents barristers in Australia while the Law Council of Australia and the Law Societies of individual states are responsible for solicitors.

While these professional bodies aim to guide and regulate the legal profession, they do not discipline lawyers. Separate disciplinary bodies operate in most jurisdictions. For example, in the US, each state has its own disciplinary body, as is the case in Australia. One example mentioned earlier in this chapter is the Queensland Civil and Administrative Tribunal, which hears cases of 'serious misconduct,' and the Legal Practice Committee which hears cases of 'unprofessional conduct,' both of which were established under the Legal Services Act 2007 (Queensland). The 2012–2013 Annual report of the Legal Services Commission reports that during that year a total of 413 (4%) of Queensland solicitors and a total of 335 law firms (20%) were the subjects of complaint. Women were one-third as likely as men to be the subject of a complaint. While 4% does not sound like a large number, it is certainly significant, suggesting that disciplinary bodies such as these have their work cut out for them.

Pro bono work

The term 'pro bono' derives from the Latin *pro bono publico*, which means 'for the public good.' It generally refers to legal work undertaken at no cost (or significantly reduced cost), usually for low-income clients. The Law Council of Australia (LCA) defines pro bono as:

1 A lawyer, without fee or without expectation of a fee or at a reduced fee, advises and/or represents a client in cases where:
   i   a client has no other access to the courts and the legal system; and/or
   ii   the client's case raises a wider issue of public interest; or
2 The lawyer is involved in free community legal education and/or law reform; or
3 The lawyer is involved in the giving of free legal advice and/or representation to charitable and community organisations.

(LCA 1995)

According to Thomas (2006: 57), many members of the legal profession undertake a significant amount of pro bono work "in spite of the seemingly endless lawyer jokes!" He also points out that acting pro bono is not the same as acting for a client on a no-win-no-fee basis, and should also be differentiated from Legal Aid services, which provide means-tested legal advice and representation to low-income individuals.

Pro bono work is also supplemented by community legal services schemes, which usually run as not-for-profit enterprises funded by government or charity, supplemented by pro bono work among its practitioners.

Review questions

1 How is the profession of lawyers different from other professions? In particular, why should they be held to higher standards?
2 Should lawyers' duties to the court and to the law outweigh their duty to their client? How can these duties be balanced?
3 Should lawyers be immune from legal redress for negligence?
4 Small towns often only have one solicitor. Should such solicitors be able to act on behalf of both parties to a dispute or transaction; for example, in a divorce or conveyancing?
5 What would be the advantages and disadvantages of allowing lawyers to disclose confidential information under certain circumstances? Give some examples.
6 Is having an intimate relationship with a client consistent with the duties that a lawyer owes to that client? Would it make a difference if the lawyer were acting in a non-contentious real estate conveyance?
7 Should all lawyers be required to perform a certain amount of pro bono work?
8 Why do lawyers need separate regulating and disciplinary bodies?
9 What do you think about countries that divide the legal profession into various roles, such as barristers and solicitors? What are the advantages and disadvantages of that?
10 What is the purpose of trust funds in legal firms? What is wrong with lawyers just using their business account for all transactions as do medical specialists?

References

American Bar Association (2013). *Model Rules of Professional Conduct*. Available at http://www.americanbar.org/groups/professional_responsibility/publications/model_rules_of_professional_conduct/model_rules_of_professional_conduct_table_of_contents.html (accessed August 19, 2014).

Auditore, Silvio (n.d.). *Ethical Duties Owed by Lawyers*. Available at http://www.findlaw.com.au/articles/455/ethical-duties-owed-by-lawyers.aspx (accessed August 19, 2014).

Australian Solicitors' Conduct Rules (Law Council 2011). Available at http://www.lawcouncil. asn.au/lawcouncil/index.php/divisions/rpr/australian-solicitors-conduct-rules (accessed August 19, 2014).

Foote, Ian (2006). Solicitors' Professional Responsibilities to their Clients. *Proctor*, June 2006, pp. 43–46.

Goldfarb, Ronald L. (2009). *In Confidence*. New Haven, CT: Yale University Press.

Green, Bruce (2000). There but for Fortune: real-life versus fictional case studies in legal ethics. *Fordham Law Review*, 69(3): 977–996.

Law Council of Australia (LCA) (1995). Pro Bono Publico: for the public good. *Law Council Policy Statement* (Australia). Available at http://www.lawcouncil.asn.au/lawcouncil/ images/LCA-PDF/a-z-docs/ProBonoPublico.pdf (accessed October 28, 2014).

Law Society of New South Wales (n.d.). *Trust and Controlled Money Accounts*. Available at http://www.lawsociety.com.au/community/thelawyerclientrelationship/Trustcontrolled moneyaccounts/index.htm (accessed August 19, 2014).

Pfeiffer, William (2014). *Lawyer Trust Account Mistakes: 3 common lawyer trust account (IOLTA) mistakes*. Available at http://law.about.com/od/financialmanagement/a/ Lawyer-Trust-Account-Mistakes-3-Common-Lawyer-Trust-Account-Iolta-Mistakes. htm (accessed October 28, 2014).

Preston, Noel (2006). *Understanding Ethics*. Second edition. Sydney: The Federation Press.

Queensland Law Society (2014). *Misleading Evidence*. Available at http://ethics.qls.com.au/ sites/all/files/files/140311%20Misleading%20statements.pdf (accessed August 19, 2014).

Solicitors Regulation Authority (2011). *SRA Handbook*. Available at http://www.sra.org. uk/solicitors/handbook/welcome.page (accessed August 19, 2014).

Thomas, Mark (2006). Legal Ethics: regulation of the legal profession. In S. Hayes, N. Stobbs, and M. Lauchs (Eds.) *Social Ethics for Legal and Justice Professionals*. Sydney: Pearson Education Australia.

Warren, Marilyn (2011). *The Duty Owed to the Court: the overarching purpose of dispute resolution in Australia*. Available at http://www.austlii.edu.au/au/journals/VicJSchol/2011/7.pdf (accessed August 19, 2014).

Wilson, Daniel (2010). *The Toughest Call: The Lake Pleasant murder case*. Available at http:// jpm.syr.edu/the-toughest-call-the-lake-pleasant-murder-case/ (accessed August 19, 2014).

Chapter 12

Ethics and accountability in law enforcement[1]

Key terms: authority; police subculture; community policing; discrimination; discretion; conflicts of interest; deception and entrapment; bribes and gratuities

Introduction

> In 1989 two New South Wales police officers attended a fancy dress party with a 'bad taste' theme in the town of Eromanga in south-west Queensland. The off-duty officers had blackened their faces, wore imitation nooses, in a parody of Aboriginal deaths in custody, and referred to themselves as Lloyd Boney and David Gundy.
>
> (Cornwall 1992: 7)

Lloyd Boney was an Aboriginal man who had committed suicide while in custody, while David Gundy had been fatally shot by police in a raid. To say their costumes were in bad taste was a vast understatement. A private video of the party that was circulated a couple of years later caused outrage and grave concern, with critics calling the behavior "deeply offensive" and racist (Cornwall 1992: 7). A public outcry ensued that called for the sacking of both men. In spite of this, the President of the Police Association defended the two officers' behavior, saying that it was more symptomatic of failures in the system than it was of outright racism. He called on government action to address the issues.

Police officers have extensive powers in terms of their authority over citizens and their discretion in the use of force. This authoritative power to intervene in citizens' lives, combined with the visual power of the distinctive police uniform, sets police apart from other professionals. Such separation can cause ethical problems that reflect negatively on police integrity. However, police also have a duty, as professionals, to conduct themselves in ways that reflect respect for the law, the government, and citizens. Arguably, police are subject to even more stringent standards than legal professionals. In the quote above, the officers' actions were reprehensible, regardless of whether they were police officers or not. However, had they not been police officers, their racist, bad

taste attire and antics would have been condemned by some, but would probably have gone largely unnoticed. This chapter examines what sets police apart
and how their particular characteristics as a group impact on the ethical conduct of their duties. It also examines the role of external and internal oversight
bodies and accountability mechanisms that are in place throughout Australia,
the United States, United Kingdom, and Canada.

The role of police

The level of corruption in police jurisdictions is to a large extent determined by
how police view their role in society. According to Pollock, police have traditionally been regarded as "crime fighters" (2004: 134). The role of the crime fighter
is one of aggressive crime control, and this is heavily supported by the media in
television police dramas such as *Blue Bloods* and *Line of Duty*, and films such as the
Die Hard and *Bad Boys* series. In the media police are viewed as forces for good
that are often morally required to bend or break the rules to catch the bad guy.
Such 'noble cause corruption' will be discussed below, but it is clear from these
media images and from real-life reports of police conduct in contemporary news
media, that the crime fighter model of police has a long history of acceptance.

More recently, however, there has been a reconsideration of role in some
jurisdictions, most notably in Australia, Canada, and the UK, with police now
regarded more as service providers than as a 'force.' For example, in most states
in Australia, extensive police corruption has led to the establishment of Royal
Commissions which have sought not only to expose and control police corruption, but also to change the face of police work. This change of role from
crime fighter to public servant changes the focus of police work from one of
aggressive control, to one of collaboration with, and protection of, citizens for
the greater good (Pollock 2004). This service model is more focussed on procedure, community relations, and due process.

Community policing has also become popular in many locales, encouraging police to collaborate with citizen groups such as neighborhood watch to
create the phenomenon of 'third party policing' where citizens take on an
informal civilian policing role in keeping communities safe (Mazerolle and
Ransley 2005). In the US, for example, the Office of Community Oriented
Policing Services (COPS) was established in 1994 (COPS 2014). In the UK,
the City of London Police (COLP) has also recently adopted a community
policing approach (COLP 2014). These changing roles of police have had a
huge impact on the way police perceive themselves and their duties, but ethical
problems still remain an issue.

Police subculture

In Queensland, a Royal Commission, chaired by G. E. Fitzgerald, was
established in 1989 to uncover severe corruption involving bribes and graft,

prostitution, and drug trafficking. One of the findings of the Fitzgerald Inquiry was that there was a pervasive "police culture" that supported corrupt activity and took action to discourage or prevent whistleblowing (Fitzgerald 1989). In any large organization a culture will develop based on the interactions of the organization's members. It is important to understand how culture is developed in such groups in order to identify both the strengths and weaknesses of this phenomenon. People naturally identify themselves with the group to which they belong (Kleinig 1996). Fitzgerald described how the Queensland Police Force created an informal code of conduct that worked against the public interest.

> Under the code it is impermissible to criticize other police. Such criticism is viewed as particularly reprehensible if it is made to outsiders. Any criticism which does occur is kept under the control of those who have authority and influence within the Force. Any dissidents are able to be dealt with for a breach of the code, with the approval of other police.
>
> (Fitzgerald 1989: 202)

Even if the group recognizes their conduct is illegal, it is not in the group's interest for it to be made public. They prefer to 'deal with it internally' or otherwise cover up any misdeeds to protect the reputation of the group. Even if an officer did not participate in or condone corruption, their sense of loyalty might prevent them from reporting it. In addition, they might not want to share in the bad publicity that all police would suffer from disclosure of corrupt activity. Consequently, the 'clean' officers become, by omission, complicit in a cover-up of the 'dirty' officers (Kleinig 2006).

Research shows that people tend to emulate the ethics of their peers (Granitz and Ward 2001). An individual might not ordinarily succumb to unethical behavior but research has shown that a person will act against their conscience if they believe they are letting their friends down by not joining them in an unethical or even illegal act (Beck 1999: 141, 145; Grossman 1995: 153). This conclusion is supported by Weber et al. (2003) who report that theft in the workplace is more likely to occur in organizations demonstrating a poorly developed ethical culture, than in organizations with a strong ethical culture. As we saw in Chapter 10, corrupt behavior in government is more likely to occur where there is an "absence of capable guardians."

In the Queensland example, many officers were able to reconcile this dilemma through *diffusion of responsibility*; where they reduced their own guilt for not reporting by noting that no one else had reported the matter either (Baumeister 1997: 299; Grossman 1995: 152). However, while this might have reduced their feelings of guilt, it did not remove their culpability as police officers who had failed to report a crime.

Nevertheless, group culture can be just as powerful in *promoting* ethical conduct. Individuals who act as exemplars of ethical conduct might help set the standard to be emulated by other members of the group. In practice, it might be much more difficult for a lower ranking officer to act as a role model to others, especially superiors. Indeed, officers may also rationalize unethical conduct by appealing to a superior's orders.

Ethical issues in policing

As we saw in Chapters 3 and 4, there are a range of ethical theories on which to draw when considering how to act ethically. Aristotle, for example, argued we should focus on becoming a good or virtuous person, and build our character in order to become good citizens. Utilitarian Jeremy Bentham sought to develop a formula for action that produced the best consequences. In opposition to both Aristotle and Bentham, Kant claimed that an act is only ethical if we can honestly say that it would be good if everyone acted the same way. In Chapter 10, we saw that the principles of conduct for public life were essentially deontological because they require one to abide by principles and processes, regardless of self-interest or the outcome. The main guiding principles, as we have seen, are respect for others as equal moral agents and a recognition of our duties towards them.

Equal respect is exercised when you put yourself in another person's shoes, develop empathy towards them, and understand the situation from their perspective. Empathy requires that you understand the person's circumstances and the experiences that might have led them to the particular situation. When we experience empathy we are engaging our moral imagination to remind us that others' suffering could be our own, and that therefore respect for others is always required (Benn 1996). Such understanding leads one to treat others as one would like to be treated and provides the basis for ethical conduct in the professional as well as private realms. We will now consider the range of ethical dilemmas that police must face in their day-to-day duties and the principles of duty and respect in each case.

Discretion

Police officers make decisions on a daily basis as to whether or not to arrest or to proceed with a charge against a person. Certain rules apply but, ultimately, the final decision will be made by the individual officer on the scene. This power carries with it enormous responsibility. Police officers are required to treat all individuals equally under the law. However, in real life police officers have many opportunities on a daily basis to treat people differently. For example, a police officer has the choice of dispensing a fine or not when stopping a driver for speeding. Similarly they have the choice of cautioning or arresting young offenders in many situations.

Discretion requires the balancing of justice for individuals against justice for the group, which suggests that full enforcement might not always be appropriate (Pollock 2004). However, as Pollock points out, such discretion opens the door to possible unethical behavior, such as accepting a bribe in return for not arresting someone.

Discretion also becomes problematic in cases where there is no obvious outcome or solution, as in the case of domestic disputes or reports of abuse.

> Many officers agonise over family disturbance calls where there are allegations of abuse, or when one family member wants the police to remove another family member; other calls involve . . . homeless people with small children who are turned away from full shelters, and victims of crimes who are left without sufficient resources to survive. In response to all these calls, officers must decide what course of action to take and can decide to do nothing at all.
>
> (Pollock 2004: 152–153)

Respect for other cultures

Everyone deserves to be treated with dignity. However, individuals differ over what constitutes dignified conduct. This is particularly the case when dealing with people from different cultural backgrounds. Police officers are likely to come into contact with different cultures in the conduct of their duties, and it is therefore imperative that they understand the nature of those cultures.

Most people have prejudices, that is, they prejudge others based on their social group, race, gender, or age. People tend to respond to others in a 'tried and true' manner rather than approaching each situation from a considered position, and this can have adverse consequences where police are ignorant of other cultures (Douglas 2001).

The police service will usually provide training for officers involved in multicultural and Indigenous communities. Individual officers can supplement this by being open and friendly with the people in their local community and by learning the various protocols embedded in such cultures. For example, police officers who work in communities with Indigenous populations need to understand the protocols of Aboriginal etiquette if they are to interact effectively in their community.

It is easier to disrespect a person when you have *moral distance* between yourself and them. Moral distance can occur when an individual assumes they are a better person because of inherent characteristics such as race, gender, age, occupation, or socio-economic background (Grossman 1995: 161–164). Most developed nations have legislation that makes it illegal to discriminate under any of these categories. It is enshrined in law that every person has equal moral value and must be treated as one's moral equal. It is therefore illegal and unethical to devalue others by dehumanizing them, such as police referring to alleged criminals as 'grubs.' Dehumanizing others removes our empathy, allowing us to act in ways we would normally find abhorrent. These attitudes may be reinforced by the police subculture where it promotes 'stereotype consistent' information (Lyons and Kashima 2003).

Moral distance can also be created where police view themselves as the 'goodies' and suspected offenders as the 'baddies.' Moral distance has two dimensions: the *punishment justification* which requires showing the enemy is guilty of a punishable/vengeful act, and the *legal affirmation* that affirms the legitimacy of one's own cause in acting against a suspected offender (Grossman 1995: 165–167). Beck, for example, describes moral distance as manifesting when people who act violently rationalize their actions by arguing that the other person 'deserved' the mistreatment they received. They have a "cluster of anti-social concepts or beliefs" that establish that they are vulnerable and the world is out to get them (Beck 1999: 125–128). For example, negative media reports on violence in Indigenous and other non-white communities might lead police to develop a mistakenly negative view of non-white identity that may manifest in a defensive attitude towards such people in public spaces, leading to unnecessary arrests and the use of violence and force in handling suspects.

Discrimination and the rule of law

Cultural bias is a kind of discrimination. But discrimination can extend beyond cultural boundaries and it is for this reason that citizens in Australia, the US, the UK, New Zealand, and Canada are protected by anti-discrimination legislation and the rule of law. As we saw in Chapter 8, the rule of law is a fundamental principle of a free society, with one law for everyone regardless of age, gender, sexuality, or cultural background. This law requires that everyone be treated equally before the law, and that an individual is always considered innocent until proven guilty. The burden of proof is on the accuser to prove the other's guilt.

It is easy to make assumptions about a person based on their appearance. Not only is it unfair to judge a person in this way, but such judgments may also trigger pre-programmed responses based on established prejudices. You might, for example, have had a drunken relative who was violent. This experience might have created a belief that violent drunks do not deserve protection and should be treated as lesser members of society. However, even violent drunks must receive due process. The box below outlines a case study in discrimination that illustrates this problem.

A case of discrimination

Two officers were cruising along a highway when they noticed ahead of them two young men driving a late model Mercedes Benz. The young men both looked to be of African-American appearance and about

(continued)

(continued)

eighteen or nineteen years of age. They were not speeding, nor were they breaking the law in any way. However, the two police officers decided that they looked suspicious and pulled them over. Upon inspection of the vehicle, the officers found a kilogram of marijuana in the boot, so they arrested them and charged them.

What are the ethical issues in this case? Did the officers have a right to pull over the young men just because they looked suspicious? Is their action justified because in fact they did find drugs in the vehicle?

Conflicts of interest

A conflict of interest arises when one's public duty conflicts with one's private interests. What should a police officer do when one of their relatives appears to have committed an offence? Would you charge your mother with stealing? Would you charge the Police Commissioner with drunk driving? Conflicts of interest arise when officers are required to act on suspected criminality, but their personal interests reduce their ability to be unbiased.

If a police officer discovers one of their relatives in a legally compromising situation, such as running a red light, they suddenly might find that empathy is very easy to develop. They might understand that their brother can make mistakes, and that he is not normally a person who would run a red light. But should they treat their brother any differently than they would a complete stranger? If we are all equal under the law then an officer is legally and morally obliged to issue a fine to them. Similarly, if their Police Commissioner was caught drunk driving, he must be treated as the law allows. It might be argued that the Commissioner is a very important person and that the police service as an agency would be embarrassed if he were charged. However, such considerations may not be entertained by a police officer on official duty. Officers are always required to make a dispassionate judgment as to whether or not any individual should be charged.

Deception and entrapment

Deception and entrapment is also sometimes called 'noble cause corruption.' It occurs when a person acts illegally in order to bring about what they consider to be a greater good. Also known as the 'Dirty Harry Syndrome,' it bears similarities to the problem of dirty hands encountered in Chapter 4. It includes such behavior as lying, threatening, and tricking suspects into revealing information or admitting guilt (Pollock 2004). Such behavior is clearly consequentialist. Pollock (2004: 197) notes that noble cause corruption is not based on selfishness but is, rather, "a profound moral commitment to make the world a better place to live." If the noble cause is simply "getting a criminal off the street" the officer may feel justified in concocting evidence or using deceptive or intimidating means to force a "confession" (Pollock 2004: 197).

Miller and Blackler (2006: 157) claim that there are four possible conditions, at least one of which must be present in 'Dirty Harry' cases:

1 They have the opportunity to achieve some morally good end or outcome, and they aim to do so;
2 The means they use to achieve this good are normally morally wrong (they are 'dirty');
3 The use of these means is the best or perhaps the only practicable way of ensuring that this good end is realised;
4 The good likely to be achieved by using the dirty means far outweighs the evil likely to follow from their use.

(Miller and Blackler 2006: 157)

It is likely that conditions 1 and 2 will be present in many situations in which police officers use immoral or illegal means. However, the fact that the aim of the immoral or illegal behavior is towards some greater good in no way justifies acting illegally or against due process, as we will see in the case below. Miller and Blackler (2006: 157) point out "[T]here is a strong presumption that moral ends do not justify the use of immoral means." This presumption may only be overridden in certain exceptional circumstances, such as when condition 4 prevails, and even then, only rarely. For example, an officer might be morally justified in lying to a suspected criminal in order to save a life.

Case Study: Entrapment[2]

When police raided an R-rated mail-order house, they found Keith Jacobsen's name and address, as well as the information that he had ordered two magazines: *Bare Boys I* and *Bare Boys II*, neither of which had been determined to be obscene material by any court. They created a fictitious company called "The Australian Hedonist Society" and sent Jacobsen a membership application and questionnaire. He joined and indicated an interest in pre-teen sexual material. In other mailings over the course of three years, the government represented itself as 'Midway Data Research,' 'Hartland Institute for a New Tomorrow,' and Carl Long, an individual interested in erotic material. Finally, a mailing from the government posing as the 'Far Eastern Trading Company Ltd' resulted in an order from Jacobsen, for *Boys Who Love*. He was arrested by federal police after he accepted receipt.

What are the ethical issues here? Is it ethical to lure someone into committing a crime? Jacobsen committed a crime by ordering a pedophile magazine, so shouldn't he be charged with that crime?

(Adapted from Pollock 2004: 201)

Methods have now been introduced into most jurisdictions to prevent situations in which deception and entrapment can be perpetrated. The most common method used is audio or video taping of interviews. A video can establish that a person was not coerced into providing a confession and was not maltreated during the interview. Such mechanisms also protect police from false claims of coercion.

Use of force

Often police officers are required to use force to detain offenders or suspected offenders. Indeed, no other public figure possesses greater authority over personal destiny than police. As Pollock (2004) points out, even judges and juries have less power when it comes to making decisions about how to deal with crime. A jury, for example, can be involved in judging offenders for the most heinous crimes, but they are required to deliberate over a period of time, sometimes days or even weeks, and are required (in most cases) to reach consensus over the verdict. Judges also must undergo substantial deliberation and must deal with both the limits of the law and personal conscience before sentencing offenders. Police, however, "[I]n a split second, without the benefit of law school or judicial roles or legal appeals, acting as judge, jury and executioner, may [enact the death penalty]" (Pollock 2004: 134).

The possibility of enacting this final punishment is not the only responsibility police face when it comes to the use of force. The use of capsicum spray or tasers, for example, has the potential to cause pain and damage beyond the requirements of the situation. Perhaps even more damage is possible when police hit with batons, or hold down suspected offenders with an arm lock. As Prenzler (2006) notes, "the split second nature of many of these actions makes them even more acute." Here, police codes of conduct should specify strict guidelines for the use of force and associated sanctions that may be employed when officers engage in gratuitous violence.

Bribes and gratuities

In Queensland in 1989 the Fitzgerald Inquiry found evidence of rampant corruption in the Queensland Police Force (now Queensland Police Service). Much of this corruption stemmed from police receiving bribes and gratuities from drug dealers and illegal brothel owners. Prior to that time, in the 1970s and 1980s, police were faced with a growing presence of illegal drugs and prostitution, particularly in the state's capital, Brisbane. Instead of using their power and authority to bring such lawless behavior to justice, many police chose to engage in deals that afforded them a comfortable extra income in return for turning a blind eye (Fitzgerald 1989).

Queensland is not an isolated case. At the time of writing, the Independent Police Complaints Commission is conducting an inquiry into police corruption in the UK over a 1993 botched murder case over suggestions there were payments made between a detective and the gangster father of the suspect (Dodd 2014). In the US, a Fresno detective is awaiting trial for allegedly accepting a $20,000 bribe (Montanez 2014). Police have a responsibility to act in the public interest regardless of the temptations of bribery and gratuities. Even accepting a free meal or cup of coffee can be dangerous because it violates the "principle of equitable service" whereby police are required to treat all citizens with equal consideration (Prenzler 2006: 129).

Personal life

To what extent should police be held more accountable than the average citizen for what they do in their private lives? Police hold a special position of power in the community and therefore are regarded as role models (Prenzler 2006). Is it more serious, for example, when a police officer is convicted for drink driving and should such a conviction result in instant dismissal? It has been argued that sometimes the private actions of public figures such as police may "bring the profession into disrepute" and that this justifies more serious sanctions (Prenzler 2006). In response it can be argued that the law should apply equally to all citizens regardless of their special rank or position. Nevertheless, how would you feel if your local police were regularly seen partying and engaging in obnoxious (but otherwise legal) behavior at a local hotel in their off-duty hours? Furthermore, should an off-duty officer face harsher penalties for speeding than other citizens? Surely, such behavior does little to instill respect for the law or those officers who enforce it? Or does 'off-duty' mean that they should no longer be judged by their profession?

Accountability measures

There are four common methods employed to ensure greater accountability of police: code of conduct; external oversight bodies; internal professional standards unit; and evaluation of police integrity. We will now explore how each of these measures ensures ethical policing.

Code of conduct

As is the case for public servants, as we saw in Chapter 10, law enforcement agencies are required to develop a code of conduct. Such codes aim to describe the role and ideal characteristics of law enforcement officers, as well as what is acceptable or unacceptable conduct, and the range of sanctions legally available to address transgressions. New recruits are usually required to undergo training in the code of conduct and to formally acknowledge their understanding and acceptance of the code. In some states such codes are required by law. For example, in Queensland the Public Sector Ethics Act 1994 states that all public sector agencies, including police, must develop and regularly review their code of conduct. The Office of the High Commissioner for Human Rights (OHCHR) of the United Nations developed a *Code of Conduct for Law Enforcement Officials*, which was adopted by the General Assembly in 1979, which refers specifically to how police treat suspects and other members of the public. A survey of jurisdictions in the US, UK, and Canada indicates that police in almost all states and counties have also adopted codes of conduct, whether legislated or not. In the main, they adopt similar principles as those outlined above.

External oversight bodies

In many states, external bodies provide independent oversight of police. In Queensland, the Crime and Corruption Commission (CCC), the third rendition of the oversight body first established under the Fitzgerald Inquiry, provides oversight over the Queensland Police and other public agencies as well, while New South Wales has the Independent Commission Against Corruption. Canada has two federal oversight bodies, the Military Police Complaints Commission, and the Commission for Public Complaints against the Royal Canadian Mounted Police (RCMP), and each state also has at least one external oversight body for their state and local police. Police in England and Wales are overseen by the Independent Police Complaints Commission.

Unlike other places in which state and federal authorities provide law enforcement, policing in the US is usually a local, municipal function.

> Although there are federal police such as the Federal Bureau of Investigation (FBI), the Border Patrol, and the Drug Enforcement Administration (DEA), their jurisdiction is limited to defined federal crimes. Individual states within the United States do have statewide police forces, such as the California Highway Patrol or the New York State Troopers, but their jurisdiction generally extends only to patrolling the roads and highways in the state. Overwhelmingly, municipal street patrol and other basic police services are provided by local authorities, including both police and local sheriff's departments.
>
> (Bobb 2014: 1)

In the US, police oversight is for the most part tied to local governing bodies, or through citizen review boards, and monitors. In a particular jurisdiction— for example, a city—the Police Chief might be accountable to an elected official who has oversight of the police department. In the case of Sheriffs, who are elected law enforcement officers, the oversight is provided through budgetary oversight and the citizens of a county, via elections. Exceptions to this include the Arkansas State Police Commission, the Chicago Police Board, and the Boise Office of the Community Ombudsman (PERF 2007).

Ethical standards units (internal)

Most law enforcement agencies in Australia, Canada, the US, and the UK have an internal unit that regularly monitors the professional/ethical standards of its officers. In Queensland, the Ethical Standards Command of the Queensland Police Service receives complaints about police, which are then passed on to the CCC. In most cases, except for very serious offences, the Crime and Corruption Commission (CCC) instructs Ethical Standards Command to investigate the matter internally and report back. Thus the internal accountability body is, itself, monitored by an independent body of the CCC, creating a double layer of accountability.

In the US, "law enforcement agencies enjoy a high level of autonomy in deciding how to self police" (Bobb 2014: 17). Many law enforcement agencies have "Internal Affairs" units, which investigate allegations of misconduct by police officers. In most jurisdictions, however, the Police Chief has the authority to determine if Internal Affairs have proved their case. Recently, however, some Internal Affairs units have come to be overseen by civilians, as in the example of Los Angeles (Bobb 2014: 18), and as such have achieved a greater level of independence.

Professional Standards Units are responsible for developing and monitoring the agency's code of conduct, as well as for training and induction of all officers into the code. Most codes reflect the principles of those developed in the *Law Enforcement Code of Conduct* by the International Association of Chiefs of Police (Prenzler 2006), which include respecting confidentiality, restricting the use of force, and treating all citizens equitably, as well as the more obvious requirement to refrain from accepting bribes and gratuities.

Evaluation of police integrity

There is substantial research and reporting on police integrity, especially over the past decade, in the wake of the Royal Commissions of Inquiry into police corruption carried out in Queensland, New South Wales, and Western Australia. The NSW ICAC and the Queensland CCC, for example, both report regularly on police complaints and how they have been addressed. In its report on *Project Dresden II*, which undertook to monitor the quality of NSW police internal investigations in 2003, the Police Integrity Commission (PIC) found that internal monitoring was hampered by loyalty issues. While officers ranked at Senior Constable and above were more likely to be the subjects of complaints of serious misconduct, almost 11 percent of these were being investigated by officers who were junior to the subjects of the complaints. In addition, over 55 percent of subjects were investigated by officers from their own work unit. The PIC (2003: ix) reports: "five percent of investigations were 'very satisfactory,' 64.3% were 'satisfactory,' 27% were 'unsatisfactory,' and 3.7% were 'very unsatisfactory'."

Compared to a similar 2000 report, the PIC found that there was a notice-able decrease in the numbers of 'satisfactory' and 'very satisfactory' investiga-tions and a noticeable increase in the numbers of 'unsatisfactory' and 'very unsatisfactory' investigations, although there were improvements in other areas such as timeliness (PIC 2003).

More recently the CMC conducted an inquiry into policing in Indigenous communities in Queensland (CMC 2007). The inquiry was the result of a series of events in which police in remote Indigenous communities were sub-ject to serious complaint and subsequent media attention. A death in custody at Palm Island in 2004 gave rise to serious allegations about police brutality in the area. In early 2007, an alleged assault on a man at Arukun was investigated but no charges were made. Both of these cases resulted in protests and the CMC was charged with reviewing policing in remote Aboriginal and Torres Strait Island communities, and making recommendations for change. Public submis-sions to the inquiry closed in June 2007 and the report was made available in early 2008.

Conclusion

It has long been recognized that police are subject to special risk when it comes to experiencing ethical problems. The past two decades in Australia have seen a massive overhaul of police integrity systems in several states. Ongoing moni-toring of these changes must be maintained if they are to continue to show improvements in accountability practices of police and supporting civilian staff, and in police culture, especially since investigations continue at a relatively high rate in most states. While this might be a reflection of an increase in reporting, we must continue to be vigilant in monitoring police integrity in the face of ongoing temptations, pressures, and opportunities for corruption.

Review questions

1   What is it about policing that creates ethical issues? Name some of the issues that routinely arise.
2   What are some basic principles that should guide police in their decision-making?
3   What kinds of accountability mechanisms are available to police? Which of these seem most effective?
4   Should police be held accountable for their off-duty behavior?
5   What are the arguments for and against police accepting gratuities?
6   What kinds of corruption can occur in police services?

(continued)

(continued)

7 Are spies and integrity tests ethical ways of obtaining compliance? What are some arguments against use of these tactics?

8 Should police be held to stricter standards of behavior than other professionals? For example, they are public servants, so shouldn't they be subject to the same standards as other public servants?

9 What is meant by 'entrapment'? Give an example.

10 What are the characteristics of police subculture that most often cause corruption?

Notes

1 This chapter draws on material from Hayes, S. and Lauchs, M. (2009) *Oversight, Accountability and Ethics*. In Roderick Broadhurst and Sarah M. Davies (Eds.) *Policing in Context*. Oxford: Oxford University Press. Reproduced with permission from OUP.

2 Adapted from Pollock (2004: 201).

References

Baumeister, R. (1997). *Evil: inside human violence and cruelty*. New York: Henry Holt and Co.

Beck, A. (1999). *Prisoners of Hate: the cognitive basis of anger, hostility and violence*. New York: Perennial.

Benn, S. I. (1996). *A Theory of Freedom*. Cambridge: Cambridge University Press.

Bobb, Merrick (2014). *Internal and External Police Oversight in the United States*. Los Angeles, CA, Police Assessment Resource Centre. Available at http://www.parc.info/client_files/altus/10-19%20altus%20conf%20paper.pdf (accessed August 21, 2014).

City of London Police (2014). Community Policing. Available at http://www.cityoflondon.police.uk/community-policing/Pages/default.aspx (accessed August 21, 2014).

Community Oriented Policing Services (COPS) (2014). *About COPS*. Available at www.cops.usdoj.gov/ (accessed October 28, 2014).

Cornwall, D. (1992). Anger over Transfer of Racist Police. *Sydney Morning Herald*, March 14, 1992, p. 7.

Crime and Misconduct Commission (2005). *Fraud and Corruption Control: guidelines for best practice*. Brisbane: Crime and Misconduct Commission.

Crime and Misconduct Commission (2007). *Inquiry into Policing in Indigenous Communities*. Brisbane: Crime and Misconduct Commission.

Dodd, Vikram (2014). Stephen Lawrence murder: new inquiry launched into police corruption claims. *The Guardian*, June 3, 2014. Available at http://www.theguardian.com/uk-news/2014/jun/03/stephen-lawrence-ipcc-inquiry-police-corruption (accessed August 21, 2014).

Douglas, K. (2001). Playing Fair. *New Scientist*, March 10, 2001, pp. 38–42.

Fitzgerald, G. E. (1989). *Report of a Commission of Inquiry Pursuant to Orders in Council*. Brisbane: Criminal Justice Commission.

Granitz, N. and Ward, J. (2001). Actual and Perceived Sharing of Ethical Reasoning and Moral Intent Among In-Group and Out-Group Members. *Journal of Business Ethics* 33: 299–322.

Grossman, D. *On Killing*. Boston: Back Bay Books.

Kleinig, J. (1996). *The Ethics of Policing*. Melbourne: Cambridge University Press.

Lyons, A. and Kashima, Y. (2003). How are Stereotypes Maintained Through Communications? The influence of stereotype sharedness. *Journal of Personality & Social Psychology* 85(6): 989–1005.

Mazerolle, L. and Ransley, J. (2005) *Third Party Policing*. Melbourne: Cambridge University Press.

Miller, Seumas and Blackler, John (2006). *Ethical Issues in Policing*. Aldershot: Ashgate.

Montanez, Rick (2014). Fresno Police Detective Accused of Accepting $20,000 Bribe. *ABC News Fresno*. Available at http://abc30.com/archive/9471671/ (accessed August 21, 2014).

Police Executive Research Forum (PERF) (2007). *Report to the Task Force on Governance and Cultural Change in the Royal Canadian Mounted Police: examination of external oversight bodies of police forces*. Available at http://www.publicsafety.gc.ca/cnt/cntrng-crm/tsk-frc-rcmp-grc/_fl/archive-xtrnl-vrsght-eng.pdf (accessed August 21, 2014).

Police Integrity Commission (2003). *Project Dresden II: Special Report to Parliament on the second audit of the quality of NSW Police internal investigations*. Sydney: Police Integrity Commission.

Pollock, J. (2004). *Ethics in Crime and Justice: dilemmas and decisions*. Fourth edition. Belmont, CA: Wadsworth.

Prenzler, T. (2006). Ethics and Accountability in Law Enforcement. In S. Hayes, N. Stobbs, and M. Lauchs (Eds.) *Social Ethics for Legal and Justice Professionals*. Sydney: Pearson Education Australia.

Weber, J., Kurke, L., and Pentico, D. (2003). 'Why Do Employees Steal?' *Business and Society* 42(3): 359.

Chapter 13

Ethics of corrections and punishment

Key terms: retributivism; just deserts; capital punishment; deterrence; naming and shaming; selective incapacitation; rehabilitation; restorative justice

Introduction

In the opening chapter of *Discipline and Punish*, Michel Foucault (1977) describes a scene of punishment in eighteenth-century France. The man being punished had murdered the king:

> On 1 March 1757 Damiens the regicide was condemned "to make the *amende honorable* before the main door of the Church of Paris," where he was to be "taken and conveyed in a cart, wearing nothing but a shirt, holding a torch of burning wax weighing two pounds"; then, "in the said cart, to the Place de Grève, where, on a scaffold that will be erected there, the flesh will be torn from his breasts, arms, thighs and claves with red-hot pincers, his right hand, holding the knife with which he committed the said parricide, burnt with sulphur, and, on those places where the flesh will be torn away, poured molten lead, boiling oil, burning resin, wax and sulphur melted together and then his body drawn and quartered by four horses and his limbs and body consumed by fire, reduced to ashes and his ashes thrown to the winds."
>
> (Foucault 1977: 3)

As recently as the eighteenth century, torture such as this was common in France and the rest of Europe. At that time, the emphasis was on public spectacle, with executions occurring in the public square and drawing the attention of many onlookers. 'Regicide' refers to the killing of a king, no doubt one of the worst crimes of that or any other time, and the punishment, which was performed almost as public theater, was meant to serve as a cautionary tale to one and all. Within a century, however, the nature of punishment had changed dramatically. Incarceration became the norm, and prison the seat of all sanction. Foucault explores how we moved from the violent and chaotic public torture of Robert-Francois Damiens described above, to the highly regimented and disciplined schedule of the nineteenth-century prison. He suggests that the motivation was not to create a more humane method of punishment, or to rehabilitate. Rather, it was to allow greater and more complete control over rebels, wrongdoers, and other deviants; that is, to allow more effective governance of them. The public spectacle of torture had unintended consequences—creating sympathy for the 'victim' and transference of guilt to the executioner, not to mention that such events often sparked riots against the sovereign. Over the following century, the spectacles became more subdued and controlled, with smaller spectacles and chain gangs. Foucault argues that during this time, which was also the time of industrial revolution, our ideas about the role of labor changed, leading to a new 'technology of discipline.' The prison entrenched state power over its subjects by providing surveillance, at first externally, so that discipline was achieved through oversight. Eventually, through new technologies, discipline became more internalized—state power and surveillance wielded from within (Foucault 1977).

Before we can understand the need for punishment and what can be considered 'ethical punishment,' we need to examine why we have sentencing laws, penalties, and prisons and what purpose they serve. The law allows social control to be maintained and helps in regulating citizens' behavior. The purpose of the law is to prevent social chaos, like a social contract of sorts that helps to prevent harm being done. The state is the fundamental controlling body and exercises a monopoly on the right to punish. This chapter explores theories of punishment, including retributivism, just deserts, and deterrence, the role and impact of corrections, and what current research reports about the viability and utility of certain forms of punishment. It also examines the role of rehabilitation and considers current debates around whether certain groups of offenders are incapable of being rehabilitated. Finally, it explores alternatives to traditional criminal justice responses to crime, including restorative justice and Indigenous justice.

What is punishment?

While Foucault describes punishment as the imposition of state power and technology in disciplining its subjects, the concept can also be found in psychology. In operant conditioning experiments, punishment is used to deter rats from certain behaviors, and is described as "any change that occurs after a behavior that reduces the likelihood that that behavior will occur again in the future" (Cherry 2014). In the sense that punishment is used as a *deterrent* to future offending, it is a utilitarian concept. However, the philosophical definition of punishment tends to align more with Foucault's view. Bedau (2010), for example, defines it thus:

> [T]he authorised imposition of deprivations—of freedom or privacy or other goods to which the person otherwise has a right, or the imposition of special burdens—because the person has been found guilty of some criminal violation, typically (though not invariably) involving harm to the innocent.

This definition is less definitive of the source of the punishment than Foucault's. The legal definition, however, is not. *Black's Law Dictionary* defines it as:

> [A]ny pain, penalty, suffering, or confinement inflicted upon a person *by the authority of the law and the judgment and sentence of a court*, for some crime or offense committed by him, or for his omission of a duty enjoined by law.
>
> (2014; my emphasis)

Such punishments typically take the form of incarceration or confinement for serious and violent crimes, while lesser crimes may receive a fine or other penalty. The study of punishment for crimes is called *penology*, or in some cases *corrections* (Stohr et al. 2008: 2), giving the impression that state-sanctioned forms of punishment are corrective in nature.

Reasons for punishment

What these definitions fail to offer, however, is a *rationale* or justification for punishment—a 'why?' if you will. There are many different theories concerning how or why individuals should be punished. For example, the theory of just deserts claims that those who offend *deserve* to be punished. The punishment must therefore match the crime—more severe punishments have a greater deterrence value and are more likely to prevent recidivism.

What about rehabilitation? Should punishment have the purpose of rehabilitating the offender to prevent them from reoffending? For example, many crimes are committed because of alcohol or drug abuse. In such cases should their punishment include psychiatric treatment for their substance abuse problem?

Compensation is another issue in sentencing and punishment. Putting people in prison or fining them might deter them from reoffending or might 'give them what they deserve,' but what about the victims of crime—should they be compensated in some way for their loss?

Traditionally, punishment is enacted for reasons of *retribution, just deserts, deterrence, societal protection,* and/or *rehabilitation.* More recently, however, corrections has become influenced by the use of methods and practices intended to be *restorative*—that is, to restore the balance of justice that has been dislodged through the committing of a crime.

Retribution and just deserts

Retributivism also seeks to restore the moral balance between victim and offender, but where restorative justice aims to mediate between victim and offender, retributivism aims to make offenders 'pay for their crimes.' This kind of justification is based upon revenge against the criminal for crimes against the innocent and/or against society and is deontological in spirit. In times past—although still occurring in some few nations today—the rationale would be described as 'an eye for an eye.' Thus, the thief will have his hand cut off, the sexual offender will be castrated, and so on. Since these are not considered to be viable or justifiable punishments in our society, we use incapacitation instead. This form of punishment is deontological because it addresses the breaking of rules and laws, and the committing of harms.

Retributivism focuses on the rights of the victim to seek justice, and justice is not achieved until the offender has been appropriately punished. The criminal is the author of his own punishment, because he has chosen to commit the crime, and now must pay the consequences. It has been argued that deviant acts often trigger group action and that retributivism responds to the need for group or community healing. Erikson (1996: 88), for example, argues:

> The deviant act, then, creates a sense of mutuality among the people of a community by supplying a focus for group feeling. Like a war, a flood, or some other emergency, deviance makes people more alert to the interests they share in common and draws attention to those values which constitute the "collective conscience" of the community.

In a study conducted by Bastian et al. (2013), they found that retributive attitudes towards offenders who intentionally harmed 'innocents' occurred in the presence of dehumanization and moral outrage, regardless of type or severity of crime. Offenders were dehumanized in direct proportion to the moral outrage felt regarding their crimes. Consider the box below.

Moral outrage and retributivism

When criminal behavior brings harm to innocent people it has the capacity to arouse strong affective responses in third-party observers. Consider Bill Clare, who was found guilty of repeatedly raping a 6 year old girl and her 3 year old brother. The 3 year old died from the associated trauma. He was sentenced to 39 years in prison and was the target of renewed calls for the death penalty for pedophiles. Just the thought of Clare's crime evokes a visceral response, not only to the criminal act, but to Clare himself.

(Bastian et al. 2013)

It does not take much moral imagination to understand the kind of outrage reserved for such crimes. The "visceral response" elicited by moral outrage calls for an eye for an eye (or its contemporary equivalent), and has a decided malice to it. *Just deserts*, on the other hand, while also focusing on the criminal getting what he deserves, is almost without malice; that is, it seeks to punish proportionate to the crime, but only to see justice done rather than to satisfy any personal moral outrage.

Capital punishment

While capital punishment has been eradicated in many countries, including Australia, Europe, New Zealand, Canada, and most of South America, it still exists in many parts of the United States, Japan, China, Malaysia, India, and other nations—although there continue to be calls for its eradication globally. Thus, as perhaps the ultimate punishment available to governments, it must be considered from the perspective of ethics, particularly since Kant most famously argued for the death penalty for violent crimes (Yost 2010).

Kant rejected the utilitarian argument that the purpose of punishment was for deterrence or rehabilitation, because such arguments consider the individual as instrumental to the social good, something that Kant always argued vehemently against. Recall that the categorical imperative states that we must never use others for our own ends. Instead, Kant argued that punishment accrued as a direct result of committing the crime and should therefore be proportionate—in the case of murderers, this means the death penalty (Yost 2010).

However, the implementation of the death penalty in many societies raises important moral questions, such as, 'What is the value of a human life?' For Kant, the murderer forsakes his own right to life in the killing of another. However, it is often at this point that the absolutism of deontology begins to demonstrate its flaws. Arguably, for example, life imprisonment or hard labor would also be proportional punishments for murder, without us having to 'play God' by taking another life.

The ethics of the death penalty is further complicated by research showing that more men than women and more minorities than whites are sentenced to capital punishment (The Sentencing Project 2013). In the United States, for example, in 2013, 59 percent of executions were of non-white people, although this figure dropped slightly in 2014 (Death Penalty Information Centre 2014). In spite of this clear discrimination in death sentencing, recent research by Peffley and Hurwitz (2010) indicates that whites in the United States think the justice system is "colour-blind." The problem of the ethics of capital punishment thus overlaps with professional ethics, including the ethics of courts, law enforcement officers, and lawyers, not to mention the social ethics surrounding the disparities in life chances between whites and non-whites in that and other countries.

Objections to capital punishment

While the possible objections to capital punishment ought to be very clear from ethical points of view, it does raise numerous questions. For example, does the period of incarceration prior to execution (and indeed the execution itself) constitute a form of torture, or ritualized and state-sanctioned killing? Does that teach society that killing is wrong—or right? Also, is it ethical to institute a form of punishment that cannot be revoked? For example, many people on death row have subsequently been found to be innocent, raising the question of how many have been wrongfully executed. While wrongful imprisonment can be compensated for after the fact, capital punishment cannot.

Deterrence and prevention

Utilitarians argue that offenders should be punished in a way that deters them from reoffending (*specific deterrence*) and also as an example to the general public to deter others from committing crimes (*general deterrence*). Arguably, punishment deters the particular criminal, it deters others and, therefore, allegedly improves society. However, studies on recidivism to date have shown that there is mixed deterrence effect in incapacitating criminals. Wright (2010) for example, reports that certainty of punishment is more of a deterrent than tougher sentences. Also, it is difficult to determine the deterrent effect of punishment if only those who are not deterred are sentenced.

In the 1980s, it was suggested that selective incapacitation of criminals based on a prediction of likelihood of future offending would reduce crime rates and rates of recidivism (Greenwood and Abrahamse 1982). Usually it is applied to those who have committed serious serial offences, have shown little remorse, and are therefore predicted to be at high risk of committing future violent offences. Such offenders are incapacitated for a longer time than the average. This is meant to have a higher deterrent effect and also to protect society from future crime. However, the effects of selective incapacitation too, have been thrown into doubt by subsequent research (Blumstein 1983).

The ethics of selective incapacitation are also questionable, even from a utilitarian standpoint. The difficulty of predicting future offences based on past offences ignores the ways in which long-time criminals spontaneously desist for a variety of reasons. It is also arguably biased by race and gender, since non-white males form the largest portion of offenders in almost every category except white-collar crime. Even utilitarians must object to sacrificing one racial group for the benefit of society because such action would definitely be anti-social and anti-productive to a coherent multicultural society long-term.

Get-tough juvenile justice reforms: The Florida experience

Get-tough reforms aimed at juvenile offenders have become commonplace in the United States. In the last decade, almost every

(continued)

(continued)

state has modified laws relating to juvenile crime in some way, and the direction of the reforms has been very clear. States are getting tougher on juvenile offenders either by shifting away from traditional rehabilitation models to punishment-oriented juvenile justice or by legislating new or expanded legal means by which greater numbers of juvenile offenders may be moved to criminal court for adult processing and punishment. The present study focuses on a major set of juvenile justice reforms in Florida and the impact on actual practice. Florida is unique in a historical sense because it has transferred large numbers of juveniles to criminal court for two decades, and, currently, because it has more juveniles in its prisons than any other state. Despite incremental get-tough reforms, the new transfer provisions have had a negligible impact. The effects of Florida's get-tough laws and practices should be instructive for those other states that have begun such reforms more recently.

(Frasier et al. 1999. Reproduced with permission from Sage Publications.)

Not only does the case study above refute the call for tougher sentences in reducing crime, it calls into question our obligations to young people in our society. Considering most young people who offend 'grow out of it' by the age of 25 or so, many have argued that we would do better by them and society at large by diverting them from the criminal justice system (Hayes 2005), and into alternative forms of 'punishment' such as restorative justice. Restorative justice is discussed in more detail below, but first we need to consider trends toward naming and shaming and rehabilitation.

Naming and shaming

Recently in Queensland, parliament has been debating about whether to institute a law allowing the naming of youth who commit crimes in that state. Proponents argue that this will shame offenders and deter potential offenders from committing crimes. Critics condemn the practice, however, in light of research showing that most youth desist from offending before adulthood, claiming that a better response is to divert them from the courts and official conviction. In this way, their chances of reoffending are reduced and their life chances are improved. The idea that shaming of offenders will lessen recidivism is not new. Braithwaite (1989), for example, conducted studies in the 1980s that demonstrated how shaming may lead to effective reintegration. He argued that the breakdown of communities meant that offenders were no longer shamed and that cultures that put higher value on community—such as Indigenous peoples—have lower rates of crime in those communities. However, this is quite different to the idea of shaming being advocated by Queensland politicians. According to Braithwaite, shaming works only when offenders are shamed within a close-knit community. Shaming young offenders by naming them in courts and public forums is effectively doing the opposite. Indeed, Braithwaite's work provided the basis for a movement towards diverting young people from the courts and into community conferencing. More on community conferencing will be discussed in the section on restorative justice.

Another form of general deterrence, but also considered to be protective of society is the establishment of publicly available sex offender registers. In the US, public registers were established under what is colloquially known as Megan's Law, which was established in 1994 at the Federal level as the Sexual Offending (Jacob Wetterling) Act 1994. This law requires child sex offenders to notify local authorities of any change of address and provides community access to both registrations and notifications. However, while research shows a general deterrent effect for sex offender registers—fewer new offenders are committing crimes—public registers do not reduce recidivism (Letourneau et al. 2010; AIC 2007). In Australia, except for Western Australia (which implemented the law in 2012) serious sex offenders are put on a register that is only available to law enforcement authorities as a way of keeping track of offenders (AIC 2007). There is considerable evidence demonstrating that public registers drive offenders underground because they are unable to find housing or re-establish themselves in the community (Parker and Emerson 2011). The ethics of sex offender registers is utilitarian; however, the maintenance of the registers in spite of research showing they do not work as intended is purely retributive.

Rehabilitation

While rehabilitation is often considered among other punishments, many ask if this is really a punishment at all? Its intention is to make a positive impact on someone's life in order to help them avoid situations in which they may commit future crime. However, some suggest it does not go far enough, and is not the appropriate response to someone who has violated the law. Nevertheless, many incarcerated offenders undergo rehabilitation as part of their sentence; for example, sex offenders are often required to undergo intensive therapy and rehabilitation before being released back into society. However, there has been little high-quality research into whether such rehabilitation works (Franklin 2013). Some argue that pedophilia is a sexuality (Cantor 2008), and as such cannot be rehabilitated. If this is the case, it would be unethical to try to rehabilitate them. But would it be ethical to keep them incarcerated indefinitely? Having a sexuality and acting on it are two very different things; therefore, we cannot assume that a pedophile will reoffend. A utilitarian would argue that, until there is evidence either way, we should err on the side of caution.

Some further critiques of rehabilitation have been proposed. To begin, it is assumed that seeking to rehabilitate someone after they have committed a crime assumes that they had a diminished moral capacity when committing the crime. This can be seen by some to mean that punishment is not as severe as it ought to be, and that people are excused for offending behavior. At the same time, it can mean that important circumstances leading to a criminal act are recognized. Additionally, rehabilitation can be an expensive procedure and quite resource-intensive, with few guaranteed positive outcomes. As such, it is not an option available to all (particularly in remote communities or in women's prisons, for example), and many see its expense as unjustified. (However, given that prison is horrendously expensive and has demonstrably little positive effect, this argument does not carry a lot of weight!) Finally, however, as prison and other retributive forms of punishment are divisive of populations, there is a strong argument for rehabilitation as a way of drawing communities together, and at least making an attempt to positively address offending behavior.

Restorative justice

Restorative justice is an alternative response to offending that attempts to address crime outside of the traditional criminal justice system, and is based on First Nations people's responses to justice. According to Braithwaite (2004: 28) restorative justice is

> a process where all stakeholders affected by an injustice have an opportunity to discuss how they have been affected by the injustice and to decide what should be done to repair the harm. With crime, restorative justice is about the idea that because crime hurts, justice should heal. It follows that conversations with those who have been hurt and with those who have inflicted the harm must be central to the process.

Programs aim to involve the victim and to encourage the offender to apologize and express remorse. Programs reflecting restorative justice will respond to crime by:

1 identifying and taking steps to repair harm;
2 involving all stakeholders; and
3 transforming the traditional relationship between communities and their governments in responding to crime (Restorative Justice Online 2014).

Restorative justice dates back thousands of years, but its recent adoption by developed societies is based on practices adopted from First Nation Peoples of Canada, the US, and New Zealand (Zehr 2005). For example, in New Zealand (Aotearoa), prior to European settlement, Maori peoples had *Utu*, a highly developed system of justice that was community based. Zehr (2005:

271) remarks that, "[I]n many ways, restorative justice represents a validation of values and practices that were characteristic of many indigenous groups [which were] often discounted and repressed by western colonial powers."

One type of restorative justice that has become prominent in Australia is community conferencing, which addresses youth crime especially by bringing young offenders, victims, and their respective families together to talk about a crime and how it affected the victim. Often the offender will show remorse and the victim will feel some closure in accepting the offender's apology. Research shows that community conferencing has a positive effect on all stakeholders. Research is still being conducted into whether community conferencing reduces the risk of reoffending for those who take part (Daly and Hayes 2002). However, a survey of conferencing participants in Queensland in 2011 revealed high levels of satisfaction among participants as well as lowered levels of reoffending among young people (AIC 2014). From a utilitarian perspective, then, it is unclear whether community conferencing and other forms of restorative justice ought to be used instead of the conventional courts. Nevertheless, there may be a case for restorative justice, especially in dealing with young people. The case study in the box below shows why we should never underestimate the power of victim–offender mediation and restorative justice.

Letters of apology

The following letter was written by one of two boys to an elderly woman they attacked, knocked over and whose handbag they stole.

Dear Mrs. Smith,

I had a family meeting last week. The statement you made was read out, the statement was hard to listen to for me and my parents. Made me think how badly you was affected, I understand physically you had banged your head, forgetting things, bad legs, lost weight and affected sleep. And emotionally scared of young people and maybe another attack, and maybe feeling isolated from society and lonely. I am very sorry what happened that day and regret it deeply, Me myself has never been in any form of trouble myself apart from that time and never again. In the family meeting we discussed my future, I want to go into computers and stay out of trouble, I have started a course already. I don't understand why we did it but I do try and it will never happen again and I am sure of that. The action we took was so wrong and it will be in my head for the rest of my life. Hope you can go back to your old routine, and feel safe again. I will write to your friend and explain my apologies.

Sorry Ian

(Crossland and Liebmann 2003)

As we saw above, young people who commit crimes often desist before adulthood, and it is widely agreed among criminologists that they should, therefore, be diverted from the courts and traditional sentencing to avoid convictions, which might affect their life chances. This is particularly pertinent in the case of Indigenous youth in Australia and New Zealand, and non-white youth in the US and the UK, who are disproportionately overrepresented in arrests, convictions, and in prisons. Restorative justice is not only an ethical response to young people, but to structural discrimination against disadvantaged youth.

Review questions

1 Imagine you are the victim of a violent assault, such as the one committed against the elderly woman in 'Letters of apology.' How would you like the young boys to be dealt with? Would you consent to participating in a conference with them? Why or why not?

2 What is the difference between *retributive justice* and *just deserts*? What ethical theory underpins these perspectives?

3 Research demonstrates that the death penalty does not reduce violent crime in those states in the US that adopt it. Why do you think they continue to employ the death penalty?

4 What are the main aims of restorative justice?

5 What would a deontologist say about the ethics of publicly available sex offender registers? Would you agree with them?

6 What are some criticisms of rehabilitation and treatment programs?

7 Explain the difference between general deterrence and specific deterrence. Which ethical theory advocates punishment for deterrence?

8 Is selective incapacitation an ethical practice in sentencing serious serial offenders? Why or why not? Which theory best illustrates your position?

9 What do we mean by 'naming and shaming'? Under what circumstances might it be ethical?

10 What are some objections to capital punishment? Do you agree with them?

References

Amnesty International Norway (2013). *Death Penalty Case Studies*. Updated September 2, 2013. Available at http://www.amnesty.no/aktuelt/flere-nyheter/arkiv-bakgrunn/death-penalty-case-studies (accessed August 21, 2014).

Australian Institute of Criminology (AIC) (2007). Is notification of sex offenders in local communities effective? *AICrime Reduction Matters No. 58*. Available at http://www.aic.gov.au/publications/current%20series/crm/41-60/crm058.html (accessed August 21, 2014).

Australian Institute of Criminology (2014). *Restorative Justice in Australia.* Available at http://
www.aic.gov.au/publications/current%20series/rpp/121-140/rpp127/05_restorative.
html (accessed August 21, 2014).

Bastian, B., Denson, T. F., and Haslam, N. (2013). The Roles of Dehumanization and
Moral Outrage in Retributive Justice. *PLoS ONE* 8(4): e61842. doi:10.1371/journal.
pone.0061842. (accessed August 20, 2014).

Bedau, Hugo Adam (2010). Punishment. *The Stanford Encyclopedia of Philosophy.* Available at
http://plato.stanford.edu/entries/punishment/ (accessed August 20, 2014).

Black's Law Dictionary (2014). What is Punishment? *Black's Law Dictionary Second Edition.*
Available at http://thelawdictionary.org/punishment/ (accessed August 20, 2014).

Blumstein, Alfred (1983). Selective Incapacitation as a Means of Crime Control. *American
Behavioral Scientist,* 27(1): 87–108.

Braithwaite, John (1989). *Crime, Shame and Reintegration.* Sage.

Braithwaite, John (2004). Restorative Justice and De-Professionalization. *The Good Society*
13(1): 28–31.

Cantor, James (2008). *Biological Influences in Pedophilia.* Available at http://jamescantor.com/
myres_ped.html (accessed August 21, 2014).

Cherry, Kendra (2014). What is Punishment? Available at http://psychology.about.com/
od/operantconditioning/f/punishment.htm (accessed August 20, 2014).

Crossland, Paul and Liebmann, Marian (2003). *40 Cases: restorative justice and victim-offender
mediation.* London: Mediation UK.

Daly, K. and Hayes, H. (2002). Restorative Justice and Conferencing. In A. Graycar and
P. Grabosky (Eds.) *The Cambridge Handbook of Australian Criminology.* Cambridge, UK:
Cambridge University Press, pp. 294–331.

Foucault, Michel (1977). *Discipline and Punish: the birth of the prison.* Trans. Alan Sheridan.
New York: Vintage.

Franklin, Karen (2013). Efficacy of Sex Offender Treatment Still Up in the Air. *Psychology
Today.* Available at http://www.psychologytoday.com/blog/witness/201309/efficacy-
sex-offender-treatment-still-in-the-air (accessed August 21, 2014).

Frazier, Charles E., Bishop, Donna M., and Lanza-Kaduce, Lon (1999). Get-Tough
Juvenile Justice Reforms: the Florida experience. *The ANNALS of the American Academy
of Political and Social Science* 564(1): 167–184.

Greenwood, Peter W. and Abrahamse, Allan (1982). *Selective Incapacitation.* Santa Monica
CA: Rand Publication Series.

Hayes, Hennessey (2005). Assessing Reoffending in Restorative Justice Conferences.
Australian & New Zealand Journal of Criminology 38(1): 77–101.

Letourneau, Elizabeth J., Levenson, Jill S., Bandyopadhyay, Dipankar, Sinha, Debajyoti,
and Armstrong, Kevin S. (2010). *Evaluating the Effectiveness of Sex Offender Registration
and Notification Policies for Reducing Sexual Violence against Women.* Report to the NCJRS.
Available at https://www.ncjrs.gov/pdffiles1/nij/grants/231989.pdf (accessed August
21, 2014).

Parker, Gareth and Emerson, Daniel (2011). *More Flak for Sex Offender Register.* Seven News.
Available at https://au.news.yahoo.com/a/11470982/more-flak-for-sex-offender-register/
(accessed August 21, 2014).

Peffley, Mark and Hurwitz, John (2010). *Justice in America: The Separate Realities of Blacks
and Whites (Cambridge Studies in Public Opinion and Political Psychology).* Cambridge:
Cambridge University Press.

Restorative Justice Online (2014). *What is Restorative Justice.* Available at: http://www.restorativejustice.org/university-classroom/01introduction (accessed August 21, 2014).

Stohr, Mary, Walsh, Anthony, and Hemmens, Craig (2008). *Corrections: A Reader.* Sage Publications.

The Sentencing Project (2013). *Report of The Sentencing Project to the United Nations Human Rights Committee Regarding Racial Disparities in the United States Criminal Justice System.* The Sentencing Project. Available at http://sentencingproject.org/doc/publications/rd_ICCPR%20Race%20and%20Justice%20Shadow%20Report.pdf (accessed August 20, 2014).

Wright, Valerie (2010). *Deterrence in Criminal Justice: evaluating certainty vs severity of punishment.* The Sentencing Project.

Yost, Benjamin (2010). Kant's Justification of the Death Penalty Reconsidered. *Kantian Review* 15(2): 1–27.

Zehr, Howard (2005). *Changing Lenses: a new focus for crime and justice.* Third edition. Scottsdale, PA: Herald Press.

Chapter 14

Where to from here?

This book has been structured to provide a guided journey through criminal justice ethics from theoretical foundations, to social ethics, to applying ethics in the criminal justice system. The overarching framework for study has been the exercise of moral imagination in thinking about justice and the legal system, public life, and professional responsibility. As we saw in Chapter 1, the moral imagination encourages us to step back from our personal prejudices and values and yet it also asks us to personally and professionally embrace the values of empathy and impartiality. The measure of a criminal justice professional is in their ability to engage with the moral imagination outside of their socially pre-scribed milieu, to appreciate the point of view of those most unlike themselves. Appreciation of that which is in many ways alien to us leads us to understand what we also share in common with them, namely, our moral agency.

The journey began with a meandering tour through the ethical theories, from consequentialism to non-consequentialism. Utilitarianism taught us that sometimes personal sacrifices must be made for a higher social good, and that sometimes we might even have to act against our personal principles for that good, and accept the consequences of our actions, no matter how dire. It might have seemed strange for an 'ethical' theory to ask us to 'dirty our hands' for a cause, and that goes a long way towards illustrating the variety of grey areas that crop up in ethical deliberation. Utilitarianism demands much of us, but in return it offers—theoretically at least—the prospect of a more prosper-ous and harmonious society and the chance to contribute to a greater good.

Egoism, on the other hand, taught us that there will be times when looking out for number one is paramount, not least in the courts, which pit prosecutor and defender against each other. In the adversarial system, we are not searching necessarily for truth, which is often difficult to find, but for the most persuasive evidence. Each side must therefore fight their cases for themselves, without regard for the fate of the other or whether the truth might end up a casualty of the process. Whether this system is itself wholly ethical remains under debate. Our comparison between the adversarial system and the inquisitorial system raised some concerns about the value and integrity of 'competing' for justice.

Deontology taught us that acting according to personal principle means maintaining one's integrity regardless of the outcome. In the case of Jim and Pedro in Chapter 4, Jim was a victim of moral luck in encountering the plight of the poor condemned villagers. He did not take them prisoner; his encounter with them was purely accidental. Deontology tells us that Jim was therefore not morally responsible for their deaths at the hands of the military leader. It might have seemed harsh to argue that Jim was morally permitted—even required—to walk away from the situation without any pang of conscience, but if we consider ourselves responsible for every injustice perpetrated by others, then we would constantly be sacrificing our principles against an unsure outcome. The Categorical Imperative requires that all such sacrifices are able to be universalized. That is the lesson of deontology—*pace* the utilitarian. It is one of the conundrums of philosophy that two such different theories can both have something valuable to say.

Was Aristotle right then, in suggesting that instead of looking for guiding principles or formulae, we should focus our moral imaginations on being a certain kind of person? That kind of person takes seriously their status as a citizen of civil society and works towards improving themselves and their environment through the practice of virtues and through kind consideration of, and forbearance towards their fellows and communities. As we saw in Chapter 4, Aristotle argued that we are constituted just as much by the social, professional, and political groups to which we belong as we are by the individual beliefs and values that we hold dear. Virtue ethics has taught us that the seat of the moral imagination does indeed lie both within and outside ourselves and that we are capable of and have a propensity towards flourishing both as moral agents and as citizens of a global society.

As current or potential criminal justice professionals, then, our aim is to use our moral imaginations to achieve justice in a world in which there is much injustice. The role of a criminal justice professional is not only defined by the code of each profession or occupation, but also by one's ability and propensity to act with integrity, even outside the code. In a world in which we are constantly exhorted to pamper and indulge ourselves to an extent that would make Aristotle turn in his grave, this is not easy! It is hoped that the foregoing chapters have worked their magic on your moral imaginations in ways that will give you courage on the path towards ethical conduct. To conclude, I leave you with yet another quote—this time from the inspiring African-American author and poet, Maya Angelou (1988):

> One isn't necessarily born with courage, but one is born with potential. Without courage, we cannot practice any other virtue with consistency. We can't be kind, true, merciful, generous or honest.

. . . to which I would also add, "or just."

References

Angelou, Maya (1988). Interview with USA Today, March 5, 1988. Cited at http://www. usatoday.com/story/news/nation-now/2014/05/28/maya-angelou-quotes/9663257/

Index

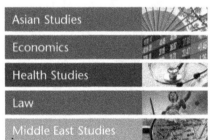